Amory Howe Bradford

The Pilgrim in Old England

A Review of the History, Present Condition, and Outlook of the Independent

Churches in England

Amory Howe Bradford

The Pilgrim in Old England
A Review of the History, Present Condition, and Outlook of the Independent Churches in England

ISBN/EAN: 9783337004149

Printed in Europe, USA, Canada, Australia, Japan

Cover: Foto ©ninafisch / pixelio.de

More available books at **www.hansebooks.com**

ANDOVER LECTURES ON CONGREGATIONALISM

THE

Pilgrim in Old England

A REVIEW

OF THE HISTORY, PRESENT CONDITION, AND OUTLOOK
OF THE INDEPENDENT (CONGREGATIONAL)
CHURCHES IN ENGLAND

BY

AMORY H. BRADFORD
AUTHOR OF "SPIRIT AND LIFE"; "OLD WINE: NEW BOTTLES," ETC.

NEW YORK
FORDS, HOWARD, & HULBERT
LONDON: JAMES CLARKE & CO.
1893

Copyright in 1893
By AMORY H. BRADFORD

DEDICATION

TO

ALEXANDER MACKENNAL, B. A., D. D.,

PASTOR OF THE CONGREGATIONAL CHURCH AT BOWDON, CHESHIRE, ENGLAND; CHAIRMAN OF THE CONGREGATIONAL UNION OF ENGLAND AND WALES IN 1887; SECRETARY OF THE FIRST INTERNATIONAL COUNCIL OF CONGREGATIONAL CHURCHES IN 1891; SECRETARY OF THE FIRST CONGRESS OF FREE CHURCHES IN ENGLAND IN 1892; DISTINGUISHED AS A PREACHER, HONORED AS A LEADER, AND BELOVED AS A PASTOR,

THIS VOLUME IS DEDICATED, WITH ADMIRATION AND GRATITUDE

PREFACE.

THE title of this book has been chosen not without the consciousness that its propriety may be questioned. The name "Pilgrim," technically, belongs to those who left England, went to Holland, and afterward came to America in search of religious liberty. But the name also belongs to an intellectual and spiritual movement of which the migration to the New World in the "Mayflower" was but a small part. It applies to those who remained in the old country, and who there, under circumstances quite as perilous as fighting Indians and the endurance of cold and hunger, fought for, and in a measure achieved, their rights as citizens of a spiritual commonwealth. It is the privilege of those who live in the United States to revere the memory of the men who founded the Plymouth Colony, and who more than any others were the fathers of our liberties; but it should never be forgotten that not all the heroes left England, and that while some of the "finest of the wheat" came to Plymouth, enough remained on the other side of the sea to insure a harvest of spiritual life and of practical righteousness which for vitality and vigour has been unsurpassed in the history of Christianity.

The descendants of those who worshipped in the Separatist assemblies in Elizabeth's time are to be found in both the Old World and the New: they have the same spiritual lineage, the same legacy of doctrine and tradition, the same memories of holy ancestors who have dared to do and to die for the faith as they have understood it, and they are still working for broader liberty, and for the incorporation of the life of Christ into the life of humanity. In the full conviction that the descendants of those who held the Pilgrim faith in the elder days are, in all spiritual things, in the same fellowship as their fathers; and that as the children better understand one another they will be able better to co-operate in hastening the Kingdom of God by showing and realising the liberty of the sons of God, these Lectures were given, and are now published.

Without the kindness and courtesy of many friends in England the facts herein considered could never have been gathered. It is not easy for me to distribute my obligations, but I have no difficulty in making a beginning, for before all others I must acknowledge the generous treatment which was extended to me in 1884 by Rev. Andrew Mearns, Secretary of the London Congregational Union, to whom I owe my introduction to the English churches, and without whose aid I could not have pursued my studies concerning the ecclesiastical and social condition of England. To Andrew Mearns I am deeply indebted. If I am not mistaken, the habit of being helpful to young ministers is an old one with him, and many in the United States, as well as in England, would gladly join with me in acknowledging his goodness. Side by side with the name of Andrew Mearns must be placed that of Alexander Mackennal, of Bowdon, whom all Americans who attended the International Council will long remember with love and gratitude, and whose helpfulness in the way of wise suggestion and courteous advice can hardly be exaggerated. Drs. Dale, Fairbairn, and Revs. J. Guinness Rogers, Robert F. Horton and F. Herbert Stead have also been of much assistance in the way of suggestion. A different obligation, and one second in importance only to that to Mr. Mearns and Dr. Mackennal, belongs to Rev. P. T. Forsyth, of the Clarendon Park Congregational Church in Leicester, and to Rev. Bryan Dale, Secretary of the Yorkshire Congregational Union. Mr. Forsyth is one of the most accomplished scholars and one of the ablest thinkers among English Nonconformists, and to him I am greatly indebted for the extreme care which he took in writing to me most exact information which is embodied in the chapter on "The Present Condition." Mr. Dale has done more than any one else in helping to make this book accurate. Without any previous acquaintance, he graciously consented to revise my work, and the patience and thoroughness with which he examined it in the manuscript places me under a debt of lasting obligation to him. I beg those who may read these pages to give Mr. Dale credit for much of the accuracy in detail which they may possess, and wherein they may be found incorrect to believe it is because I have ventured to disregard his suggestions.

In this recounting of those to whom my thanks are especially due are named only those who have directly helped in the preparation of this work. If I were to attempt including all those whose courtesies I have received among the good people of the Congregational Churches in England my list might be longer than my book.

It remains only to say that the substance of the following chapters was delivered in the course of my regular duties as Southworth Lecturer on Congregationalism at Andover Theological Seminary, in the spring of 1892. The chapter on "Creeds" was delivered in the course on "American Congregationalism," in the same Seminary, in 1893; and the chapter on "Doctrinal Conditions of Church Membership" was read before the International Congregational Council in London in 1891. The portions of these two chapters concerning the faith and practice among American churches, like many other similar passages, have been included in the belief that, by comparing the development of the same vital principles in the different environments of the Old World and the New, a better understanding of both could be arrived at.

This book is not intended to be an exhaustive study of ecclesiastical polity, nor a history of the rise and growth of an ecclesiastical order, but rather an exposition of the working of the principles which are taught and illustrated in the Independent, or Congregational, Churches of England. If anywhere in these pages there seems to be an assumption that the faith of the Pilgrims concerning the Church is the only true faith, or, indeed, that there is any Divine order of church polity, I desire distinctly to disclaim such meaning. Each man is a fraction; each division of the Christian Church is of necessity fractional; and although emphasis is here placed on those truths which best commend themselves to us, we recognise that the Truth as a unit is too large for the comprehension of any individual or sect. The claim of any section of the Church to be the true and only Church of Christ is too absurd for refutation.

> " Our little systems have their day;
> They have their day and cease to be:
> They are but broken lights of Thee,
> And Thou, O Lord, art more than they."

In the full recognition that the faith of the Pilgrims is that which Providence fitted them to emphasise, and that the Kingdom of God is to be realised, not by any denomination making light of its distinctive principles, but rather by the loyalty of all to that which is most clearly revealed to them, this attempted contribution toward a better understanding of those principles, as they are illustrated in the history and present condition of The Pilgrims of Old England is now offered to the public.

AMORY H. BRADFORD.

First Congregational Church,
Montclair, New Jersey.

CONTENTS.

I.

LIFE AND FORM. 1

How to study the Church—No institution perfect at its beginning—Organisation a product of life and environment—Growth necessitated by life; form determined by circumstances—Early life influenced by environment—The early Christian Church—The Church a fellowship of those who have the Divine life—The primitive Church subordinated form to life—Forms best for one age may not be best for another—Forms best for one class may not be best for another—The polity of the Apostolic Church not necessarily the best for all time—The truths which distinguished the Pilgrims and their churches: A personal relation between the Divine Spirit and the individual human spirit; the Church composed only of regenerate persons; the Church a brotherhood of believers; the Bible, interpreted by the Spirit, contains all truth necessary to righteous life here and salvation hereafter; creeds of secondary importance—The Church of the future a spiritual commonwealth; how its coming may be hastened. . . . .

II.

BEGINNING AND GROWTH. 33

Christ's teaching concerns a Kingdom, not a Church—The Apostles a brotherhood rather than a society—After the Master's death, the believers gradually organised for more efficient work—The Apostolic Church—Increase in numbers compelled greater organisation—The church at Rome, the capital city, becomes the Imperial Church—Christianity, the religion of the Empire—Contest between Church and State—External prosperity causes decrease of spirituality—The primacy of Peter as a basis for Roman supremacy—The division into Greek and Roman—Creeds and liturgies supplant dependence on the Spirit—Supremacy of the State—The Protestant Reformation spiritual rather than ecclesiastical—Luther's contention—Calvin, and his new ecclesiastical order—The English Church severs its relations with Rome—Protestantism persecuting as Romanism—Church of England established by law—The difference between Puritans and Separatists—An Episcopal *versus* a Calvinistic State—Cromwell and the Parliamentary army—Temporary separation of Church and State—Modern Congregationalism in Great Britain—The "Brownists"—Early martyrs to liberty of conscience—Emigration to Holland and America—Leaders among the Pilgrims—English Colonies in the New World—Character of the Pilgrims—Increase of toleration—Nonconformists in Great Britain—Gradual change in Independent theology—Congregationalism in the United States—Congregationalism a principle, not an organisation—The spiritual life the only reality with the Pilgrims—Tolerance of the Independents—Theological divergence of their descendants—Congregationalists' faith in the present efficiency of the Living Spirit—The Separatists men of prayer—The Pilgrims' ideal of the Kingdom of God.

III.

CHURCH AND STATE. 83

The English Church a part of the Government—Authority of the State over the Church—The Established Church and Nonconformity—Introduction of Christianity into the British Isles—Supremacy of the Roman Church—Transition from Paganism to Popery—Cooperation of civil and spiritual authorities—Separation of Church of England from Rome—The Church a part of the Government, and Henry the Eighth its head—Papal control under Queen Mary—Authority of the Crown reasserted by Queen Elizabeth—The Puritan Revolution—Conformity to Prayer Book required; defection of Puritan clergy—Common membership in Church and State—The State in ecclesiastical matters—Laws concerning Church property—Patronage and simony—Various measures passed since the Restoration—Union of Church and State—Points of failure in the English Establishment—Some advantages of a State Church—Facts concerning Nonconformists—A theocratic State a beautiful ideal, but difficult of realisation—Disestablishment inevitable—Difficulties—Separation of Church and State better, even for the Episcopal Church in Great Britain—Ultimate Disestablishment to come rather as result of spiritual life within than of agitation without.

IV.

THE PRESENT CONDITION. 123

How to study ecclesiastical systems—Recognition won by Nonconformists—Numbers, influence and social standing of Congregationalists—Statistics from the Year Book of 1892—The kind of work English Congregationalists

PAGE

are doing: In local churches; in Foreign Missions; in Home Missions; in City Missions—Theology coloured by study of social problems—Poverty of the Free Churches in country districts—Independence of the Local Church —Method of entering the ministry—Change from one parish to another—Certification of ministerial standing—Basis of union between the churches—Organisation of churches—The County Unions and the Congregational Union of England and Wales—Difference between the Congregational Union of England and Wales and the National Council of the United States—Concerning reception of members in churches—Matters of discipline—Emphasis on spirit and life rather than government and authority—Doctrinal schedules in Trust Deeds—Belief in an educated ministry—Nonconformist academies—Points of weakness in English Congregationalism—Elements of strength—Influence of the Congregational Union of England and Wales—Organisation for work in the English churches—Change of emphasis from independency to fellowship—Importance of Sociology—Death of Rev. Henry Allon, D.D.

V.

CREEDS. 177

No general creed possible for all Congregational churches —Local churches formulate their own Confessions of Faith—The usage in the Baptist Church—The elements in the Puritan Revolution—The Westminster Assembly (1643)—The Savoy Assembly (1658)—Congregational Union Creed (1883)—Superiority of creeds of Westminster and Savoy as compared with later productions—The Savoy Confession of Faith—Difference between Westminster and Savoy standards—Dr. Stoughton's testimony on creeds—Change in the doctrines held by

English Christians—Confessions of Faith in New England—The Westminster Standard adopted in New England by Synod of Cambridge (1648)—Adoption of the Savoy Confession by Synod of Boston (1680)—Synod of Saybrook endorses action of former synods (1708)—Burial Hill Confession (1865)—First National Council at Oberlin, O., (1871)—The Oberlin Declaration—Creed of the National Council Commission (1883)—Difference between creeds of Congregationalists and those of other denominations.

VI.

DOCTRINAL CONDITIONS OF CHURCH MEMBERSHIP. 225

Existing usage in admitting members to local churches—Testimony concerning the usage in English churches—Testimony concerning usage in the United States—Summary of usage on both sides of the water—Reasons for the American usage—Arguments in favor of doctrinal conditions: They preserve soundness of doctrine; they bind in unity the whole membership—Arguments against doctrinal conditions: They violate the spirit and letter of Scripture; they hinder progress in knowledge and growth in spiritual life; Christ made no such conditions; knowledge of the truth necessary for intelligent assent to them is the fruit of the Christian life; requiring assent to them cultivates intellectual dishonesty; they misrepresent Christianity; they bar from the means of grace many who most need the help and who give evidence of the Christian life—Questions of doctrine cause contention and division—No basis for such requirement in Scripture—The assumptions of such tests—Doctrinal conditions passing away.

VII.

THE PULPIT. 249

The power of Protestantism in the Christian pulpit—Importance to preachers of the study of work and methods of other pulpits—The three most conspicuous Dissenting preachers in the seventeenth century: John Robinson, John Howe and John Owen—The two greatest spiritual forces of the eighteenth century: Watts and Doddridge—Nonconformist preachers of the present century—Long pastorates—John Angell James, Robert S. McAll, Samuel Martin, James Parsons, Thomas Binney, James Baldwin Brown, Henry Allon, Joshua Harrison, Edward White, J. Guinness Rogers, Prin. Fairbairn, Alex. Mackennal, George S. Barrett, Robert F. Horton, Charles A. Berry, John Hunter, C. Silvester Horne, Robert W. Dale, Joseph Parker—Preachers of English Congregationalism compared with those of the Establishment—Responsibility of the ministry for moral life of the State—Influence of Nonconformist preachers in England—Possible influence in the State of the ministry in all lands—The ministry a potent force in solving social problems of England—Growing social conditions in the United States call for the same work—Great pulpit orators of England and America—The pulpit not losing its power.

VIII.

THE OUTLOOK. 295

Natural correspondence between doctrine and life in each age—Emphasis has passed from theology to sociology—Revival of interest in Theology—Theological agitation in England and in the United States—English theology influenced by social conditions—English theologians—

Education of the Independent ministry in England—Advance in the direction of Christian unity and coöperation—"The Nonconformist Conscience"—Consciousness of imperial relations—Movement of English Christians toward federation—Theological outlook in English churches—Doctrinal beliefs of English churches: Papers read before the International Council of 1891 by Principals Simon and Fairbairn, Rev. Dr. Conder and Rev. George S. Barrett—The author's own impressions of the English theological *status*—The preaching practical rather than theological—English teachers have little time for theological investigation—Continuous Inspiration—The Atonement—Last Things—Strong men in the English pulpit—Independents to lead in the future religious development of England—Movement toward Disestablishment—Influence of Congregational principles—Relation of English Congregationalism to the Church of the future—Mutual relations of England and America.

INDEX. 335–344

I.
LIFE AND FORM.

"If the churches of Christ exist for the religion of Christ, then their polities must be looked at through its nature and ends, spirit and purpose. The polity that best interprets and realizes these is the best church polity."—PRINCIPAL FAIRBAIRN.

"Such was the mild and equal constitution by which the Christians were governed more than a hundred years after the death of the Apostles. Every society formed within itself a separate and independent republic; and, although the most distant of these little states maintained a mutual as well as friendly intercourse of letters and deputations, the Christian world was not yet connected by any supreme authority or legislative assembly."—GIBBON.

"All the churches in those primitive times were independent bodies, none of them subject to the jurisdiction of any other, for, though the churches which were founded by the Apostles themselves frequently had the honor shown them to be consulted in difficult and doubtful cases, yet they had no judicial authority, no control, no power of giving laws. On the contrary, it is clear as the noon-day that all Christian churches had equal rights, and were in all respects on a footing of equality."—MOSHEIM.

I.

LIFE AND FORM.

In beginning this study of spiritual life and ecclesiastical polity in England our attention should first be directed toward the nature of the Christian Church, and the processes through which it has passed from its primitive simplicity to its modern complexity.

"Churches and societies," says Principal Fairbairn, "like men, ought to be studied in their actual histories, but through their distinctive ideals. The most prosaic person has in him a vein of poetry which must be found if his behaviour in the higher and more critical moments of his life is to be understood, and the most utter church of the Philistines has its ideal elements, were it only the memory of its ancient or recent feuds with the people of God."* The ideals of the various denominations can be learned only from a study of their history. In tracing the line along which they move we catch hints of the goal toward which they tend. Each branch

---

* "Jubilee Lectures," p. 11.

of the universal Church contains within itself some reason for its existence, but that reason can be understood only by an examination of the relations of the parts to the whole. Clear views concerning the Church are necessary to an appreciation of the true spirit of that fraction of it which we call Congregational. But the Church is an external and visible society; it exists in the world in the midst of other institutions, as Societies and States. This describes not the ideal but the actual Church; not any one denomination, but all who profess and call themselves Christians, and who are associated, in whatever way, for the promotion of Christian ends. As a society, the Church has certain features in common with other societies. It is composed of men, governed by laws, operated according to methods, has members, and clearly defined conditions of membership. In these respects it resembles a State, or a mutual improvement society. Yet the Church is in a real sense divine, and clearly separated from all other institutions. That separation is found in something behind the external organization,—in its life, for there is a corporate as well as an individual life, a life which fuses the individuals in a common and indivisible unity.

We do not expect to find any institution perfect at its beginning. The law of growth holds sway among Societies and States as distinctly as among human beings. The doctrine of development has influenced the study of history not less than the study of science. The present cosmic order is the result of long processes of evolution. Similar processes have operated in the development of history. If the scientist would understand, as well as classify, physical phenomena, he must have some clear idea of life. If the historical student would have a philosophy of history, he must know the principles whose development he traces in institutions. And if the theologian would understand the Church, he must have some accurate knowledge of the life which thrills in its members and makes their union an organism rather than a mechanism. Therefore, since ecclesiastical polity, so far as it has the slightest claim upon the thought or veneration of Christians, has it because of indwelling life, the present inquiry concerns Spiritual Life and Ecclesiastical Polity.

Life always precedes organization. Without life there is no change. A stone is a stone to the end of time, except as it is modified by external forces. There can be no organization, no co-operation between stones. Organization and co-operation presume life, and yet life is dependent on organization for manifestation. Abstract life—life apart from substance and form—so far as we know has no existence.

But organization is a product of two factors, namely, life, which determines the necessity and kind of growth; and environment, which determines the form of growth: and a large proportion of all environment is itself the organized product of life. Therefore it is accurate to say that an organization is chiefly a product of indwelling life, and of life manifesting itself in other organizations with which it has come in contact. The life determines that a tree shall be an oak or a maple, and impels it to grow, responding to the attraction of the sun and the influences of the air and the soil: the environment determines how it shall grow—whether it shall be sturdy, with roots reaching deep; whether it shall havè free expanse for its limbs, or whether they shall be dwarfed and bent. The environment of the tree is the clear sky, full of light; the generous clouds, with abundance of rain; the soil from which the roots gather moisture, and the forest or field of which it is a part. The life is neither the sky, nor the soil, nor the rain: yet it uses and is affected by all in producing the tree. The life organises the human body and determines whether it shall be of one race or another; but environment determines whether that life shall make for itself a body from abundance and comfort, with every opportunity of perfect development, or whether it shall draw from poverty and limitation, with no opportunity of development along lines of healthfulness and beauty. A State is a product of human life; it is more than a congeries of individuals: it is that, plus some common energy which works toward unity. But circumstances modify States as well as men, and have much to do with the form which they actually assume. The ideal in the minds of the founders of the American Republic was a free government, of the people, by the people, and for the people, but the actual form is in many cases an oligarchy, masquerading in the garments of democracy. That ideal has proved a blessing where there has been intelligence and lofty character. but a curse where it has been degraded, and made the occasion for a mob usurping the throne of rule. The final form of the republican theory of the State will be a joint product, of the principles of our fathers and of the circumstances in which those principles have been developed.

What is true of trees, human beings, and States, is equally true of the Church. A tree is life manifesting itself in forms of matter; a man, life manifesting itself in humanity; a State, life manifesting itself in forms of government: and the Church is the Divine Life manifesting itself in the society of redeemed souls. The Church, like the State, the human body, and the tree, is a joint product of life and environment. Its beginning was the life that was in Christ, and which was imparted to those who accepted Christ as Master and Lord. The growth of the Church is necessitated by its life, but the forms in which it has actually been manifested—as in individuals and communities—have changed with its circumstances. At first it was limited to a few unlettered fishermen and devout Jews who instinctively, under a common impulse, associated in simple forms of fellowship. Afterwards it appeared in many lands, under different skies, in men with different tendencies, different conditions, and different ideals. The church in Corinth, having the same general characteristics, was yet very unlike the church in Jerusalem. The latter strongly emphasized the law and the sacrifices, and constantly tended to revert to them; the former, situated in the midst of a corrupt but splendid heathenism, was more or less influenced by pagan customs and corrupt social standards. A little later the Divine Life which was in the Master and the Apostles, having invaded Europe, conquered the Empire, and in turn was modified by it, until the simple beliefs and ecclesiastical methods of the early Christians well-nigh disappeared in heathen rites and practices, in secular theories and aims. A tree cannot be the same on the summit of the Sierras as in the valley of the Amazon. On the heights the growths go deep and take firm hold on the rocks; tempests blow and lightnings play, but the forests remain companions with the mountains for thousands of years. So the Church, when it has been exposed to persecution and has had to struggle for existence, has developed a strength, and its members a grandeur of character, unknown in prosperous times. Spiritual life manifests itself through organization, which is a product not only of indwelling life but also of environment. Necessarily, therefore, the pure and perfect life will be long in freeing itself from its impure and imperfect environment. As a matter of fact, for centuries the Church was more and more pervaded by corrupt and secular elements.

At first life is largely influenced by environment, but later it becomes nearly impervious to surrounding influences. The body of a child may be dwarfed, but no power can put a full-grown man back to childhood. When the constitution is firm and strong it easily resists that to which before it would have yielded. Society in primitive conditions is made up of individuals who are influenced not simply by air and light, but whose thoughts are coloured by every mood of the sky, and whose characters are moulded by every sound which they hear. Then superstitions are prevalent; but with the years life asserts itself, progress changes the conditions, and superstitions are sloughed off. The State originally was only a mob in which the strongest had precedence. It has grown through various stages to an organization in which the will of the people is expressed through law. Civilized nations are now co-operative institutions, composed of individuals working together for purposes of mutual protection and advancement; and all nations which have not reached this stage are in the throes of a more or less evident and serious revolution.

As individuals, society, and the State reach higher conditions through successive eras of civilisation, gradually mastering unpropitious circumstances, so the Church moves slowly toward the realisation of its ideal. The perfect Church is far in the future. When it appears the life of God will have unhindered manifestation in and through redeemed humanity. But before that altitude can be reached there must be co-operation between what is called spiritual life and its environment; the life must subject the environment to its sway, eliminating and casting off what is false and corrupt and appropriating for its own growth what is healthful and good.

Such a movement is in progress—all too little emphasized—and consequently society itself is in process of transformation. As individuals are regenerated, their new ideals and customs modify old usages and institutions. Society is becoming more Christian. As an illustration of this, the code of duelling has disappeared from most civilised lands simply because Christian principles have begun to prevail. In the State there is a gradual but sure movement toward international arbitration, not because the nations are yet regenerate, but because they have felt the influence of Christian principles. Institutions are improving and customs changing, and the world is different to-day from what it was a century ago, because the "redemption of society" is going on coincident with the conversion of individuals. The spiritual life is transforming society, both by the regeneration of individuals, and by the influence of their example and teaching on others, which makes a new and favourable environment in which the Divine Life may advance more swiftly.

And now we come to a question which needs but little consideration here—What is the Church? This is not so much a question about a term (no real light is gained from Hebrew or Greek etymology) as about the social relations of men who have life. Our Lord said: "I am come that ye might have life." He said next to nothing about the Church, but very much both before and after his resurrection about the spiritual and social relations of believers. The word "Church" is mentioned but twice in the four gospels. Christ said much about the Kingdom. "Kingdom" he used in a large way, as indicating the fellowship of those who have the life, and with him the Church and the Kingdom seem to have been practically synonymous terms. In the Acts and the Epistles is a still clearer recognition of the Church as "the fellowship of those who have the life."

In the New Testament there are to be found no formal rules concerning the government of churches, and yet there are many principles and precedents applicable to the Church in all time. Christians had many gifts, and it was made clear that there was a place for their exercise in the new society. There is little in the New Testament that is definite concerning offices in the Church. There were officers—pastors, elders, teachers, deacons—but the office was of less importance than its duties. The spheres of work were not strictly defined, and not much stress was laid on offices, or officers, of any kind. Only one thing is unquestionable: the most honourable position was that of servant. The Apostolic office was temporary; and but two officers were general and permanent, namely, bishops (overseers, care-takers) or pastors, and deacons. It must be said, however, that many believe that there were three grades of service in the early Church, and that there are also three in the modern Church, so far as it is Scriptural and Apostolic. If these questions had had any importance in the minds of the Master and the Apostles they would have been stated with greater precision and fulness. The disciples sought to bring men to Christ, and, having accomplished that, left them to themselves and the Spirit of Truth, content that the life in each should manifest itself in its own way. How different the tone of the Scriptures when dealing with moral and spiritual subjects! The Epistles show a realisation that their writers were in a life-and-death contest with heathenism, whose vices were threatening the corruption and defilement of the new society. Concerning ethical subjects there is a clearness and precision not found when questions of polity are treated.

Principal Fairbairn says: "Paul writes to many churches, and many churches confess him their founder and teacher, but his letters are expository or expostulatory, hortatory or biographical, and as far as possible from speaking with legal or political authority. No man ever had a doctrinal system so carefully articulated, or labored more to make it intelligible or credible to the societies he formed; yet no man ever so carefully avoided building the societies he erected at Galatia and Rome, Ephesus and Colosse, Philippi and Thessalonica, Corinth and Athens, into a political corporation. His unity of the faith did not mean 'organised uniformity.' And the same is true of the other apostolic writers." *

What Dr. Fairbairn has said concerning "organised uniformity" of faith might also have been said concerning the nature and growth of the Church. Spiritual life is not imparted by baptism. There may be baptism and no life, and there may be life and no baptism. Life is known by fruit. The Master spoke to his disciples; the disciples repeated the message to others, and left it to do its own work. As the story was told in distant lands those

---
* "Jubilee Lectures," pp. 21 and 22.

who had lived in vice and crime felt their hearts burn within them, new aspirations were started, old habits laid aside, and they were impelled, like Saul, to "join themselves to the church"; and thus gradually the Christian society has grown. If it be said that this exposition is inadequate because it makes no place for the children of believers, our reply is, that they are born into the kingdom in which their parents are, and are to be regarded as included in the fold of the Church unless they choose to go out. But they are not made Christ's by being "christened"; they are "christened" because they are already Christ's by reason of the organic unity of the family. Ideally, the Church in a community is all the individual Christians in that community, whether in formal fellowship or not; the Church in a State, all the Christians in that State; the Church in the world, all the Christians in the world. But that ideal is slow of realisation, and consequently in the minds of many the Church is composed of such Christians in each community as agree in their intellectual beliefs concerning the nature and operation of the Divine Life. Because these beliefs differ there are various denominations, each calling itself a Church. But the life is at work, and gradually individuals who have experienced the new birth are coming together; clearer and more correct conceptions of truth are resulting, and by the agency of the Spirit there is slowly coming into realization what has always been impossible to human ingenuity,—something like a real and vital unity.

As a result of this study we are brought to a conclusion already stated, but which we now more fully develop—that the *ideal* Church is not yet in sight. At this point a few principles require emphasis:

(*a*) What is best for one *age* may not be best for another. In the nature of things, while the Church can never cease to be a free brotherhood of believers, the institutions through which it operates will in the nineteenth century be no more like those of the first than the clothing of a full-grown man is like that of an infant. Principles are eternal; institutions fluent and flexible. There has been progress in every department of life. The world is both larger and smaller than when the Apostles lived. Lands of which the wisest of that age never dreamed are now centres of population and civilisation. The great Empire has been dismembered, and new Empires greater still have arisen. The democratic principle has come to the front, and by it all political policies are moulded. No institutions are the same now as then, and least of all the Church. That which was best for a few scattered communities in the midst of heathenism, presumptively would not be best for the nineteenth century, when Christianity from being "a despicable superstition" has become the mightiest of forces. Growth within always necessitates change without. This principle is illustrated in Hebrew history. Laws which were necessary in the Exodus were laid aside long before the Advent. What was imperative for the government of a rabble of newly emancipated slaves would have been useless if applied to their descendants fifteen hundred years later. The Jewish church, after the priestly system had done its work, after the prophets had thrilled and inspired it with almost preternatural eloquence, after the psalmists had breathed into it the breath of immortal music, was little like that which was preceded by a pillar of cloud by day and a pillar of fire by night. If the Apostolic Church was Congregational, Presbyterian, or Episcopal, it would not follow that any one of these forms would be best in the nineteenth century; nor is it at all probable that the rites and order standing to-day will be desirable when nineteen centuries more have passed. The Divine Life has always adjusted itself to its environment, and always will. It may be enveloped by corruptions and superstitions; if so, its growth will be temporarily thwarted and hindered, but as the environment becomes purer the life will have freer manifestation. " A form of government which was the best possible organisation for the church of the first century may perhaps have been the worst possible for the organisation of the third." *

---

* Dale's " Manual of Congregationalism," p. 5.

(*b*) What is best for one *class* may not be best for another. Dean Stanley has illustrated this with eloquence and force in his sermon on " Diversity in Unity." He says: " So far from diversity being contrary to the genius of Christianity, it was involved in the religion of our Divine Founder from the very beginning; and so far from its being a reasonable obstacle in the way of its reception it ought to be one of the chief commendations of it to the reception of those to whom it is addressed." * The Dean then shows how diversity of creeds has resulted in emphasis on different but equally important truths ; that it was Ulfilas, the Arian Bishop, who evangelised the Gothic tribes of Northern Europe, and that from him was derived the first translation of the Scriptures into our modern tongue; that he was the precursor of Augustine, Boniface and Adelbert; that the first missions through the whole of Central Asia were established by the followers of the once persecuted, exiled and detested Nestorius; that the boatmen of Madras, as they dash through the perilous waves which encircle their weather-beaten shore, still invoke the name of Francis Xavier, the representative of the most repulsive and offensive phase of the Roman church—the Society of Jesuits. The Dean might have gone farther in his illustrations concerning the influence of doctrine, but he preferred to show how diversity of organisation has adjusted

---

* " Westminster Sermons," p. 344.

itself to different nationalities, and with a fine enthusiasm, and beautiful charity, has not failed to acknowledge that the Divine Life has been manifested in many ways in many lands. On the other hand, Dr. Dale, in his address before the International Council, with a charity equally fine, said: "Among the men from whom we are divided by cruel conflicts, but from whom our hearts should never be estranged, we recognise a saintliness shining with a glory that has its fountains in God. In their very contention and argument for errors which seem to us to obscure the light and impair the power of the Christian gospel we catch an accent which is the sign that they, too, are the children of the Eternal. If they maintain with passionate earnestness a doctrine of the Priesthood and of the Sacraments which appears to us to be irreconcilable with the whole spirit and substance of the Christian faith; if they regard those who reject and assail this doctrine as the worst enemies of the human race, it is because for them the Sacraments when duly administered are the appointed means by which the grace of God first originates and then sustains the Divine life in man. It is this which in their judgment makes the sacramental and sacerdotal controversy so critical, so awful . . . . They are contending for the sacredness and efficacy of the institutions by which they believe that the eternal life of God is made the actual possession of mankind."

(c) It follows of necessity that the form of church government which prevailed in Apostolic times may not be best for *all* time. There were seven deacons in the early church, and while that may indicate that the office of deacon is essential, it is no indication that there should not be more or less than seven in modern churches. At one time the twelve Apostles were ministers of the church in Jerusalem, and while that may indicate that the ministry as a distinct office is desirable, it does not imply that each church now should have twelve ministers. It would hardly become us, who believe that our polity is most like to that of the Apostolic age and has most hope for the future, in any way to belittle the church of the Apostolic Era. Rather let us emphasise its excellences. It was a *free spiritual brotherhood*, where men lived in the spirit and walked in the spirit. " Clergy and laity did not stand sharply opposed to each other, distinguished and divided by official (which are ever fictitious) sanctities. Nay, clergy and laity did not even exist. The most eminent distinctions were moral, the best gifts spiritual, and possible to all. The man who lived nearest to God stood highest among men; he who loved most lived the best. Office carried with it no special sanctity; sanctity only qualified for office." *

While to us it seems as if, whatever the changes

---
* Fairbairn, " Jubilee Lectures," p. xlvi.

of the future, the ideal of a "free spiritual brotherhood" could never be surpassed, as if it would grow young without ceasing, we cannot think of insisting that it contains all the glory of the ultimate church. That, like the New Jerusalem, has still to descend from God out of heaven. Concerning the constitution of the Church, "God has yet more light to break from his Holy Word."

While we have at the best dim and uncertain hints concerning the Church which is to be, we may yet ask, How may we best help toward its realisation? Our reply is, Each individual Christian will do most toward hastening the "Church of the future" by being loyal to the principles which he believes to be true, and seeking to give to them fullest and most perfect expression. When the foundations of that noble Church are laid, and its walls raised in fair colours, it will be found to combine something both of the doctrine and polity of widely differing and perhaps even antagonistic denominations. Toleration does not imply disloyalty to principle. It has been said that sectarianism necessitates toleration. It were better said that clear views of individual limitations promote toleration. The members of each denomination of Christians are selected for the purpose of cutting and finishing separate stones in the Christian cathedral, and the structure will be completed and glorified not by each one neglecting his own distinctive principles, but rather by all doing their work, emphasising the special revelations given to them, and, at last, bringing that which has been put into their hands, finished and beautiful, for the Master's use.

Therefore, in no spirit of denominational rivalry, we turn to what may be regarded as the truths which distinguish the Pilgrims and their churches. Church polity is a part of religion, though an inferior part. If there is any real religion it will manifest itself more or less in ecclesiastical institutions. Life must ever move on the world by means of form. If there is vital piety among Christians there will be something to stimulate spirituality in the institutions through which they work. It is one thing to affirm that there is somewhat of religion in our institutions, and very different to declare that there is nothing of it in the institutions of others.

(I.) The Pilgrims and their children on both sides of the Atlantic have ever recognised a personal relation between the Divine Spirit and the individual human spirit. This has never been more clearly stated than by Jonathan Edwards in his sermon entitled, "A Divine and Supernatural Light immediately imparted to the Soul, shown to be both a Scriptural and Rational Doctrine." In that sermon he says: "What I would make the subject of the present discourse from these words is, that there is such a thing as a spiritual and divine light

immediately imparted to the soul by God of a different nature from any that is obtained by natural means." Sacerdotal systems have put priests and sacraments between the individual and his God. "Church polities may be divided into two great great classes—the monarchical and the republican." *
The episcopal and the prelatical forms are monarchical. What are known as the "Free Churches" are more or less democratic under Christ; the fundamental principle of their faith is that the human spirit may hold personal communion with the Divine Spirit. Dr. Dale says: "The church, this is the Congregational ideal, is a society, larger or smaller, consisting of those who have received the Divine life, and who, with whatever inconsistency and whatever failure, are endeavouring to live through the power of it. All that is characteristic of Congregationalism lies in that ideal."† Over and over again Dr. Dale reiterates the fact that both the Church and the regenerate individual are the temples of the Holy Ghost. The same truth is emphasised by Dr. Dexter: He says: "Our system attaches itself—so, reverently, to speak—directly to God without intermediate machinery. It holds that the Great Head of the Church dwells in every true believer, to prompt and shape his acts. It holds that He pre-eminently dwells in every church of such believers,

---

* Fairbairn, "Jubilee Lectures," p. 17.
† Address at "The International Council, London, 1891."

giving definite promise of guidance to them in their associated capacity in answer to their united supplication. It holds especially that He pledges His peculiar presence by His illuminating Spirit when those churches humbly and reverently confer in council, desiring His light in darkness and His calm in storm. And so what the hierarchical organisations seek through their hierarchy, and the presbyterial congregations look for through their graded courts, Congregational believers seek—and rightly seeking find—at first hand, directly from the inspiration of God within their own souls, and the supervision of God over their Congregational acts."*

These two passages fairly state the fundamental Congregational principle. Liberty of conscience is its direct and necessary outgrowth. The Pilgrim Fathers revolted from the old church more because fallible human authority presumed to usurp the prerogative of the Divine Spirit, and to require what, in their view, was contrary to the Scriptures of truth, than because of dissatisfaction with current customs and ceremonies. The history of Puritanism has been one prolonged assertion that the individual may open his heart directly to the Divine Spirit, and without the mediation of priest, or sacrament, receive messages from the Eternal Light. That principle has led to apparent differences, but the differences in the end have helped to advance the

---

* "Congregationalism as Seen in its Literature," pp. 706-7.

Kingdom. Loyalty to it divided the Independents into Congregationalists and Baptists. In these days of doubt and panic concerning the possible results of criticism, the utterance of Dr. Dale rings like a bugle-note. He says: "I should like to ask whether in our relations to the controversies of our times the Congregational idea of the church has exerted its proper and adequate influence. We believe that a church is a society of men possessing the life of the Eternal Son of God, and having direct access through Him in the power of the Spirit to the Father; of men knowing for themselves at first hand the reality and glory of the Christian redemption; of men to whom the truth of the Christian Gospel is authenticated by a most certain experience—the experience not of the individual life merely, but of a society. Is this consistent with the agitation, the heat, the panic created by the assaults of critics on the historic records of the Jewish and Christian Revelations? We of all men should keep calm... For us every church is a society of original and independent witnesses to the grace and power of Christ." *

(II.) Congregationalists insist that the Church is composed only of regenerate persons. "The apostolic churches consisted of those, and of those only, who made a personal profession of their faith in Christ, and who, on the ground of this profession,

---

* International Council Address, 1891—London.

were received into the Christian assembly. They are therefore addressed in the apostolic epistles as 'faithful brethren' and as 'saints in Christ Jesus.'"*

This principle has always distinguished Congregationalism, and this is its chief contention with the Establishment. In an Erastian church all citizens of the nation would be members of the church; although the High Church party in the Anglican Communion would limit church membership to baptised citizens. Citizenship, and not Christian character, would thus become the condition of entrance into the fold of Christ. During the Commonwealth the Independents, as distinguished from the Puritans, maintained the doctrine that the Church is composed only of regenerate persons. The English Congregational churches lay even more stress upon this point than the American, because they are daily brought in contact with that system of church polity which not only includes believers in the Lord Jesus Christ, but which also has a place for those who deny him in word, and belie him by vileness of character. In the United States, conditions of church membership have been doctrinal rather than ethical; in the free Churches of England, ethical rather than doctrinal. I do not mean that we have not emphasised morality, but rather that the emphasis has been put upon belief. In England no formal doctrinal tests of church membership are allowed.

---

* Dale's "Manual," p. 6.

"When such a creed has been once adopted and emphasised a church is no longer under the immediate control of the Living Christ. Its freedom and its independence are lost : it is governed not indeed by the decrees of an external council or synod, but by the decrees of the dead."* The freedom of the spirit is fundamental with English Congregationalists, and it is that which leads them to decline to make doctrinal tests of church membership, while at the same time they insist with a rigour unknown elsewhere on regenerate character. That doctrine is fundamental, because Congregationalists believe that "acceptance of Christ" and the " new birth " are vital and not merely formal processes.

(III.) Congregationalists hold to the theory that the Church is a brotherhood of believers. " The Anglican emphasised the idea of the church, its unity, authority, order, but the Independent emphasised the idea of religion, the personal relation of God to the soul and the soul to God. . . . The Anglican made obedience to the church a question for the magistrate, bound the sovereign and the church in relations which placed the sovereign above its discipline, and placed the church under his authority; but the Independent made obedience to God the distinctive characteristic of the religious ; the church independent of the magistrate, the sovereign able to exercise no authority over it, with no standing in it

---

* Dale's " Manual of Congregationalism," p. 187.

as a prince, only as a man, as such amenable to it for his conduct, liable like other men to censure for ungodliness, or to honour if he did well."* Rev. Bryan Dale has tersely condensed the same idea as follows: "The Anglican says, Hear the Church! the Congregationalist, Hear ye *Him!*"

In the Pilgrim polity there is no place for caste or any distinctions not resulting from spiritual character. Its motto is—"One is your Master, even Christ, and all ye are brethren." The minister is not one exalted above the others, but one called to special service because of peculiar gifts, and no more entitled to honour for the work he does than the care-taker of the church, or the humblest member who can do little except pray and wait. Wealth gives no standing, culture no authority; all are one in Christ.

A necessary corollary of this truth is that the whole body of believers constituting a local church should be trusted. Not to the committee, or to the deacons, or to any company of elect spirits, do the affairs of the church exclusively belong, but to the whole membership. That was clearly true in the Apostolic times. When a successor of Judas was selected he was chosen by ballot, not by the Apostles, but by the believers in Jerusalem. And when the first strife arose in the Jerusalem-church concerning the care of the Grecian widows, Peter said, "Choose ye out for yourselves"—in other

---
* Fairbairn, "Jubilee Lectures," pp. 54-55.

words, the deacons were not elected by the Apostles, but by the whole membership. This principle is fundamental, but can be preserved only by constant vigilance. Wealth and power seek influence for themselves. He who has a large place in the world naturally expects a large place in the Church. Selfish, and sometimes even vicious men import into the religious community methods which savour of the caucus and the exchange. In a society of regenerate persons the only distinctions which can be recognised without peril are those which result from character and spiritual discernment; in other words, which result from the recognition that some have given more generous hospitality to the Spirit of God than others.

These three truths, then, may be called the foundation-stones on which the Congregational fabric has been raised:—the personal leadership of the Divine Spirit; regenerate character the condition of reception into the Church; the brotherhood of all believers.

(IV.) The Pilgrims from the first held that the Bible, interpreted by the Spirit to each individual, contains all the truth that is necessary to righteousness in this life, and salvation in the future. Loyalty to the Word of God as interpreted by the Spirit of God characterised those who founded the Free Churches, and that loyalty has been equally prominent in their descendants. The Independents differed from the Puritans, in the time of Cromwell, not so much in their loyalty to the Bible as in their insistence on the duty and privilege of private interpretation. The Presbyterian and prelatical churches by their representatives presume to extract from the Word of God its meaning, to put it into other forms, and to insist that their interpretation shall be accepted as of inspired authority. The Thirty-nine Articles and the Westminster Confession are the statements of what Episcopalians and Presbyterians believe to be the teaching of the Word of God. Congregationalists as a whole have never had any general Confession. The Savoy Confession never had any such relation to the Independent churches of England as the Westminster Confession has had to Presbyterian churches of England, and the world. The Creed which appears in the Year-Book of the Congregational Union of England and Wales is expressly said to be published only as a statement of what is *believed* to be the doctrinal position of the churches. Few local churches in England have formal Confessions of Faith; but there is as great loyalty to the Word of God in Congregational England as in Presbyterian Scotland. The first article in the unwritten creed of Congregationalists affirms that every individual Christian may open his heart to the Divine Spirit, and by him be led to the knowledge of the truth.

The Spirit may guide to the adoption of different forms from those which are prominent among us to-day, but the time will never come in which Christians will not be spiritually receptive in proportion to the earnestness of their consecration to God; in which they will not recognize that the Christian Church is composed of the brotherhood of believers, that the whole Church may be trusted, that only the regenerate should compose it, and that the written Word contains all the truth that is necessary for the life that now is and to lead to that which is to come. These principles are not formulated, nor is their acceptance made a condition of fellowship. Where there is real loyalty to the fundamental truths of the Christian revelation, our polity necessitates toleration of the opinions of others. That is inevitable where men believe that the Spirit works in His own way leading the pure in heart to knowledge of the truth. Hence even in the terrible struggles of the Puritan Revolution, when Cromwell and his Independents came into power, the right of all to do their thinking for themselves was fully respected. The Presbyterian party desired to substitute the Presbytery for the King, and also the Presbyterian Church for the existing Establishment. It sought to change the rulers, but proposed to leave the government as it was. Cromwell and his Independents, on the other hand, sought to put in the place of the Establishment the recognition of the Spirit. Whatever abuses, harshness of judgment, and attempted tyranny of thought there may have been in those days received little countenance from the great Protector. After the battle of Dunbar the defeated expected severe treatment at his hands, but he told them to worship God as they pleased, only not to attempt to impose their forms on those who differed from them. "The new ideal of religion proclaimed the rights of the individual conscience; the new idea of the Church, its duties and obligations. The main matter was no longer uniformity, but reality—not organisation of religious forms, but the conversion of the soul and the regulation of life by truths directly believed and completely obeyed. And the significant matter is that, save on this ground, toleration can never be, and has never been, logically claimed and defended by a man believing religion to be true... The Independent idea is the only sure basis for a theory of toleration, and in practice its only complete realisation."*

There are many prophets in the modern Church, and the gift of prophesying seems to exercise itself chiefly in attempting to describe the Church of the future. These prophets speak in many tongues, words which at times are strangely contradictory. There will, no doubt, be a Church of the future. Some time the City of God will descend out of heaven and fill the earth. Nay! that city is already here, having descended when the Master came, and it is growing before our eyes, although they are so holden that it is not clearly discerned.

---

* Fairbairn, "Jubilee Lectures," pp. 64-5.

What its glory will be no man can foretell. Enough for us to know that the Church of the future will be not only a Church but a State in the spirit. Gradually the life of the Divine Spirit is becoming the life of humanity. At last the spiritual commonwealth and the spiritual church will be one.

In the meantime, with nothing of sectarian rivalry; in no confidence that our puny faculties can discern and hold all truth; with perfect toleration for those who, under the guidance of the one Spirit, are led by different ways, we, children of the Pilgrims, should be loyal to the principles which have come to us, which our fathers loved, for which they died, and which have played so large a part in the development of Christian history. We can best help to rear the Church of the future by giving full and consistent expression to those truths which most commend themselves to us, which are known as " Pilgrim principles," which have received the Divine approval in many ages and in many lands, and which in the future as in the past will help very much in hastening the coming of that Kingdom which is the " realisation of righteousness in the life of humanity."*

---

* Mulford's " Republic of God," p. 168.

II.
BEGINNING AND GROWTH.

"Our spiritual forefathers may not have been perfect men, but my impression is that, take them for all in all, neither the world nor the church has seen such men elsewhere in modern times."

—Dr. Robert Vaughan.

"Their blood was shed
In confirmation of the noblest claim—
Our claim to feed upon immortal truth,
To walk with God, to be divinely free
To soar and to anticipate the skies.
Yet few remember them. They lived unknown
Till persecution dragged them into fame
And chased them up to heaven. Their ashes flew—
No marble tells us whither. With their name
No bard embalms and sanctifies his song;
And history, so warm on meaner themes,
Is cold on this."

—Cowper.

"So no man is prepared to do justice to that intense religious element which gave its main peculiarity to the character of the Puritans, who has not faithfully studied those emotive forces which the peculiar conditions of that English life into which they were born had generated and brought to bear upon them."

—Dr. Henry M. Dexter.

II.

BEGINNING AND GROWTH.

ON the thirteenth day of July, 1891, there assembled in London, in the Memorial Hall, Farringdon Street, adjoining Fleet Street, and near Fleet "Ditch"—now completely covered over—the first International Council of Congregational Churches. Memorial Hall is on the site of the old Fleet Prison, in which many martyrs of liberty were confined, and from which they were led to the flames of Smithfield. Not far distant is all that remains of the Bridewell Palace and Prison—which may be called the birthplace of English Independency. Hardly more than a stone's throw from it is the City Temple, whose first pastor was Thomas Goodwin, near to which "Richard Baxter ascended to the Saint's Everlasting Rest,"* and "John Bunyan fell asleep in Jesus."

The Council convened in the large hall. At the back of the platform was a stained-glass window

---

* Joseph Parker, D.D., Address International Council, London, 1891.

representing the Sailing of the Pilgrim Fathers. Here and there, their folds peacefully intertwined, were draped the flags of many nations. On the platform and in the assembly were delegates from every part of the world,—representatives from the ancient churches of England, from the American churches, from Canada and South Africa, Australia and Japan, Madagascar and Tasmania, New Guinea and India,—all nations and all races were there. That first International Council represented a world-wide and constantly developing spiritual power.

The contrasts of the occasion were many and striking. One hundred and one Pilgrims left the Old World for New England in the *Mayflower*, suffering for many weeks at sea the cold and storms of winter, seeking a place in which they could worship God according to their consciences. One hundred and one of their descendants from the richest land under the stars made the reverse journey in a single week, on a summer sea, in comfort and luxury. There were delegates from lands undiscovered when the Pilgrim Fathers sailed for New England. Black men, red men, day-labourers, and millionaires, sat side by side. Ten days were passed in mutual fellowship and conference concerning the affairs of the Kingdom; then the Council adjourned, and its influence, still as the movement of light, went forth among the churches. The contrast between those meetings, in such an environment, and the time when in the same districts the fires were burning at Smithfield, and the Bridewell and Clink were crowded with those who were charged with no crime save loyalty to conscience and fidelity to Christ, was inspiring and encouraging. That International Council is our starting-point in an attempt to sketch the beginning and growth of modern Congregationalism.

The churches which to-day have missions in every land, have come to their present position of greatness and service by a road stained with tears and blood, lighted by martyr fires, and along which have echoed shrieks of anguish, mingled with thanksgiving and praise. Beginning from that Council we might go backward, step by step, along the way which has been traversed by the churches of our order from the days of the Apostles. Or we may avail ourselves of the study of others, and starting from the childhood of the Christian Church, advance step by step to the present day. For our purpose the second course is preferable.

Dr. Bacon, in his "Genesis of the New England Churches,"* says: "In the beginning Christianity was simply Gospel." When Christ came He found a church—the Jewish—already existing. He said very little about doing away with the old church or founding a new one. He promised to be with the two or three gathered in His name, and that is His

---
* Page 17.

most distinctive teaching on the subject. The passage in Matthew about dealing with offences, and the reference to St. Peter, are all that the four gospels contain on this point. Only twice is the word "church" used by the evangelists. There are frequent references to the founding of a kingdom, but few to the founding of a church. The Kingdom of God is the perfect state which our Lord in His own person brought to the earth; the Church the means by which that Kingdom is advanced. The Master gathered about Him a few ignorant men, who were yet capable of responding to spiritual attractions, impressed them with His own personality, trained them by His example and conversation, left them, so far as we know, no written word—but many facts and truths well known, to which they were to testify,—disappointed all their earthly hopes, and then, having promised them in clear language the leadership of the "Spirit of Truth," He was crucified. That was the beginning of the Christian Church. In the modern sense of an organised society, with doctrinal tests of membership and elaborate rules and ritual, there was no church: there was a company of people—believers, disciples, brethren, apostles—devoted to the Teacher. There seems to have been some organisation among the Twelve, for Judas was the treasurer. Beyond that there are no signs of a society; only of a brotherhood. There were no formal articles of faith, no covenant, no rules of order, but there were strong beliefs, bonds of love, the words of Jesus, and the mighty attraction of the person of Christ. Because they must needs live they appointed one of their number to manage their finances, as a company of students often select a fellow-student as steward of the commons.

Directly after our Lord went away the idea behind the word "church" became more distinct. At first it referred to the company of believers who were united to Him by faith and love, and by love to one another. As years passed converts were made in various localities. One characteristic of those early Christians is conspicuous. All who lived in one city met together and had all things in common. Even then the Early Christians were a spiritual democracy. They had officers, but there is no recorded command as to how those officers should be appointed. They recognised the duty of mutual helpfulness, and they met together for the purpose of being instructed in the things of Christ. The Apostles could not be with them all the time, therefore teachers were appointed. But the teachers could not also manage the finances, therefore deacons were appointed. Thus gradually and naturally the new life began to assume appropriate, simple, efficient, social form. Dr. John Brown of Bedford says*: "The early churches were simply brotherhoods of believers exercising self-

---

* "Historic Christian People," p. 120. Address before Congregational Union of England and Wales Oct., 1891.

government under the over-lordship of Christ, the laws of Christ being administered by officers chosen by themselves." In the early Christian document known as "The Teaching of the Twelve Apostles" the brethren are thus charged : "Appoint for yourselves bishops and deacons worthy of the Lord, men who are meek and not lovers of money, and true and approved."

Two things are evident concerning these early churches. First, the officers were nominated or "appointed" by the Apostles, but elected by the people ; and, second, there was but one church in one city. In this statement there is reference only to organisation,—there were often many places of meeting, while there was but one fund for the common use, and one Bishop for the common administration. "The organised church in the primitive age of Christianity was always a local institution—never national, never provincial or diocesan. . . . . Each local church was complete in itself, and was held responsible to Christ for its own character, and the character of those whom it retained in its fellowship."* In that age no one church had authority over another. When the church in Antioch appealed to that at Jerusalem it was not in recognition of a right to dictate, but as seeking more reliable knowledge. It was a request for information. Yet the churches in many lands and many cities had a

---

* "Genesis of the New England Churches," Bacon, p. 25.

bond of unity, and that bond was neither creedal, liturgical, nor governmental, but the common life of love and service which followed acceptance of Christ as Master and Lord. Moreover, for membership in those churches nothing was required except evidence of genuine repentance, a confession of faith in the Lord Jesus Christ as Master, and willingness to receive the rite of baptism. In the Apostolic period there were no complicated organisations, no formulated creeds, no express covenants, no superior officers—save the Apostles. The church in each place was a brotherhood of believers. The simple life of the early Christian communities has undergone startling changes. Such changes were to be expected. That early fellowship of believers of which hints are given in the "five hundred brethren," and the "one hundred and twenty" who were commanded to "tarry at Jerusalem," was in no sense an organised ecclesiastical body. It was simply the brotherhood of those who believed in Jesus, and from Him had received the Divine life. Our Master left His followers free men, evidently expecting that those who had the mind of Christ would adjust themselves to varying conditions in all lands and times.

The life of the Divine Spirit never has had uniform manifestation; that always has been as diversified as the men through whom it works. The process by which the simplicity of the early Church passed into the complexity of later ages may be quickly sketched. As the number of Christians increased, and it became impossible for all to worship in one assembly, additional places of worship were added. In turn there had to be readjustment of the relations of the worshippers. In each church there was also a necessity for more organisation, and, consequently, (as the "love of power" was not wholly eradicated) a tendency was manifested on the part of some to be "lords over God's heritage." When the Apostles died it was natural that the persons who had seen them and known them best should be consulted by the various churches concerning disputed questions of order and doctrine. Moreover, there is always a subordination of the country to the city. Thus the churches in small towns and outlying districts became subordinate to those in the cities, and the churches in the smaller cities, where the Apostles had been but a little time or to which they had written no letters, naturally turned to those in the larger cities. Thus gradations of rank and authority appeared. There was a whole century at least when the Bishop of Rome was no more than the ordinary pastor of a local church, and when the diocesan bishops had no existence at all. The outlying church districts coming under the influence of the larger cities gradually developed into what is now known as the Diocese, and Rome being the largest of all the cities and the centre of imperial power, the church at Rome became, by the process of evolution, the Imperial Church.

When it was proclaimed to be the religion of the Empire, Christianity as an institution was appropriated by the Empire, and thus began the long contest between Church and State, between spirit and form, which continued until the time of Luther, and indeed has continued until this day. While Rome remained the capital of the Empire the church of Rome without dispute was the chief church. But the secular power invaded and transformed the Christian community. The first churches were select and spiritual ; later they became comprehensive and secular.

"The increase of the external prosperity of the church and the decline of its spiritual life went on together. There were now [in time of Constantine] some eighteen hundred Christian Bishops, of whom about eight hundred were seated in the Latin province of the Empire. These rulers had not yet altogether emancipated themselves from the necessity of popular election, but such election was in process of extinction, and had already very much changed its character. The elections to the higher offices of the church—now that they appealed to the love of lucre and the aspirations of ambition— were more real, but were entirely governed by worldly considerations. Not only the inferior clergy, but senators, nobles, men of property, the common people, joined in voting the ecclesiastical dignity to some candidate, who usually desired it for the rank it gave him in the State, rather than from any religious motives. Often these elections were as riotous as the most angry political contests, and bribery and intimidation were called in to assist in the choice of the true successor of the Apostles."* At first the election of Bishops was in the hands of the people; then it was transferred to the clergy; then to the Pope; and then, as the wealth and power of the Church increased, the controversy began as to the right of appointment to the chief offices in the Church.

When the seat of the Empire was changed from Rome to Constantinople, the supremacy of the Roman church was threatened and it became necessary to find some other basis on which to rest its claim to authority. Then the primacy of Peter was put forward. He was asserted to have preached, and suffered martyrdom, in that city, and also to have founded its church; therefore, as our Lord had said that He would found His Church on Peter, it was maintained that the Roman should be the supreme and sovereign church. But the Emperors who had transferred the capital to the Bosphorus would not yield the primacy, and thus commenced the schism between the Eastern and the Western churches, or the Greek and Roman, which continues to this day.

---

* Parkinson's "State Churches," p. 68.

Long before this absorption of the Church by the State, episcopal authority had taken the place of the simplicity of the early Church. Its officers were no longer appointed by the people. Dependence on liturgies and creeds had supplanted dependence on the Spirit. At first the Church was composed of those who accepted Jesus Christ as Master, and held their hearts open to the leadership of the Spirit of Truth. All Christians who were resident in one place came together as naturally as drops of water. In proportion as they were near to the Master there was among them unity of spirit and life. "Where the Spirit of the Lord is there is liberty." It is often said that among rude and uncultured people liberty is impossible. In the childhood of the Church liberty was universal. Even in the second century the authority of the Church under Christ rested with the people. Tertullian is explicit on this point: "That which has constituted the difference between the governing body and the ordinary members is the authority of the Church." And in the same chapter he adds: "Where three Christians are, though they be laymen, there is the church."

Dr. John Brown says: "These early churches were very much like our own, made up of men and women of varied position, culture and enlightenment. Many of them were in humble life; some were even slaves; but all alike were held to be entitled to a voice in Church affairs, for, possessing a Divine life in their souls they were held to be the subjects of Divine enlightenment on spiritual things. . . By and by changes came. The simple Church life of the earlier time suffered sorrowful eclipse as transition from self-government to government by a hierarchy was slowly but surely made. The encroachments upon the liberties of the Christian commonalty were like those of a glacier moving inch by inch down the slopes of a Swiss valley. . . . First, as controversies arose which threatened to endanger the faith, creeds were formulised. Then jealousy for the formulised creed began to supersede watchfulness over the spiritual life, which had once been the bond of brotherhood. If a man held the creed he was deemed eligible for the Church whether he had the life or not. . . . One step prepared the way for another. It was next contended that if the Church had the truth she also had the Spirit, which those outside had not. Whoever therefore would be secure of salvation must come into the Church. And men did come in, not because they had found salvation but in order that they might get it. The natural result followed. Unspiritual, unrenewed men came into the fellowship, and holiness ceased to be the distinctive note of the brotherhood. . . Then, again, when the unity of the Church had come to mean unity of faith it was contended that the bishops were the appointed guardians of the faith, and that with the faith of the Apostles they had received the power and authority of the Apostles. By the time the second half of the third century was reached it was no longer sufficient to hold the Catholic faith in order to enter the Church. The supremacy of the Bishops must also be recognised; they must be obeyed. Thus the circle was now complete: The doctrinal faith is all-important. You cannot have Christ unless you have that: you cannot have that unless you are in the Church, and you cannot come into the Church except through the Bishop. So it came about that the Church, which was at first a community of saved men, became an institution for saving them, and the condition of salvation, was ecclesiastical submission. The authority, once in the hands of the people, thus passed over to the Bishops; the communion table was turned into an altar to which the people were denied access; the chancel was jealously railed off from the church, and so far as the government of the Church was concerned the Christian commonalty vanished out of sight."*

We have now before us the facts concerning the early Church, and the process by which it became complicated and corrupt. The Apostles taught that each individual may open his heart to the Divine Spirit; that all who do that become free men in Christ Jesus; that the Church is composed of those

---

* "Historic Christian People," pp. 12-14. Address before Congregational Union of England and Wales, 1891.

who are thus made free by the indwelling Spirit. The simple teaching of Apostolic times disappeared. The Church converted the Empire, and the Empire, in turn, conquered the Church—but could not kill the individual spiritual life. The new ecclesiastical system which resulted from the supremacy of the State over the Church, was a compound of Christian words, Pagan institutions and practices, and secular associations, methods and aims. Here and there individuals were sensitive to the Spirit, but in a gigantic mechanism there is no room for freedom and the assertion of individual rights. When strong souls attempted to speak the word which the Spirit had spoken to them, the wheels of the machine ground them to powder; but among the commonalty were many too insignificant to be noticed, and among the nobility some not too forward in speaking their thoughts, in whom the Spirit worked until the Reformation gave them freedom of utterance. But from Constantine to Luther it was 1200 years.

The Reformation was a protest against the assertion of spiritual authority by Rome; against the sacerdotalism which had little if any place for the Scriptures. Ecclesiastical principles, as such, did not come to the front. The Protestant Reformation was spiritual rather than ecclesiastical. The Church having been transformed into a secular organisation could be restored only by the co-operation of secular powers. The idea of absolute democracy in religion would have meant the same in the State, and that would not have been tolerated by the allies of Luther. It would have undermined the authority of those on whom he depended for success, and there is little evidence that he had thought much about questions of Church polity. He resisted the Pope as a representative of error rather than because the order and usage of the Church were unspiritual.

Yet, even before Luther, there was at least one prophet who spoke with no uncertain sound concerning the rights of the people under the guidance of the Spirit to think and act for themselves. In 1327 John Marsiglio, of Padua, published a book entitled "The Defender of Peace," in which he asserted the principles of modern religious liberty. "The *regulator* of the community he held to be the judicial or governing class, whose province it is to enforce the laws, but the *legislator*, or lawmaker, is, he says, 'the people or community of the citizens, or the majority of them, determining by their choice or will, expressed by word in a general assembly, as to what should be done or should not be done regarding man's civil acts.'"* He maintained that the true Church is the community of all who believe in Christ, for all—priests and laity

---

* "The Historic Christian People," pp. 17, 18, John Brown, Address before Congregational Union of England and Wales, 1891.

alike—are churchmen, because Christ redeemed them with His blood. If a man is to be separated from the Church he ought first to be judged, not by the priest but by the whole body of the faithful or their representatives. "'How is it,' he asks, 'that some unscrupulous flatterers dare affirm that every Bishop has received from Christ a plentitude of power even over his own clergy, to say nothing of the laity? The Apostles never presumed to arrogate to themselves any such authority. They who say this should be laughed at. They should not be believed, much less should they be feared, for the Scriptures plainly tell us quite the contrary. He is the successor of Peter and the rest of the Apostles who comes nearest to them in copying their lives and their holy manners.'" Marsiglio, like John the Baptist, was a forerunner; he was "the voice of one crying in the wilderness."

After him came John Wycliffe, Martin Luther, John Calvin, and the leaders of the new day. Luther asserted the right of private judgment and the duty of loyalty to conscience; and yet the truths which he proclaimed were not applied to the Church and the State by him, but by Calvin. Calvin organized a new ecclesiastical system, and Geneva became the centre of its propaganda. John Knox, Thomas Cartwright, and many of the English thinkers, after being associated with Calvin at Geneva, carried back to England and Scotland the new Presbyterian order. They sought to free the Church both from the supremacy of the State and from the Bishops, and at the same time to compel the State to protect and enforce the authority of the Church.

As the result of his contest with the Pope, Henry the Eighth became the head of the English Church. The difference between that Church under Henry and the same Church under the Pope was a difference only in the name of the organisation, and in that of its head. The English King took the place of the Roman Pontiff; otherwise the ecclesiastical system remained substantially unchanged. Henry contended for the liberty of England against the arrogance of Rome; but he did not attempt to secure to the English people individual independence in matters of religion. The work begun under Henry suffered eclipse in the time of Mary, and in her reign the Pope became again the head of the Church, while many of the Calvinists in the English Church took refuge in Germany, and there adopted the Genevan Prayer-book. But when Elizabeth ascended the throne the English Church once more, and finally, severed its relations with Rome.

The separation of the Church in England from the Church in Rome was one step in a long process. When it was taken new parties were gradually formed. Some thought that the Reformation had not gone far enough. The bonds had been cut between England and the authority of Rome, but not between England and what was regarded as the idolatry of Rome. The union of Church and State was not attacked, but various rites and usages of the Church sanctioned by the State were openly condemned. Thus began what is known as the Puritan Reformation. The otherwise splendid era of Queen Elizabeth—the most glorious in the history of Great Britain except the Victorian—is stained by terrible cruelty against those who refused to conform to the rules and ceremonies of the English Church. In 1558 Elizabeth ascended the throne, and the first act of Parliament in her reign was the Act of Supremacy, by which her headship of the Church was established. The second act of her reign was the Act of Uniformity, by which it was made sedition to question the Queen's spiritual supremacy. It was afterward made felony. Nonconformity was absolutely prohibited to Romanists and to Protestants alike. The Calvinistic refugees who returned from Germany found Elizabeth as "bloody" as Mary. Romanism was superseded by an equally persecuting Protestantism. The only alleviation in the tyranny was that the State resorted to hanging the victims of ecclesiasticism instead of burning them. The Thirty-nine Articles of Religion were agreed upon by Convocation in 1562, adopted by Parliament in 1571, and the Church of

England was then, by these and other Acts of Parliament, completely established by law, and continues so until this day.

At this point observe the difference between the Puritans and those then called Separatists. The Presbyterian-Puritans objected to many practices of the Church as to discipline, liturgy, ceremonies, but wished to simplify the Church according to the "pure" word of God, not to separate themselves from it. The name "Separatist" primarily distinguished those who insisted on separation from the world and sin rather than from the State Church. Quickly and logically, however, they insisted on the separation of Church and State, because they had come to believe that the union of the two was worldly and sinful. This distinction must be kept in mind. All the Puritans alike contended for pure doctrine and holy living; all were united in their opposition to what was merely formal in worship: but the Separatists were opposed to the union of Church and State, while the Presbyterians believed in that as loyally as did the friends of the Establishment. At that time the Separatists were few. They were called "Brownists" from one Robert Browne, nephew of Lord Burleigh—an eccentric, excitable, but able man, who preached and published the doctrine of nonconformity to the State. He was himself exiled to the Continent, but afterward returning, having made his peace with the Church and the

State, was given a "living," and died in the service of the Church. "The difference between the Puritans and the Separatists was wide, fundamental and irreconcilable. It involved nothing less than the whole question of enforced or free religion; of religion by act of the State, or freedom of conscience; of religion as an act of obedience to the rulers, or as an act of conscience toward God,—the difference, in truth, which separated and still separates the State Churches from the Free Churches all the world over." *

In the reign of Elizabeth the Separatists were comparatively few in number, and were easily persecuted and driven out by the State. There were the churches at Southwark, in London, and at Gainsborough and Scrooby; there were men like Robinson, Brewster and William Bradford, who led the people in their assertion of individual liberty, and preached the doctrine that the State had no right to interfere in matters of religion. But the Separatists did not quickly become a power in English life. With the death of Elizabeth, and the beginning of the reign of James I., began a long controversy between the King and the Parliament —Parliament fearing that James would attempt to restore the supremacy of the Roman Church, and gathering into its party all the Puritans of every kind. That controversy was continued after James died

---

* "The Pilgrim Fathers," Scott, p. 18.

and Charles the First became King. The conflict lasted during all the reign of that most unfortunate monarch, who seems at first to have been the dupe of his favorite, Buckingham, and always the slave of his own passions and prejudices, until, after eleven years without any Parliament, what was known as the "Long Parliament" convened, and there began the struggle which culminated in the overthrow and execution of Charles. The contest in the time of James and Charles was not between the Separatists and the Established order, but between the Presbyterian Puritans and Separatist Puritans on the one side, and the Established order on the other side. Knox in Scotland, and Cartwright in England, represented the ideals of Calvin in opposition to the ideals of the Pope. The English Church retained what were thought to be idolatrous rites and ceremonies, and the rule of the Bishops. The Puritan Presbyterians wished to do away with everything which reminded them of the supremacy of Rome. They decided to make a new church, but not to separate the Church from the State. "The conservatism which loves to preserve ancient institutions was arrayed against a conservatism which loves to preserve spiritual and mental beliefs."* Charles stood for the union of Church and State on the Episcopal basis. The Puritans wished to make the whole State Presbyterian, and they insisted on

---
* "The Puritan Revolution," Gardner, p. 132.

uniformity of doctrinal belief. The order of the controversy was concerning (1) papal ceremonies; (2) church government; (3) doctrinal beliefs: in all, the Scriptures *versus* the Pope. Charles wished an Episcopal State; the Puritans a Calvinistic State.

There were many other elements in the controversy, but those mentioned were the most prominent. When discussion and dissension grew into war, at first the Royalists were victorious; but, gradually, that hitherto hardly known country squire, Oliver Cromwell, destined to become the chief figure in English history, came into prominence. A rough and sturdy member of Parliament, captain of a troop of horse, colonel, lieutenant-general,—he rapidly attained ascendency by force of character and military genius. As defeat followed defeat Cromwell advanced the idea that the Parliamentary army was beaten because it was composed of inferior men. He organised a cavalry troop of Independents or Separatists,—a heterogeneous collection of Anabaptists, Congregationalists, Mystics, claiming freedom to serve God as taught in the Scriptures and by the Spirit. The troop grew to be the invincible "Ironsides" regiment, whose perfect discipline permeated the whole army. Step by step Cromwell became the leader of the Parliamentary side. It could not do without him. At length Charles was overthrown, and Parliament was supreme. Cromwell was then the acknowledged chief.

The Parliamentary forces were no longer a mass of unwieldy ignorance, but a gigantic debating society, a company of independent, self-confident, bigoted, but consecrated and splendidly disciplined men— although the last class in the world in which discipline would be supposed to be possible. In matters of religion, they stood for personal godliness, individual and direct fellowship with the Spirit, and, very soon, for the separation of Church and State, the necessity of which they had not at first appreciated.

The Independent members of the Westminster Assembly convened by Parliament in 1643, in which the Presbyterians greatly predominated, never declared in favor of Separation. They did not at first assert universal toleration. Sir Harry Vane, the republican nobleman of the Parliamentary party, a member of the Assembly, appears to have led the advance toward absolute freedom. He said: "The Province of the Magistrate is this world and man's body, not his conscience and the concerns of Eternity." Soon the public weal seemed to demand that Parliament, which had deteriorated into an assembly of busy-bodies, should cease to exist. It was put to an end by the Independents, or Separatists, under the lead of Cromwell. The Revolution, which had been a revolt against the unscriptural and popish practices of the Established Church, and which was led by those who sought to have a Presbyterian rather than an Episcopal State, was ended by the Independents, and resulted for the time in the separation of Church and State.

We are thus led to the beginning of what may be called Modern Congregationalism in Great Britain. Among a few obscure pupils of the Spirit, faith in liberty and individual reponsibility had always existed. They had ever insisted on the importance of the guidance of the Spirit rather than on obedience to ecclesiastical law. Long before their number was large enough to attract much attention in the State, these people had quietly promulgated their teachings, and been getting ready for their mission in the world.

The Separatists had established themselves in numerous little companies in England before the time of Cromwell. New England had already been colonized at Plymouth. Let us return to the movement which brought the Pilgrim Fathers to New England, always being careful to draw a sharp line of distinction between the Pilgrims and the Puritans. The Pilgrims were the extreme Puritans—they followed the principle of separation to its logical end.

As we have seen, Queen Elizabeth ascended to the throne in 1558. The first act in this drama was the assertion by Elizabeth of the primacy of the Throne in the Church; the second, the securing of the passage of the Act of Uniformity, requiring all persons to worship according to the State liturgies, and in the parish churches. In 1571 the work was completed by the adoption of the Articles of Religion, and from that day, the Church of England being completely established by law, we may conveniently trace that *Separation* which with more or less distinctness can be found through all subsequent English history, and never more so than at the present day. The contention of the Independents was that neither the Pope nor the English Queen was the true head of the Church, but rather the Lord Jesus Christ himself; that everything which He commanded should be observed, both in doctrine and ritual, and everything contrary to His word should be refused hospitality.

The first evidence I find of the organisation of the Separatists is in 1567, when a company of Christians is mentioned as meeting at Plummer Hall, in Laurence Poultney Lane, London. The meetings, held with the greatest secrecy, were discovered by the alert police; one hundred persons were arrested, and the minister and the deacon, with twenty-four men and seven women, were committed to the old Bridewell Prison in Blackfriars. This has been called the birthplace of the Free Churches. Richard Fytz, the minister, and Thomas Rowland, the deacon, died of the plague, in prison. In one form or another, however, the meetings were continued.

The next step brings us to Robert Browne. The Separatists were originally called, in derision,

"Brownists." Browne returned to the State Church, but there were others more faithful to continue the work. Robert Harrison preached the doctrine of Separation, until in 1580 it was made treason to worship except as prescribed by law. Then he escaped to Middleburgh, in Zealand, and became pastor of a church of refugees. He also wrote a treatise on True Church Government. In the country districts in England it was difficult to execute laws against illegal gatherings of people for worship, and the cause of liberty grew in secret places. The works of Browne and Harrison were published in Holland and surreptitiously circulated in England. In 1576 John Copping and Elias Thacker were arrested for distributing Separatist literature. After being imprisoned several years they were brought to trial, as the result of which Sir Christopher Wray, Lord Chief Justice, wrote that "they were condemned to die and were to be executed immediately, not waiting for the possibility of a reprieve."* They were interred in 1583 at Bury St. Edmonds. Their crime was that, while they acknowledged Elizabeth as Queen in civil matters, they looked to Jesus as sole Master in the spiritual realm.

The next names that meet us are those of John Greenwood and Henry Barrowe. Both were men of fine culture and lofty character. In 1586 they

---

* "The Pilgrim Fathers," etc., Benjamin Scott, p. 23.

were incarcerated in "The Clink," a prison in Southwark. While there they wrote scraps of manuscript which were secretly conveyed outside, sent to Dort in Holland, and there printed and circulated. Barrowe and Greenwood were executed at Tyburn in 1593. While they continued in prison (1586-1593) little companies of Separatists met in the open air, and in private houses in and around London, and in country districts. They had among them twelve or fourteen expounders of Scripture, and conducted their services in the simplest manner. One of their meeting-places was the house of Roger Rippon in Southwark, who in due time was arrested and imprisoned with many others. In 1589 there were fifty-nine persons in various prisons, and these united in signing a petition to Lord Burleigh, setting forth their hardships and pleading for a fair hearing. Associated with them was one Francis Johnson, originally a clergyman, who had been converted to Separatist principles by reading the books which he had intended to destroy, and who still later, 1592, was associated with Greenwood as pastor of the Separatist church in Southwark.

From the darkness of those terrible times, when independent thought was a penal offence, and the worship of God according to individual conscience more likely to be punished than robbery or murder, another name rising into light is that of John Penry. He was educated at Oxford, and his crime was the terrible heresy contained in these words: * "That men by whomsoever ordained—whatever prelate or bishop or presbyter's hand had been upon them—who did not do the work of an evangelist, but neglected to preach God's word to the people, were no true ministers of Jesus Christ." When charged with having used these words he replied: "If it is heresy I thank God that He has taught it me from His Word." Archbishop Whitgift answered: "I say it is heresy, and thou shalt recant it." "Never, God willing, so long as I live," was the reply. Nothing gives a clearer idea of the bigotry of those otherwise bright Elizabethan days than the fact that a man of a spirit so exalted, having fled to Scotland, should have been followed thither by an autograph letter to the Scotch King from Queen Elizabeth, insisting on his extradition. He was charged with treason, and in 1593 condemned to death. The character of John Penry may be judged by his answer when pressed to save his life by recantation: † "If my blood were an ocean sea, and every drop thereof were a life unto me, I would give them all for the maintenance of this my confession. Far be it from me that either the saving of an earthly life, the regard which I ought to have to the desolate outward state of a friendless widow and four poor fatherless children, or any other thing, should enforce

---

* "The Pilgrim Fathers," Benjamin Scott, p. 26.
† Penry's "Protestation," Land's MSS.

me, by denial of God's truth, to perjure my own soul." John Penry was the last Separatist to suffer martyrdom for his faith.

Thus in merest outline we have followed the Separatists from 1567 to 1593. The idea of escaping persecution in some foreign land originated with Barrowe and Penry, the former of whom left a legacy "to aid the persecuted church in the event of their emigration"; while Penry in his last letter urged the brethren "to prepare for banishment in an unbroken company." Francis Johnson, already referred to, petitioned Lord Burleigh in 1593 that the members of the church in Southwark might have leave to emigrate. In 1597 we find the Brownists, falsely so-called, petitioning under that name the Privy Council to be allowed to go to Canada. Permission was given, but restricted to the island of Ramea. The voyage was unsuccessful. The ships "Chancewell" and "Hopewell," were not suffered to land. Some of the voyagers went to Newfoundland and some went to Holland. Francis Johnson became pastor of those pilgrims in Holland. John Smyth, a fellow of Cambridge and pupil of Johnson, after having been imprisoned for his views, was liberated because of ill-health, and he, retiring to Gainsborough in Lincolnshire, founded there in 1602 a Separatist church, and became its pastor. A second or branch church was established at Scrooby in Nottinghamshire, on the borders of Yorkshire.

The meetings were held in the Manor House occupied by William Brewster. In April, 1608, the church at Scrooby had been brought into some order, and in that month Brewster was fined £20 as a Brownist. The first pastor of the church at Scrooby was the venerable Richard Clyfton. In 1608 persecution became unbearable, and the little congregation, with their pastor and teacher, determined to flee to Holland, at that time the freest country in Europe. Amid dire distress, and much cruelty inflicted by the officers of the government, at last the refugees succeeded in reaching Amsterdam. While in that city if they assembled by themselves for worship, instead of meeting with their brethren who had previously reached there, they had the same officers as at Scrooby. But when they determined to make another removal, Clyfton, being aged and infirm, decided to remain in Amsterdam. After halting for about one year in that city the Scrooby people moved to Leyden, where John Robinson was elected successor to Richard Clyfton in the pastoral office. Brewster, who had been received into the church at Scrooby under the ministry of John Robinson, went with the Pilgrims to Holland in 1608, and then came with them to the New World in 1620.

The story from this point is well known to all students of American history. The three most conspicuous leaders among the Pilgrims were Robinson, Brewster and Bradford. In 1620 that little company of heroes, possessing the spirit of Apostolic times, crossed the North Atlantic and landed in the New World to face the terrors of a New England winter. They were not Presbyterian Puritans. Those remained in England, having no conscientious scruples against a State Church, although quite as much as the Separatists opposed to Episcopacy and all usages and ceremonies that seemed to have a Roman flavor. In less than a decade, however, the oppression became so severe that many of the Puritans also felt compelled to leave England, and these coming to the New World founded the Massachusetts Colony.

The English colonies in the New World were established in the following order: First, the colony in Virginia in 1607, whose settlers were exclusively Episcopalian. Second, the colony of the Pilgrim Fathers at Plymouth in 1620, who were Separatists. Third, the colony at Salem and Boston, planted by Puritans in 1630, that party having in turn come under the persecuting hands of Laud. "It was these Puritans of Boston who contended for Church-and-State connection, who passed the act against the Quakers, and were guilty of whippings, brandings, tongue-piercing and selling into slavery; which cruelties have been ignorantly charged to the account of the Pilgrim Fathers." * Later, the Puri-

---
* "Pilgrim Fathers," Benjamin Scott, p. 40.

tans themselves were converted to Separatist principles; but when they came to the New World they believed in a State Church and tried to found one here.

The Pilgrims, compared with others of their times, were broad and liberal men. They emphasized individual responsibility and the right of private judgment in religion. What they asked for themselves they accorded to others. The Puritans, on the other hand, emphasised the authority of the State, and tried to coerce individual thinking and acting into harmony with ecclesiastical rules ordained by a secular society. Roger Williams was expelled, not by the Pilgrims of Plymouth, but by the Puritans of Salem and Boston. He was received by the Pilgrims, and by them given generous and Christian hospitality.

After the death of Cromwell and the restoration of the monarchy, Charles the Second at first granted religious toleration, and the friends of liberty had great hopes of better times; but soon he dropped his mask and attempted by force to suppress freedom of thought and worship. That, however, was an impossible task. Liberty had been won by the splendid eloquence of Pym and Hampden, and the more splendid victories of Cromwell, and was too firmly established to be overthrown. The Protector died and his work seemed to perish; yet it did not perish. The principles for which he fought continued to spread. Toleration, even when established by law, was not kindly received by large classes of the English people. The Church and the State seemed to belong together. Those who dissented were regarded with suspicion and distrust: but they were earnest, strong, consecrated men, although somewhat fanatical. They had in them the stuff of which heroes are made.

From the time of the Commonwealth there has been advance, but it has been by no means rapid or constant. At one time the "old Dissent" was drowned in rationalism, in Arianism, in Unitarianism; and but for the "Evangelical Revival" Congregationalism in England would have become nearly extinct. After the Restoration, Independents and Presbyterians became practically one. Under the Toleration Act they held meetings in private houses, and by the year 1700 had built a thousand meeting-houses. Soon after this began the decline. Those who acted on Presbyterian principles largely fell away into Arianism and Unitarianism; but those who acted on Independent principles kept to the faith, and felt the impulse of the new life kindled by Wesley and Whitefield, who labored under the shadow of the toleration won by the fathers of independency. The "Evangelical Revival" commenced about 1770, and the life and strength of Modern Congregationalism is the outcome of that Revival. At the same time the old principles have been more fully asserted, and religious liberty gradually extended, in opposition to the dominant Church.

But liberty has been won at great cost. The Separatists have had to pay dearly for their faith. Even to this day their ministers are unrecognised by the State, save as the Toleration Act protects them and their meetings. This statement applies to all dissenters. The Nonconformists combined are more numerous than the adherents of the Establishment; and yet in the eye of the State there is but one Church, and that the Anglican. The Congregational was the first Nonconformist denomination in Great Britain. A little later, and a part of the same movement, came the division into the regular Congregationalists and Baptists. The growth of the Baptist Church finely illustrates the power of the principle at the basis of Congregationalism,—each individual must think for himself. Some men finding in the Bible, as they believed, that our Lord taught immersion as the true and only mode of baptism, made that an article of their faith. The Baptist branch of the Congregational churches exists because men have thought and acted for themselves. In England the branch is much smaller than the trunk; in the United States, vastly larger.

Step by step, however, the advance toward liberty has been made. Parliament makes now no religious tests of membership. The Universities are now open to Nonconformists. The descendants of those who two centuries ago were cast out of the Established Church, fined and imprisoned, and who three centuries ago worshipped in barns and caves and were executed for loyalty to conscience, now form great and honoured branches of the Christian Church. On this side of the Atlantic, children of the same martyrs and witnesses founded our Republic, and started influences which are transforming all the nations. The upper-middle class in England largely belongs to the Established Church, because of its "respectability" and prestige; the lower, to the Congregationalists and Methodists. Of late the Free Churches have been gathering the "masses" rather than the "classes," seeking to influence the democracy of the future, and they are succeeding to a surprising extent. They have colleges at many important centres. Even into the midst of Oxford itself has gone Mansfield College, which has already proved a potent force in the life of that great university. Fytz and Rowland were the first martyrs; Barrowe and Greenwood were executed as criminals; Penry was torn from his wife and children and brutally murdered because of his loyalty to truth as he understood it;—but in these days the successors of Fytz and Rowland, Barrowe, Greenwood and Penry, sit in Parliament and have prominent places on Royal Commissions. Their churches are among the most splendid in the Kingdom; they have an assured position ; their influence has permeated all the life of the State, and the missionaries whom they are sending are leading the English armies around the world, and going where the English armies do not go.

Originally the Puritans and Pilgrims in England were intensely Calvinistic. Knox in Scotland and Cartwright in England were 'pupils of Calvin. The Genevan theology inspired the Puritan Revolution. The " Invincibles" of Cromwell were theologians of a severe type. Gradually the theology of the Independent churches has undergone a change, and the steps in the process are not difficult to trace. First, there was the influence of rationalism, 1720–1770; second, the influence of Methodism, 1800–1856,—Wesley exerting a more positive and lasting influence than Whitefield; and third, there has been the effect of recent activity in science, criticism, and the study of sociology. The best elements of the old Calvinism remain—such as loyalty to the Scriptures, to conscience, to the living God and the person of Jesus Christ : but, with increase of knowledge ; with a clearer understanding of the Word of God, with the pressure of social problems; and, most of all; under the guidance of that Spirit which the Pilgrims have always honoured, and to which their hearts have always been open, have come larger conceptions of the Fatherhood of God, a more vital realization of the life and teaching of Christ—of the redemptive purpose of His work, of His spiritual presence and power,—a truer appreciation of the brotherhood of man, and a deeper conviction of the duties and responsibilities necessitated by clearer views of these regulative facts. Congregationalism in England to-day is not Calvinistic, but it was never more distinctly evangelical,—never indeed so distinctly evangelistic. Its leaders seem inspired with almost Apostolic earnestness, and not since the days of the Apostles has the truth of Christ been proclaimed with greater enthusiasm and more convincing power than in its pulpits. But the doctrinal tendencies and pulpit peculiarities of these churches will be more carefully examined at a later stage of our study.

It is not our purpose in this connection to trace with care the development of Congregationalism in the United States. At first there was the contest between Puritan and Pilgrim principles in New England. The Puritans soon became Separatists, and the dividing lines nominally disappeared. A longer time, however, was required to accomplish the actual unity of the two parties. Indeed it may almost be said that the line of cleavage between the Pilgrim and the Puritan exists until this day. The Puritan emphasises authority—the authority of organisation and fellowship; the Pilgrim emphasises individuality—the duty of each to open his heart to the Spirit of God, and "stand or fall to his own Master." The Puritan principles lived longest perhaps in the State of Connecticut, where for a while there was union of Church and State, and where the Consociation differed but little from the Presbytery of regions farther to the West. One of the earliest ecclesiastical controversies in this country concerned the Half-Way Covenant, by which citizenship and membership in the church were made synonymous; but that was a relic of the older controversy between Pilgrim and Puritan. In the old days it was often said, even at Andover and New Haven, that New England belonged to Congregationalism, while the Middle States and the West should be left to the Presbyterians; but those who spoke thus little dreamed of the proportions to which this Republic would grow. The institutions which the Pilgrims founded have moved northward to the Canadian line and westward to the Pacific. As men have been educated and trained to independent thought they have in all lands asserted the truth for which the Separatist contended in the old battle with the Establishment, namely, that each man is individually responsible to God alone for his faith and worship.

The Congregational churches have multiplied and extended themselves over America. The Methodists, the Baptists and the Presbyterians are more numerous, but it must not be forgotten that Congregationalism is primarily a principle and not an organisation. Its growth and influence cannot be estimated from the membership of the churches which bear the Congregational name, even when it is remembered that Baptists are Congregationalists. Congregationalism is an atmosphere, or, perhaps better, it is like the invisible forces of nature, whose presence is detected only by the changes which they work. Its influence is seen in the decadence of the supremacy of the episcopate in Methodism, and in the growing independence of the individual church. Its progress is seen in the gradual transformation of the Presbyterian denomination, in which there is appearing the recognition of the fact that however much the local churches may combine for aggressive work no power can force into uniformity the thinking of their members. The movement in Presbyterianism on both sides of the water, first, for the revision of the Westminster Confession and then to supplant it with a short and credible creed, is distinctively a triumph of Congregational principles. If the Presbyterian churches of a whole State were to become nominally Congregational the victory would not be more evident.

It has been said that democracy in church polity will do very well in the Millennium, but not before. On the contrary it is the polity for men who think, and who recognise individual responsibility, here and now. It has been called "a rope of sand," but no carefully welded ecclesiastical chain holds its members more closely to pure religion than does that "rope of sand." Prophetic fingers in our time point toward a day in which union in organisation will be subordinate to the unity of the spirit and yet realised through it; in which men will act and think as they have light and guidance from the Spirit of Truth; in which the principles that impelled the Pilgrims to leave their fatherland, and for which Barrowe, Greenwood and Penry suffered martyrdom, will have a large and regulative influence on all ecclesiastical thought and life.

This study of the Beginning and Growth of modern Congregationalism has brought into clear outline certain great facts. Of the Puritan Revolution Carlyle says: "I will call it a section once more of that great universal war which alone makes up the true history of the world—the war of belief against unbelief! The struggle of men intent on the real essence of things against men intent on the semblance and forms of things."* By that sentence Carlyle has illuminated the heart of the controversy between Independency and a State Church. It has been all along a part of the great struggle between belief and unbelief—between reality and appearance. The Separatists, the fathers of modern Congregationalism, believed in the sovereignty of God, the deity of Christ, and the immediate touch of the Divine Spirit on the human spirit. To them

---
* "Heroes," p. 189.

the life of the spirit was the only reality. Because they believed that could they open their hearts to God and have Divine guidance they cared little for human leadership. They were men with a Calvinistic creed, and they believed in the Bible as few men have ever believed in it; yet they believed, too, in the right of each individual to interpret the Bible for himself, and to do his own thinking. The Presbyterian Puritans believed also in the Book, but in it as interpreted by Calvin, and they attempted to compel all others to think as they did. Since the Restoration they have had a small place and comparatively little influence in England. Scotland has been the home of the Presbyterians.

The text which inspired the faith and fortitude of our fathers more than any other is, "Ye have an unction from the Holy One, and need not that any man should teach you." They laid broad and deep the foundations not only of a new social order, but also of a new spiritual order. They were the progenitors of that modern progress in theology which is not satisfied with negations, but is positive and constructive.

In England the Separatists were more conservative of the old Calvinism than the Presbyterians, for the latter fell away into Unitarianism, and yet the doctrine of the Independents made them tolerant. Their God was too great to be fully comprehended by any school of thinkers. "Religion is never intolerant, but only religious systems."* The Plymouth Pilgrims had a home for Roger Williams, and chose for their military leader one who has been supposed to have been a Roman Catholic. Sternly Calvinistic themselves, they yet insisted that the Word of God is the sufficient rule of doctrine and of life, and that the Holy Spirit is its only true interpreter. As a necessary result there is a wide divergence of theological attitude manifest in their descendants. Among them emphasis has been placed upon the spiritual life rather than upon uniformity of doctrine. Those who study the ways of spirit do not forget that as the Divine Life in nature has myriad manifestations—reverberating in the thunder, flashing in the lightning, rolling in the sea, blooming in the flowers, bending in the fruitage of the trees, running in the animals of the field, singing in the birds, laughing in the joy of childhood and struggling in the strength of manhood—so the spiritual life of humanity, following the Divine impulse, will have equally diverse manifestations—appearing in profound studies of the infinite and eternal, rising in earnest prayers, voicing itself in anthem and oratorio, going out in sympathy for the weak and the afflicted, and planning enterprises for bringing the whole world under the dominion of the Master. Spirituality necessitates individuality.

    The chief difference to-day between the Congre-

---
* Pfleiderer, "Development of Theology," p, 48.

gationalists and those who believe in stronger forms of government is, that the former have faith in the present efficiency of the Living Spirit, while the latter have more confidence in His manifestation once made to those who are now dead than in His continuous ministry. They are sure that God came, but not sure that He is always coming to His people. Yet, if Robinson, Greenwood and Penry were guided by the Spirit of God, why may not the same guidance be expected under these serener skies, and in this era of unexampled progress? The fathers believed in the immediate touch of the Divine Spirit, and their children can show their loyalty to the fathers in no way so well as by keeping their hearts open and their minds pure that the same Spirit may dwell in and inspire them. We know not what the fathers believe now; we know what they believed three hundred years ago. The light and beatitude of Heaven must have wrought great changes in their knowledge of God and of His universe. In His own time the Spirit will lead their children to clearer visions and ampler knowledge.

The Separatists—the men of Southwark and Scrooby, the men of the " Mayflower " and of Plymouth—were men of faith and of prayer. Whenever they undertook a great work they turned to God for His guidance. Carlyle says of Cromwell:*
" All his great enterprises were commenced with

---
* " On Heroes," p. 201.

prayer. In dark, inextricable-looking difficulties his officers and he used to assemble, and pray alternately for hours, for days, until some definite resolution rose among them, some ' door of hope,' as they would name it, disclosed itself. Consider that. In tears, in fervent prayers, and cries to the great God to have pity on them, to make His light shine before them."

Cromwell and his soldiers were the brethren of those who first fled to Holland for freedom, and who crossed the sea to lay broad and deep the foundations of American civilisation. When the Pilgrims were about to sail from Holland they gathered in the cabin of the " Speedwell," (a vessel afterwards abandoned as unseaworthy), and their pastor, John Robinson, who was to remain behind, commended them all unto the care of Him who holds the winds and waves in His hands. The prayer of the Pilgrim pastor seems to have rested like a benediction on that company. Its answer he never saw. Its answer is not yet complete. When the " Mayflower " anchored in the harbor of Plymouth, and Pilgrim feet for the first time trod those sands, William Brewster knelt on the shore of what was then an unknown wild and invoked the blessing of Almighty God on the work then undertaken. To read the answer to that prayer one must travel from the Atlantic to the Pacific, from the Lakes to the Gulf, and he will see it in churches and schools, in colleges and universities, in villages and cities, in seventy millions of population among whom is almost realized the ideal of " a Church without a Bishop and a State without a King." For as the years passed, other colonies came to the New World. The spirit which had asserted independence in the Old World reasserted it in the New. The inspiration of the American Revolution came from the Pilgrim churches. Their preachers were prophets of the new day. They were men who believed in God, and in the manifestation of His power in the affairs of men.

The history of the Pilgrims—both in England and in the nation which they founded and their children have preserved on this side of the Atlantic—is inseparably associated with their faith in prayer and in Providence.

The Pilgrims sought to realise a high ideal of the Kingdom of God. The ideals of Rome and Geneva were of a gigantic State in which the spiritual should unite with and control the secular. The Separatists received their name because they heard and heeded the command : "Come ye out from among them, and be ye separate." Nevertheless, they recognised the Divine authority of the State. They were neither Anarchists nor Socialists. Their contention was that the sphere of the State should not dominate the sphere of the Spirit. Their conception of the Kingdom of God was of a kingdom of righteousness embodied in the lives of individuals and States. They taught that the first step toward that result would be taken when men were made true to conscience and loyal to the truth of the Bible as it was interpreted by the Spirit of God. Their heroes were Moses, Elijah and Isaiah; their favorite reading, the writings of the Hebrew prophets. They were prophets themselves.

To promote righteousness, first in the individual and then in humanity, was the object of our Lord. For that He came; for that He died; for that He ever lives. Righteousness is the life of God; it must be the life of the children of God. That ideal represents the Kingdom as vital rather than mechanical. It is entered by spiritual birth rather than by baptism. The Established Church sought to make men righteous by bringing all to uniformity in certain rites and ceremonies. The Presbyterian-Puritans sought to hasten the Kingdom by the strong arm of the law; they attempted to coerce the thinking of spirits which God had made free. Browne and Greenwood, Barrowe and Robinson, were far from mild or entirely Christlike men in their speech or conduct; on the other hand, they were often harsh, and sometimes, possibly, cruel; but their times needed strong men; and they championed a truth which has revolutionised society,—that the only way in which a man can be made righteous is for him voluntarily to submit his will and open his heart to the Spirit of God. An inspired man, a God-breathed man, in these days as in all days, will be a prophet, a priest, a righteous man.

The Separatist ideal of the Kingdom was that of a kingdom of righteousness made real through the ministry of the Spirit. The splendor of that ideal is gradually becoming more clearly recognised. The dominion of the State over the Church is in many lands practically a thing of the past. Where it has not ceased its days are numbered. Men must think for themselves. Conscience knows no master but its Author. The human mind cannot be fettered. It is an emanation from God. It cannot be bound, but it may be illuminated. The Pilgrims trusted the Spirit without so to present truth to the spirit within that it would be self-evidencing.

Not in forms and ceremonies; not in creeds and confessions; not in councils and assemblies; not in laws against heresy, nor in complicated machinery of organisation for aggressive work, is the hope of the future; but in the fact that, more and more, free men are coming to recognise that they have the sublime and inviolable privilege of seeking and realising the guidance of the Spirit of Truth. As the fathers who went before us, as the Apostles and prophets of earlier times, we may open our hearts to the Spirit of God; by Him may be inspired, may voice His messages, perform His ministries, in the midst of time, twilight, midnight and sorrow, until all enter His life and rejoice in His love, " until the day shall dawn and the shadows flee away."

It is written in the Prophets,—" They shall all be taught of God." That prophecy is nearer fulfilment in our time than it has ever been before; when it ceases to be prophecy and describes what actually is, the Kingdom of God will have come upon the earth.

III.

CHURCH AND STATE.

"Every one of the Church is made a King, a Priest, and a Prophet under Christ, to uphold and further the kingdom of God, and to break and destroy the kingdom of Antichrist and Satan. The Kingdom of all Christians is their office of guiding and ruling with Christ, to subdue the wicked, and make one another obedient to Christ. Their Priesthood is their office of cleansing and redressing wickedness, whereby sin and uncleanness is taken away from amongst them. Their Prophecy is their office of judging all things by the Word of God, whereby they increase in knowledge and wisdom among themselves."—ROBERT BROWNE.

"The main ground for settling episcopal government in this nation was not on any pretence of Divine right, but the conveniency of that form to the state and condition of this Church at the time of the Reformation."—BISHOP STILLINGFLEET.

"The highest authority was in the people, or whole body of Christians: for even the Apostles themselves inculcated by their example that nothing of any moment was to be done or determined on but with the knowledge and consent of the brotherhood (Acts i. 15; vi. 3; xi. 4. xxi. 22). And this mode of proceeding both prudence and necessity required in those early times."—MOSHEIM.

"In the first ages of its history, while, on the one hand, it was a great and living faith, so, on the other hand, it was a vast and organised brotherhood. And, being a brotherhood, it was a democracy."
—EDWIN HATCH.

III.

CHURCH AND STATE.

A STUDY of Pilgrim principles would be incomplete without an examination of the relation between Church and State in England. The religious problem there is very different from what it is in the United States. In America the voluntary system is universal; in England, however, the Church is as much a part of the government as the Crown, or the Judiciary. The three estates of the realm are not, as is sometimes erroneously supposed, the Crown, the Lords and the Commons, but the Lords Spiritual, the Lords Temporal and the Commons.

The Church is the State on its spiritual side, and the State is the Church on its political side. All the officers of the Church are officers of the State, and are not amenable to any authority inherent in the spiritual body, but to the spiritual powers inherent in the State. The Queen is the head of the Church because she is head of the nation. The Church as such has no voice in the conduct of civil affairs. There are Convocations, Congresses and

Lambeth Conferences, Archbishops, Bishops, Deans, etc., but these are all for the discharge of duties clearly defined by the civil power. Moreover, the ecclesiastical authorities are all appointees of the civil authorities. The reverse is never true. The Bishops never designate the occupant of the throne, but the reigning monarch always determines who shall be Bishop. The King may be an infidel, or a debauchee, and still have the responsibility of appointing the most distinguished and important officials of the Church. That difficulty is not theoretical. The throne expresses its will through the Prime Minister, and more than once both Sovereign and Prime Minister have been men utterly unfit for the discharge of such duties.

Moreover, the laws governing the Church are made and executed by the law-makers of the kingdom—the Houses of Parliament. The House of Commons represents the whole realm, and its members are returned not only by members of the Established Church but also by Jews, Agnostics, Roman Catholics, and the various Nonconformist churches; and men like Charles Bradlaugh, Henry Labouchere, John Morley, Randolph Churchill, the Duke of Marlborough and the Marquis of Queensberry, have a voice in the decision of spiritual questions. Even the Parsee Member of Parliament from Finsbury has a vote in determining the action of the Established Church, of which he, by virtue of his political office, is a director.

In the ecclesiastical polity of England a man has no rights or privileges because of his regenerate character. His position in the Church, as in the State, is largely determined by his hereditary possessions. Nonconformist ministers of saintly spirit have neither place nor recognition in the State, and Nonconformist churches have no other standing than secular societies. A Dissenting pastor may not perform a marriage service without the presence of a Registrar. An ignorant and brainless curate is an officer of the State, while learned and venerable Nonconformists, like Dr. Dale or Dr. Allon, have no official standing.

The Establishment has not only the official recognition but also the prestige of wealth, authority and social influence. It has a monopoly of the royalty and nobility. Those who worship in the Episcopal churches look down, often superciliously, upon those who worship in the Nonconformist "chapels." The "clergymen" not infrequently assume a lordly bearing, while "ministers" in many localities are regarded by them as almost beneath contempt. This air of offensive superiority is by no means universal, and is far less common than it was a few years ago. In the cities, Nonconformity has made itself respectable. Its members have wealth, and, now that the Universities are open to them, culture also. Direct conflict between the Church and Dissent is no longer common. In many places the members of the dissenting churches have compelled appreciation; now and then they are called upon for important functions, and even appointed on Royal Commissions. And yet in the Church Congresses and other assemblies, words are often spoken even by distinguished prelates which show that the old animosity is by no means dead. In country districts, where the vicars and curates assume an almost divine authority, there is frequent ill-feeling, and sometimes open collision, while in Wales there is something resembling continual battle.

Let us now consider what may be called the Evolution of the Established Church in Great Britain. The date of the introduction of Christianity into the British Islands is unknown, and, as Parkinson says, "What account we have belongs rather to tradition than to history. Whence it came—at what period—to what extent it prevailed—are equally uncertain."* Christian churches existed in Great Britain without doubt before the arrival of Augustine (596). When the country was conquered by the Anglo-Saxons the Christians fled into the mountainous districts. "Britain," says Milman, "was the only country in which the conquest by the northern barbarians had been followed by the extinction of Christianity."† "And yet," he adds, "Christianity was driven to the mountain fastnesses

---
* Parkinson, "State Churches," p. 81.
† "Latin Christianity," Vol. II., p. 54.

of Scotland and Wales, and there it survived, a continuing, flickering existence." The history of the Church in Great Britain, however, really begins with the Pontificate of Gregory the Great and the mission of Augustine. Gregory was one of the four or five great Popes before the Reformation. His name must be ranked with those of Innocent I., Leo the Great, and Hildebrand. From the Church as introduced by Gregory and Augustine has descended the present Establishment. It has no relation to that which had existed in England a long time before. "It was born of the preaching of a monk, and its sponsors were a Pope and a King."

During the period between Augustine and the reign of Henry the Eighth the Roman Church was supreme. It converted the people *en masse*, not by a change of heart, but by winning the rulers, and then inducing them to command the conversion of their subjects. The first sermon of the monk Augustine "was a procession of ecclesiastics in the presence of Ethelbert's court; one bearing a silver cross, another a picture of the Saviour, the rest chanting litanies. The key-note of English ecclesiastical history is here sounded. It is not the willing conversion of a people to the religion of the New Testament; it is the transition by law from Paganism to Popery."* " The ecclesiastical system ' was built on the lines of the State.' The bishoprics

---

* Parkinson, "State Churches," pp. 83 and 84.

were commensurate with the kingdoms. The bishop was a magistrate of the shire, and 'he took his seat in the national council, or Witenagemot.' "* In this way Christianity was established in England. The kings of the separate nations were converted, and then they delivered their people to the Church "in blocks" to suit their fancy or cupidity. From that time to the reign of Henry the Eighth, Rome was in the ascendant in England. The civil rulers were often jealous of the spiritual, and between the two there were frequent outbreaks of violence; but the advantage was all on the side of the Church, for, however brave the King might be when facing his Bishops, he dared not defy Rome. The courts of the Church soon became more powerful than the courts of the State. The reason for this was that for disobedience the former were able to threaten not only temporal but also spiritual penalties. As a result, the civil rulers often sought the co-operation of the spiritual authorities in order that the edicts of the State might have greater force; and in turn the spiritual authorities demanded the co-operation and support of the civil rulers. " The power of the Ecclesiastical Court varied according to the strength or weakness of the character of the reigning sovereign; but it gradually increased until it became an intolerable despotism. It declared its supremacy over the temporal power." † With the growth of the spiritual power,

---

* Parkinson, "State Churches," p. 89.   † *Ibid*, p. 85.

there was also growth in riches, and the possession of wealth gave the Church ability to coerce the government. These things excited irritation, and the subsequent history of England is full of the records of the contest between Church and State which ensued. "Under the vacillating rule of John, the royal power bowed again to the claims of Church authority. The story is familiar, how the Canterbury monks with the sanction of the King designated the successor to Hubert—how Innocent III. overruled the election and appointed Stephen Langton—how the King violently maintained his right—how the Papal interdict imposed upon him the curse of the Church and freed his subjects from their allegiance—how the successor of Peter triumphed over the successor of the Conqueror, and compelled him to submission—how all England was reduced to the Roman bondage—and how, in that dark hour of degrading superstition, the Barons won from the impotent tyranny of the King the concession of the Charter which was the foundation of English liberty."*

To attempt to trace with more care the growth of the Church before the Reformation is quite unnecessary. It should not be forgotten, however, that even preceding the time of Henry many, like Wycliffe and his followers, were great and strong enough to dare to preach a spiritual Christianity of as high and pure a

---

* Parkinson, "State Churches," p. 93.

type as that which inspired the Reformation under Luther and Calvin. It is of much importance to our subject that the fact should be kept in mind that the present Church Establishment owes its origin to Augustine the monk and to Gregory the Pope, and that the claim which the Anglican Church has sometimes made that it is in a direct lineage from Apostolic times cannot be maintained.

In the reign of Henry the Eighth the Reformation was in the air. Luther had defied the Pope, and Calvin had founded his theocratic State in Geneva. It may well be doubted whether Henry, if he had lived two centuries earlier, would have dared to take the step which he did, for he possessed little of the spirit or principle of a reformer. The truth, when plainly told, is that the present English Church Establishment owes its existence to the anger of a corrupt and sensual king against the Pope, because the latter would not sanction the divorce of the King from Catharine of Aragon, and his marriage with Anne Boleyn. "The existence of the Church of England as a distinct body, and her final separation from Rome, may be dated from the period of the divorce." * Mr. Lecky speaks of the Anglican Church as having been "created in the first instance by a court intrigue." † Dr.

---

* Bishop Short, " History of the Church of England," p. 86, Sixth Edition.

† "History of Rationalism." Vol. II., p. 193.

Stubbs, the Bishop of Chester, says: "In the general legislation of the Church the English Church and nation had alike but a small share; the promulgation of the successive portions of the Decretals (the letters written by the Popes for the determining of matters of controversy, and having the authority of law) was a papal act to which Christendom at large gave a silent acquiescence; the Crown asserted and maintained the right to forbid the introduction of papal bulls without a royal license, both in general and particular cases; and the English prelates had their places, and the ambassadors accredited by the King and the estates had their right to be heard in the general council of the Church. But except in the rare case of collision with national law the general legislation of Christendom, whether by Pope or council, was accepted as a matter of course."*

Before the reign of Henry the Eighth, the State had been under the dominion of the Church. At that time the Church as a separate organisation had no existence. After the so-called Reformation under Henry it was a separate, independent National Church, " having no connection with the Church of Rome; declaring in its articles that some of the distinctive doctrines of that Church are 'blasphemous fables and dangerous deceits,' and regulated

---

* "Constitutional History," Vol. III., p. 348.

in all its procedure, as it was founded, by the action of the legislature.*"

In 1532, the Statute of Citations was enacted, which made it impossible for the King's subjects to be summoned to the Archbishop's Court in London except at the request of the Bishop of the diocese. The next Act, 1533, attacked the authority of the Pope himself. It was called "An Act for the Restraint of Appeals," and was passed in order that Queen Catharine might be prevented from appealing to the Pope. The next Act, in 1534, made Henry the head of the Church, because it provided that all persons should make their appeals "immediately to the King's Majesty of this realm in the Court of Chancery, in like manner as they used afore to do to the See of Rome." † Following this was an Act which provided that the appointment of Bishops should be in the hands of the King; and that Act remains to-day as in Henry's time, and is a curious specimen of ecclesiastical mummery, for it provides that the Dean and Chapter of the Cathedral Churches, where there may be a vacancy, shall proceed to the election of the officers to be chosen, in accordance with a letter missive which they will receive, but they must always elect the person whose name is suggested by the Crown in the letter, under the penalty of a *præmunire*. In 1539 a statute was

---

* "Case for Disestablishment," p. 34.

† *Ibid*, pp. 35-36.

passed authorising the King to create new bishoprics. Then followed, in the same year, a statute by which the places of the Bishops in the House of Lords were determined, and that statute is still in force—the Archbishop of Canterbury sitting next to the Lord Privy Seal, who is the vicegerent of the King. The most important of these Acts, perhaps, was that by which the King assumed the headship of the Church, which was passed in 1534. Before Henry's time the Church had been supreme, and had practically manipulated the State ; but he asserted the supremacy of the Crown, and presumed to be the judge of the doctrine, discipline and government of the Church, and since then the Church has been simply a department of the civil government.

Under Queen Mary there was a recurrence to papal control, but with the ascension of Elizabeth the authority of the English sovereign was reasserted and permanently established. Her first Act restored to the Crown the jurisdiction over the State, ecclesiastical and spiritual, abolishing all foreign power repugnant to the same. Then followed the Act of Uniformity, 1559 which re-imposed the use of what is known as the "Second Prayer-Book of Edward VI." In 1571 the Thirty-nine Articles were adopted as they now exist. The penalty for not complying with the provisions of this Act is stated in the following words : " Every such person which shall not do as is above appointed shall be, *ipso facto*, deprived, and all his ecclesiastical promotions shall be void, as if he then were naturally dead."

The long contest resulting in the Puritan Revolution, the part which was played by Cromwell and the early Puritans, and the rise of the Separatists, need not be again traced, for, while they broke they did not destroy the continuity of the Establishment. The Church was re-established under Charles the Second, and as such has continued until the present time. Passing, then, the period of the Puritan Revolution, we come to the Act of Uniformity of 1662. That Act provides as follows: " To the intent that every person within this realm may certainly know the rule to which he is to conform in public worship, and administration of sacraments, and other rites and ceremonies of the Church of England, all and singular ministers in any cathedral, collegiate or parish church or chapel, or other place of public worship, shall be bound to use and say the morning prayer, evening prayer, celebration and administration of both the sacraments, in such order and form as is mentioned in the said book annexed and joined to the present Act, and entitled ' The Book of Common Prayer.'"* That Act, still in force, made the English Church practically what it is to-day. Two thousand ministers resigned their positions rather

---

* " The Case for Disestablishment," p. 44.

than conform to the Act. Concerning them, Green says: "With the expulsion of the Puritan clergy, all change, all efforts after reform, all national development, suddenly stopped. From that time to this the Episcopal Church has been unable to meet the varying spiritual needs of its adherents by any modification of its government or its worship. It stands alone among all the religious bodies of Western Christendom in its failure, through two hundred years, to devise a single new service of prayer or praise." *

Since the State and the Church are one, it follows as a matter of course that membership in the one implies membership in the other, and hence we find Hooker saying: "There is not any man a member of the Commonwealth which is not also of the Church of England." † And the author of "The Case for Disestablishment" quotes the *Times* of October 9, 1876, as saying: "The fact is that all Englishmen are, by law, members of the Church. It is about as difficult for any Englishman to separate himself from the Church of England as it is for the Church of England to separate itself from him. Indeed, practically, there is no such act, form, or way of separation." ‡ It is well known that the late Dean Stanley was in the habit of speaking of Dissenters as

---
* "Short History of the English People," p. 610.
† Ecclesiastical Polity," Book VIII., Sec. 2.
‡ "The Case for Disestablishment," p. 46.

"Nonconformist members of the Church of England."

From the supremacy of the State in ecclesiastical affairs it follows that the civil power has authority to create dioceses and new parishes, and within recent years many new Sees have been created by Act of Parliament, among them being Ripon, Manchester, St. Albans, Truro, Liverpool, Newcastle, Southwell and Wakefield. New parishes have been constituted in the same way, while church building is also a subject for State legislation. In 1818 no less than a million pounds sterling were set apart for the erection of churches.

Discipline in the Church of England is also determined by Act of Parliament. The "Court of Arches" is a State Court and its President one of Her Majesty's Judges. If an appeal is taken from that, it is not to the House of Bishops but to the Throne. The relation of Church and State has been well summarised in the following words: "In effect, therefore, the State controls the clergy of the Established Church by declaring what they must believe and teach, and how they must conduct their religious services; by appointing courts for the express purpose of hearing complaints against them; and by prescribing the penalties which are to be imposed upon them for any violation of the laws." *

The inquiry naturally arises, Has the spirituality

---

* "Case for Disestablishment," p. 51.

of the realm any power? Is there no Body which can speak for it? The Houses of Convocation, which are the assemblies of the Church of England for the consideration of ecclesiastical questions, have a nominal importance, and, probably, more or less influence legislation, but they are not courts of final appeal. They may convene only with the permission of the Crown, and they may pass no act without the consent of the Crown. They may not so much as discuss the amendment of a canon except with royal approval.

Convocation meets simultaneously with Parliament. England is under the spiritual superintendence of two metropolitans, the Archbishops of Canterbury and of York. Each district has its House, of which the Archbishop is the head. The House is composed of Bishops, Deans, Archdeacons, members of the various Chapters, and representatives of the beneficed clergy. Occasionally Convocation has attempted to assert its own rights, but has always failed. During the period between 1717 and 1861 no license from the Crown was granted to Convocation to proceed to business. It would meet and then be prorogued. The most it can do is to consider questions which concern the spiritual affairs of the realm, and then report them to the officers of the State for their approval or disapproval. An illustration of this is a request which was addressed to the Queen in 1865, praying that

Her Majesty would be graciously pleased to grant to Convocation her royal license to make a new canon, and to alter others on the subject of Clerical Subscription and the oath against simony. The reply of the Home Secretary stated that the government was willing to advise Her Majesty to comply with the prayer of Convocation, but as there was another bill before Parliament which might touch the case the government could not advise Her Majesty to take any definite action until it was known what course Parliament would pursue in the matters under consideration. This shows how absolutely Convocation is subject to Parliament.

Let us now turn to the laws which concern church property. The Church is one of the largest landholders in the Kingdom, and yet is not a corporation and cannot control its own possessions. The public property appropriated to the maintenance of the Church of England includes " tithes, and land set apart in lieu of tithes, glebe lands, the episcopal and capitular estates, the ecclesiastical edifices, and property in the hands of the Ecclesiastical Commission and the Corporation of Queen Anne's Bounty. In addition there are also local rates levied under special Acts of Parliament." * The tithes are a charge imposed by the State for the maintenance of the Church Establishment. They were originally received into a common fund for

---

* " The Case for Disestablishment," p. 54.

the fourfold purpose of supporting the clergy, repairing the churches, relieving the poor, and entertaining the pilgrim and stranger. Originally they were collected in produce: since 1836 there has been substituted a tithe-rent charge, which is chiefly devoted to the maintenance of the clergy. All the bishoprics and cathedrals are endowed, and many churches carry with them large incomes. The cathedrals form an important part of the public property appropriated to the use of the Church. Hon. Arthur Elliot, M. P., says: "It would be absurd and impossible to put a money value on the cathedrals, churches and chapels of the Established Church. At the same time it would be to give a very false notion of the position of the Church toward the State to omit all mention of the sources from which, as regards its edifices, the Church of England finds itself so magnificently endowed. In the main the wealth of the Church in this respect was inherited, or rather acquired, at the time of the Reformation, from the Roman Catholics, who had created it. The Roman Catholics and the English nation had been formerly one and the same. When the nation, for the most part, ceased to be Catholic, these edifices, like other endowments devoted to the religious instruction of the people, became the property of the Protestant Church of England, as by law established." † It has been estimated that

---

† "The State and the Church," p. 98.

the value of Church property in England is about £220,000,000. This property is held by the State and managed by a Board called "The Ecclesiastical Commission."

The disposition of this vast wealth has, as was to have been expected, resulted in abuses and in the growth of a worldly spirit. It is said, for instance, that Bishop Sparke of Ely, who owed his promotion to the circumstance of having been tutor to the Duke of Rutland, secured to himself, his sons and son-in-law, an income from different ecclesiastical positions amounting to £40,000 per annum. Prelates with from twenty to forty thousand pounds a year lived sumptuously in splendid palaces, while beneath them were crowds of people almost on the border of starvation, ministered to by half-paid curates, who were little better than slaves. These abuses were so great that at last an investigation was called for, and the Ecclesiastical Commission was constituted in 1836. As a result, numerous Acts were passed looking toward the equalisation of salaries, and the wise distribution of monies. Even at present the Bishops can hardly be described in the language which was applied to the Master—"The foxes have holes, the birds of the air have nests, but the Son of Man hath not where to lay his head"—for the salary of the Archbishop of Canterbury is £15,000, and that of the Archbishop of York £10,000; the Bishop of London has £10,000, the Bishop of Durham £8,000, the Bishop of Winchester £7,000, and, all things included, probably no Bishop receives much less than £5,000 a year.

The Ecclesiastical Commission is now a Corporation, made such by Parliament. It is a State Commission, engaged in the service of the State. It holds the church property and determines its use. It may take from one diocese, or one parish, which it regards as too highly endowed, such property as it may choose and bestow it upon those which are more needy,—surely a wise provision, although a civil function.

That peculiarity of the Church of England which most unpleasantly impresses an American is "patronage," or the right held by certain favoured persons, not necessarily Christians, of determining who shall hold the ministerial office in various parishes. "The right of the Crown to nominate to episcopal sees and other dignities, is, apparently, made to rest on the same foundation as the right of lords of manors to nominate to lesser benefices; namely, that the founder, in the first instance, was the patron, and that the right to present ought to descend to his successors and heirs. Such is the legal theory."*

Originally, patronage possessed no money value, but in process of time positions in the Church became articles of merchandise, and are even advertised, and sold in the auction-room. Simony, or

---
* "The Case for Disestablishment," p. 82.

the sale of livings, became so great an evil that severe measures were taken against it. As early as 1603 persons appointed to "livings" were required to make oath that they had not bought them, and in 1865 to make declaration that they had neither directly nor indirectly done anything simoniacal in obtaining their preferment. And yet the traffic goes on, and, in spite of efforts at reform, patronage is sold like any other possession. It has been estimated that there are about thirteen thousand livings in the Church of England, and that of this number seven thousand nine hundred are saleable. The effect of such a system on both churches and ministers needs no description. Ministers who secure positions by such methods stultify their consciences, and if not absolutely untruthful, indulge in mental reservations destructive of honesty and moral earnestness; while it is impossible for people ministered to by such pastors to have confidence in either their moral earnestness or their integrity. Against this evil Bishops have thundered and laws have been enacted, but it still flourishes. When noblemen, conspicuously vicious, have it in their power to name vicars who will have the spiritual care of tens of thousands of souls, what can be expected except that the owners will dispose of this property in a way that will enable them to gratify their evil tendencies, since they use all their other wealth in that way? Patronage injures both the ministry and the people. In a large city of the Midlands is one of the most beautiful churches in England, situated in the heart of a dense and terribly needy population. It ought to be a source of blessing to thousands. But the people to be reached have no part in deciding who shall be their minister; neither has the English Church as a spiritual body, for it is powerless either to nominate or remove. The right to select is in the hands of a nobleman, living at a distance, who has neither sympathy with the people nor care for them, and who gives little evidence of being influenced, in making his appointments to the pastorate of the church, by motives other than such as will enable him best to realise his own selfish ends. If the Church of England were independent, and could legislate for herself, such abuses would disappear. But it is part of the civil order, and in determining its policy the Bishops are almost as powerless as the people.

Subscription to the Articles of the Church of England, and to the Prayer-Book, was formerly a condition of holding public office, of entering the Universities, and of receiving degrees from them. The constitutional status of the Church of England, however, has been considerably affected by various measures passed since the Restoration ; the chief of these being the Toleration Act of William and Mary, 1689, the Roman Catholic Emancipation Act, 1829, the Jewish Disabilities Removal Act,

1858, and the Abolition of University Tests, 1870. Formerly, subscription to the doctrinal and ecclesiastical formulæ of the Church of England was a condition of entering Parliament, but that is no longer the case. Not until 1828 was the Act passed repealing previous laws which imposed the necessity of receiving the Sacrament of the Lord's Supper as a qualification for certain offices and endowments. Not until 1829 could Roman Catholics sit in either House of Parliament. Not until 1858 could Jews be admitted to Parliament. Not until 1866 did it become unnecessary to make and subscribe certain declarations concerning religion as a qualification for office. Not until 1869 were the governing bodies of Grammar Schools opened to all denominations. Not until 1870 were the Universities of Oxford, Cambridge and Durham freely accessible to the nation. Not until 1880 were services other than those of the Church of England permitted in parochial church-yards, and consecrated portions of cemeteries. And not until 1882 were Headships and Fellowships at Oxford and Cambridge Universities freed from clerical restrictions. Religious tests for public office, and public honour, have now been very generally abolished. The only honour which is still restricted to the Church is the degree of Doctor of Divinity, which is never by English institutions conferred upon any who are not members of the Establishment.* All Nonconformists who have received recognition for distinguished ability and achievement in theology have received it from Scotland, Germany or the United States.

This study of the relations between Church and State has disclosed a condition which is anything but satisfactory to those who live where an established Church is unknown. Theoretically, we may grant that Church and State should be one. That is but saying that the distinction between sacred and secular should disappear. Voting is as holy a service as praying; the discharge of obligations to the State is as important and as sacred as the performance of duties required by the Church. But wherever the Church and State have been united, corruption and injustice have prevailed. It has been so in France and Spain, as well as in England. There are no darker pages in French history than the persecution of the Huguenots; nothing more disreputable in the world's history than the attempt of Spain to secure uniformity in religious thought and conduct among her people. And English history, from the days of Boädicea to Victoria, records no acts more disgraceful than those by which the dominant power in the State has attempted to enforce uniformity of relig-

* Whether the degree could be conferred on any other than an Episcopalian, providing he were a resident of another country, I do not know.

ious thought and life. When humanity is perfect, the Church and the State may be one; until that day they must be independent. They cannot be coördinate, for in the nature of things the State must always be supreme in general legislation and control. It may, nevertheless, allow, as wise States always do, the utmost liberty of thought, worship, education, and the promulgation of opinion, so long as there is no interference with the common weal.

The Establishment, as such, has been a failure in England. The glorious results which have been achieved by the Anglican Church, have been in spite of, rather than because of, its union with the State. Its aim is to secure uniformity, both in belief and in worship, but there is as great diversity in doctrine and liturgy in the English Church as among Nonconformists. There is more diversity between the High Church party and the Low and Broad Church parties, than between Congregationalists and Baptists. Among its adherents every phase of religious opinion is tolerated, and almost all diversities of worship. The Establishment has failed in reaching the masses, for there are more Christians in England outside of the Establishment than within it, and the number of those who are non-attendants, both at church and at chapel, is so great as to deprive the champions of the Establishment of any ground of confidence in their system. The Establishment is a failure as a means of preserving the unity of the faith. A church which has had in its ministry within the last half century men of such contradictory teachings as Pusey and Maurice, Kingsley and Keble, Haweis and Dean Burgon, can lay little claim to success in preserving doctrinal purity, for the differences between these schools of thought are irreconcilable.

But there is another side to this subject, and the friends of Voluntaryism must not suppose that such broad and earnest men as Maurice and Robertson, Kingsley, Stanley and Farrar are loyal members of the Church of England, without good reason. They believe that the system, freed from its impurities and excrescences, is best adapted to reach the whole people; that only a State Church can be large enough to include all diversities of thought and life, and that loyalty to principle requires them to maintain that the State ought to bear witness to its faith. Their ideal of the Church is as broad as humanity, and has a place for all differences which are found in the State.*

It is argued, furthermore, that only a State Church can provide for the religious training of all the people: and there is reason for this contention. The traveller, whether he be among the bleak and barren hills of Wales, the smoke of the Black Country, or the luxuriance of Devonshire, is impressed by no fact more than that everywhere he finds the

---

* Gladstone, *Contemporary Review*, July, 1875.

Parish Church. And those churches are not little boxes built for a day, as if they were intended to fall down, but are, usually, large and architecturally imposing. Their walls are covered with ivy, which has been growing for centuries, and every pillar, every foot of the pavement, every window, yellow as gold or red as blood in the setting sun, is made sacred by memories which have been growing in that parish for generations. Around those churches the dead are buried; within them are recorded the heroic actions of those who at home and abroad, in science, religion and war, have done their part in helping to make England great. If the parish system were properly operated, I can see no reason why the whole people should not be reached and evangelised. A large and beautiful church in every parish, and the parishes arranged so as to preclude conflict, is surely desirable, and under any other system hardly attainable. The union of the Church with the State has been a blessing in providing religious privileges for the people, but it has been connected with so many abuses, and has been so unfortunately operated, that its excellences have been weakened or destroyed. If the State, without injustice to any, could provide houses of worship, and make it impossible for the crudities and puerilities of individuals to raise unseemly competition and controversy in things ecclesiastical, and then leave the administration of its affairs to the spiritual body, the history of the Church in future would record a constant series of victories.

There is, furthermore, an unquestioned advantage in general uniformity of worship as observed in the English Church. Every small town, and country district, has the same ritual that thrills and inspires, comforts and delights, those who have large wealth or fine culture in cities and university towns. Even when the preaching is poor, the lessons and the prayers, the litany and the hymns, never fail to stimulate Christian thought, and fittingly to express the devotion of those who desire either to praise or to pray.

Precisely because the Establishment has not been administered in a large and liberal way; because it has sought an impossible uniformity; because it has been managed in the interest of selfish and vicious rulers; because it has been the pliant tool of those whom it ought remorselessly to have condemned; because it has ground the faces of the poor, the Nonconformist denominations have had reason for their existence and been hastened in their growth. The Church of England, while larger than any other sect in the Kingdom, is considerably smaller than the various Nonconformist bodies united. The latter, however, are hardly more divided than the Establishment. Of the Dissenting denominations the oldest, and by far the most influential, is the Congregational, although the Wesleyan has already surpassed it in numbers, and is rapidly approaching it in influence. The third in size and importance among the Nonconformists is the Baptist. The Presbyterians, the Unitarians, the Quakers, all have more or less local strength, as have also numerous smaller branches of the great Methodist communion.

Until 1870, Nonconformists were excluded from the Universities. As a consequence England is dotted with Nonconformist colleges and seminaries. Now that the Universities are opened it is felt that these colleges are too numerous, and a movement has been started for their consolidation.

One peculiarity of the Nonconformists in England, necessitated by the fact that there is a State Church, is that even their religious life has a political bias. They have a double work: they bear witness to their loyalty to Christ, and at the same time to their faith that Christ's Church should be free. The strength of the Liberal Party is in Nonconformity. Mr. Gladstone's warmest supporters and most trusted advisers are many of them Congregational ministers, and men like Drs. Dale and Allon and Mr. Guinness Rogers, at times have largely helped to determine his policy. This political element in the Churches tends somewhat toward the secularisation of their methods. Those who are engrossed with political questions seldom have quite so much enthusiasm in evangelistic work. That English Nonconformists are as evangelistic as they are is a rare tribute to the vitality of their faith; and they are far more evangelistic than their brethren in the Church. On the other hand, opposition develops strength, and there is a rugged earnestness among Nonconformists which no doubt is largely the result of the conditions in which they have lived. Their people are often narrow, but always sincere. Shut out from the Universities, they have been compelled to seek liberal education in other ways; looked down upon by those in authority, they have been stimulated to prove their manhood by the quality of their work. Social distinctions and emoluments belong to the Church. It is rich, and its services are practically free. The Dissenters have to bear their proportion in the support of the State and consequently to do somewhat toward supporting the State Church, and in addition to build and sustain their own churches. Those who at such cost remain true to their principles are strong men, and strong men usually bequeath more or less of their characteristics to their children. The great middle class, "the bone and sinew" of Great Britain, are chiefly in the ranks of Nonconformity.

The theory that the State and Church should be one body is a beautiful one, and we may believe that it will be realised some day; but that day is far in the future. Not until the Lord is enthroned in the hearts of His people will those worthy to rule in the Church be called to positions of responsibility in the State. A Theocratic State is certainly very near to the New Testament ideal of the Kingdom of God; but the world is not ready for it yet, and thus far every attempt in that direction has been a dismal failure. The Hebrews tried it, and failed. The moment the Church in Europe was absorbed by the Empire it began to deteriorate. The Roman Catholics tried to unite the Church and the State by making the Church supreme, and they have disastrously failed. Calvin tried to revive the Hebrew ideal, and he also failed. The English Establishment has reversed the process, and is attempting to secure unity by making the State supreme, but with no better success. Every other experiment in the same line has proved that spiritual life grows more vigorously and beautifully where it is independent of civil authority. The fundamental idea of Christianity is that each individual may come into personal and vital contact with the Supreme Spirit. Union of the Church with the State presumes that the State is superior to the individual conscience, even in matters of religion. Until all are Christian the State must be composed of many not Christian, and who have an equal right with those who acknowledge the leadership of Christ in determining the nature and administration of political institutions. Their right is inalienable. But there is an inherent contradiction in the idea that those who are "worldly, sensual, devilish," should have a voice in deciding what Christians must believe, in what forms they must worship, and by what methods they should do their work. As men now are, the union of Church and State results in the weakening of both. This fact is becoming increasingly evident. The recent discussions in France have shown that the French people are nearly ready for the separation which must inevitably come. The history of religion in America, where the Voluntary principle has prevailed almost from the first, has proved that as fine and vital a type of piety is developed without State aid as where its riches and authority support the Church. And, even in the English Establishment, prophetic spirits are already beginning to recognise that Disestablishment is only a question of time, and not altogether undesirable.

And this leads to the question, Is Disestablishment in England probable? It has been hindered by many influences. The "Evangelical Revival," the indirect influence of Nonconformity, the diffusion of High Church principles, a growing sense of responsibility for the spiritual welfare of the nation, and, most of all, a far higher standard of Christian life among the leaders in the Church, have combined to delay the separation of Church and State. The

Church formerly was used as a kind of asylum for the younger sons of the nobility; and many who had no other outlook for a support in life were snugly, and often luxuriously, provided for in the priesthood without much regard to their moral character or spiritual efficiency. In this way there came into the Church incapacity, unspirituality, neglect, vice, and —what it is impossible for any genuine man to reconcile with common honesty—traffic in sermons. If the pulpit of the Established Church had been occupied by men worthy of their places the disheartening revelations of the last few years, the facts of which can be learned by reading the church papers —that ministers buy and sell sermons, using them as if they were their own—would not only never have come to the light, but never have existed. The traffic in sermons, the traffic in livings, and the misuse of the endowments which belong to certain departments of the Church, opened the eyes of the people, and those who honestly believed in the Establishment went to work with a will for its reformation. A more wonderful change than that in the English Church during the last quarter of a century can hardly be found in ecclesiastical history. The quality of its ministry has improved. Its pulpits are now largely occupied by earnest, aggressive and spiritual men. Prophetic spirits have arisen who have not hesitated to denounce abuses with an intensity worthy of the ancient prophets. I have heard Canon Farrar, appealing to the nobility of England, call them to witness that if they did not change their manner of living their memories would be as foul as those of their ancestors who were buried in the grand old Abbey in which he was preaching. Such preachers with lofty ideals of the Church and of the minister's vocation, have wrought a marvellous change, and have delayed the inevitable separation.

But in our day the agitators are not simply Dissenters. Many of the most intense and eager Episcopalians clearly see that Disestablishment is sure to come in time. The High Church party is restive under the dominance of Parliament, and with it are found also men, professing no religion, who see the incongruity of the alliance and its injustice to other denominations. The present Archbishop of York, Dr. McLagan, when he was Bishop of Lichfield, is reported to have said that the Church recognised the authority of the Crown and would be loyal to it, but as to the authority of Parliament, that was a very different thing. High Church men are rising to the conception that Jesus Christ is their only Lord, and that for unworthy and unbelieving men to presume to dictate how they shall worship, and how they shall work, is a species of tyranny not much longer to be endured. Even John Henry Newman, before he became a Roman

Catholic, saw that Disestablishment was inevitable, and declared that he welcomed its approach.*

The greatest difficulty in the way of Disestablishment seems to be in determining what is to be done with the cathedrals and the endowments. It is maintained on the one hand that both belong to the State, and should be given to the State; that the Voluntary system should be rigorously applied to all denominations; that the cathedrals should be used impartially, or, as some maintain, should be secularised, or be assigned to those churches which may be able to purchase them. There are undoubtedly questions of detail, difficult of adjustment, in the solution of this part of the problem. For myself, however, I can see no reason why the Nonconformists should not, gladly, unite in a declaration that the cathedrals had best always remain in the hands of the Episcopal Church. Its service alone is adapted to them; and its organisation embraces them. They would be of no benefit to others, and if the Church was once disestablished the cathedrals would no longer be, as they are now, used chiefly for an elect few, or for special spectacular services, but would become the meeting and rallying points of great religious movements which would start under the influence of the Voluntary principle. As to the endowments, that is a ques-

---

* See the Monograph on J. H. Newman by his brother, F. W. Newman.

tion which had best be left for adjustment until after the main principle involved has been settled.

The Nonconformists and the agents of the Liberation Society are regarded by some as prophets of discord, ministers of dissension and strife, enemies of the Kingdom of God. They are rather the prophets of the only principle by which the Kingdom of God in England can be realised. They are better friends of the Church than are the advocates of Establishment for when it is separated from the State there will probably be the greatest addition to the Episcopal Church which has ever been known in its history. The English people are devoted to their venerable institutions. Many who are loyal Dissenters love the Anglican ritual, and delight in the Episcopal organisation. Separate Church and State, and, if the evangelical rather than the sacerdotal party is dominant in its affairs, the chief reason for Dissent will disappear. I am neither a prophet nor the son of a prophet, but I am willing to predict that when the day comes, as come it will, in which there shall be separation between the spiritual and the civil powers in England, there will be such a movement from the chapels to the churches as has never yet been seen. Disestablishment will be the beginning of power for the Episcopalian Church in Great Britain.

One by one the bands that bind the Church and the State together are being broken. The Irish

Church is practically free. It cannot be long before there will be Disestablishment both in Scotland and Wales. Welsh Disestablishment is the second clause in the present Liberal programme, and the first steps towards the carrying out of that part of the programme have already been taken. When Mr. Gladstone passes away many will lift Disestablishment to the front who are unwilling to do so during his life. If he had fifty years more of active service, probably he himself, notwithstanding his early conservatism on this subject, would be a leader in the Free Church crusade. But he is too old to become the champion of new issues beyond the great one in which he is now so energetically engaged—the securing of Home Rule for Ireland.

A few years have witnessed many revolutions in England. The ballot is now in the hands of the people. Education is free and universal. With a free press, a free ballot, free schools, there need be only a free church to make England as free a nation as the sun shines upon. However long the struggle may continue, there is reason for thankfulness that it is not developing serious acrimony and strife, but greater activity and more splendid consecration. While the Anglican Church is now devoted to the advancement of the Kingdom of God at home and abroad, in city and country, among rich and poor; while she has such noble and honoured men in her conspicuous places, multitudes are more anxious to add to her efficiency than to expose her weakness. In due time Disestablishment will be realised, but unless all signs fail it will come at last hardly more because of agitation from without than as the result of the development of a truer spiritual life within.

IV.
THE PRESENT CONDITION.

"A Church is an association of the friends and followers of Christ for the profession of Christian faith, and the performance of Christian duty."—Dr. HENRY M. DEXTER.

"Congregationalism is an ideal polity. This is at once its reproach and its glory. The transcendent prerogatives and powers which it claims for the Church lie beyond the reach of Christian communities which are not completely penetrated and transfigured by the spirit of Christ. But as churches approach more and more nearly to the perfection to which Christ has called them, their authority becomes more and more august, and they enter more and more fully into the possession of the blessedness which is their inheritance in Him."—Dr. R. W. DALE.

"In the speculative delineations of this system there is something, to a free and generous mind, extremely fascinating. It supposes the existence of a virtuous brotherhood, confederated for the sublimest purposes, and acknowledging an almost universal equality of rights and privileges."—THOMAS BINNEY.

"If I might add a word on an immediately related question, it would be to the effect that our evangelism is in danger of devoting its energies almost exclusively to know what is known as 'the masses.' I must protest against this contraction, on the ground that it is as unjust to Christianity as it is blind to the evidence of facts."
—Dr. JOSEPH PARKER.

IV.

THE PRESENT CONDITION.

ECCLESIASTICAL systems, like individuals, to be understood should be studied in relation to their heredity and environment. All the Free Churches of England are materially affected by their nonconformity. A distinguished English Congregationalist, when asked concerning his impressions of religious life in the United States, replied that his first feeling was one of relief because he was in a country where he was no longer looked down upon as a Dissenter. Congregationalists, Baptists, Presbyterians, Methodists, and even Roman Catholics, in England are all " Dissenters," although by the Act of Toleration they are recognised as having a legal right to exist. The State, however, knows but one Church, and dissent carries with it more or less of the taint of conceit and narrowness. It is therefore important to remember that Independency in England, in its worship, theology, preaching, benevolences, is modified by its relation to the predominant State Church. It is a child of struggle and of war.

It had its birth in the stormy days which preceded the Puritan Revolution. Grim heroes like Cromwell stood sponsors when it received its baptism of blood. Those whose opinions are developed in persecution cling to them with a tenacity and intensity unknown in calmer times. The descendants of such people do not easily lose the qualities which were developed by the struggles through which their ancestors passed. A study of the heredity which has culminated in the English Congregationalism of to-day helps materially to account for its characteristic qualities and principles.

No man antagonises public opinion and existing institutions when there is nothing to gain, and everything but the consciousness of being right to lose, unless he is impelled by faith in a divine call. The early Separatists believed that Christ was the sole Lord of the conscience and the Church; and that each individual was responsible to his Master alone for his interpretation of the Scriptures and for his individual conduct. They believed that the Papacy was the impersonation of Anti-Christ, and if they carried their opposition to the extreme it was because they were convinced that it was a sin to make compromises with a Church which arrogated to itself claims which were both unscriptural and morally pernicious. That reverence for liberty and for the leadership of Jesus Christ; that sense of personal dependence upon the Spirit of God; that faith in the Spirit's illumination, and the consequent hostility to all attempts at dictation from the State, which distinguish the present generation of Nonconformists, are a heritage from their fathers. An English Churchman is attached to the service of his Church, and feels that worship for him is impossible except through its impressive forms. In the same way English Independents believe that acceptable worship and service are inextricably associated with those great principles of intellectual and spiritual liberty for which their fathers died, and the defence of which has been handed down to them as a sacred obligation.

The influence of environment in the development of Nonconformity is also equally evident. In England the royalty and nobility are almost all in the Establishment. Not yet has Dissent ceased to be a reproach. Nonconformist ministers are made to feel that they are endured rather than approved by the State. The Cathedrals, the ecclesiastical endowments, Universities, Parish Churches and the great schools, are in the hands of the State Church.

Only recently have even the newspapers begun to pay attention to services in " dissenting chapels." Nearly all the London dailies almost ignore Nonconformist assemblies. *The Times*, *The Standard*, *The Telegraph*, have notices of proposed services in the Established Churches, but only *The Daily News* finds much space for those in Nonconformist chapels.* Newspapers reflect popular sentiment. In the Provinces, however, many of the great dailies are conducted by Dissenters. The founders of the three principal papers in Yorkshire were Nonconformists, *viz*:—Baines, of *The Leeds Mercury*; Leader, of *The Sheffield Independent*, and Byles, of *The Bradford Observer*. Until 1870 the Universities were closed against Nonconformists, and if their children were sent to the Parish Schools they were trained in principles which were abhorrent to their parents. Consequently denominational schools and colleges were established solely because Dissenters could not patronise institutions supported by public funds without having their children indoctrinated with the religious teachings of the Established Church.

English Congregationalists are the descendants of a race of warriors who fought valiant battles for freedom of conscience and independence of State control. We honour the Pilgrims who faced the wintry sea, and the perils of an unknown continent, and laid in New England the foundations of a free State, but those Independents who remained in Old England, and held aloft the banner on which was inscribed "Freedom of Conscience: Freedom of Worship: Freedom of Speech" faced trials quite

---

* This was written in 1891. It is possible that a change in the attitude of the London papers toward Nonconformists may have been introduced since then.

as severe and fought battles quite as fierce as their brethren who took refuge in the New World. Their children live in easier times. Disestablishment may be far in the distance, but Dissenters are now numerous and influential enough to compel attention and respect. They are members of Parliament, and even of the Cabinet. In the municipalities—especially in the North of England—their enterprise and sterling character have led to their being chosen Councillors, Aldermen, and Mayors, in many of the large boroughs, more frequently than Churchmen. No political party dares to ignore them. They have grown in wealth, education, and social position, and now can well afford to care little for sneers and gibes which are manifestly inspired by prejudice. Socially, England is cleft in twain by the assumptions and exclusiveness of the Episcopal Church. The battle for freedom of thought and worship however is practically won, although much remains to be accomplished before the contest will be ended.

In the meantime ecclesiastical life is modified by the controversies of the past, and by the relics of old struggles which still remain. Even spiritual life, as has before been observed, is in many places more or less coloured by the ever-present political issue of Disestablishment. A Nonconformist minister has duties which concern not only the souls under his charge, but also other duties arising from the fact that he is bound to protest against the evils of a State Church. Of course many successful ministers never trouble themselves with politics; but as a rule Congregational ministers are active in all that concerns the welfare both of the Church and the nation. They are usually public-spirited, and also both liberal and progressive. The Wesleyans, with some striking exceptions, are much more absorbed with the administration of their polity, and have less time, and apparently less interest, in political affairs. "Clergymen" are devoted to "Church" work—which is not always Christian work—and are generally both conservative and exclusive.

This is the background against which we must study English Congregationalism. In numbers the various Methodists, if classed together, would constitute the largest dissenting denomination; but they are almost hopelessly divided, and at present the Congregationalists are second in numbers, and far in advance of all others in general influence. The members of their churches belong to the great middle class, but the "middle class" in England is gradually disappearing, and giving place to the increasing and rising masses of the people. While this "middle class" is not what it was thirty or forty years ago, it still has in its hands a large part of the wealth of the kingdom. It is composed of merchants, well-to-do mechanics and manufacturers. Many of the wealthy members of this class

THE PRESENT CONDITION. 131

have gone to the Church, for the sake of the social prestige which it confers. A common, if not a true, saying is, "He has lost his religion and gone to the Church." The dissenting churches, however are becoming identified with the "masses" rather than the "classes," and so taking the lead in the new democracy. During the last half century Dissenters have been able to secure the advantages of culture which before had been denied them. They have been educated in their own schools and colleges, and on the Continent. They were the real founders of the London University, which, while not a teaching university, is said to grant more degrees, and to have more thorough examinations for degrees, than Oxford or Cambridge. In London, Birmingham, Wolverhampton, Manchester, Liverpool, Norwich, Plymouth, and all the large cities of England, Congregational churches are strong, thoroughly manned, and doing an aggressive work along both humanitarian and evangelistic lines.

The Year Book of the Congregational Union of England and Wales for 1892 furnished the following figures: The number of churches, branch churches, and mission stations in England and Wales, is 4,652; the accommodation is estimated at over 1,666,000 sittings. There are 2,747 ministers in England and Wales; 8 theological colleges and seminaries in England, with 282 students and 38 professors and lecturers ; 3 colleges in Wales, with 92 students and 10 professors and lecturers. It is interesting to compare these figures with those of the Congregational churches in the United States, where in 1891 there were 4,817 churches, 4,619 ministers, and 506,882 communicants. The number of communicants in the English churches is not reported. In that fact is an illustration of the sensitiveness of many Free Churches, caused by the controversy between Church and State.* It is felt that inquiries concerning such subjects are an intrusion ; and that to give such information to a taker of the census, is an acknowledgment of the right of the State to enter the sphere of religion : consequently we have reported the number of sittings in the places of worship but not the number of communicants. In England and Wales 373 students are preparing for the ministry, and in the United States 577. In England there are 8 colleges and seminaries, nearly all of which are exclusively theological. In them students are usually received both for arts and theology, but instruction in the former is given in the Universities ; in the latter only at the colleges. In the United States under Congregational auspices there are 7 seminaries furnishing theological instruction only, and 27 colleges with both classical and scientific courses.

---

* An exception must be made of Yorkshire, and a few other Unions, from which a return of communicants is made. This sensitiveness is said to be passing away.

To the inquiry, What kind of work are the English Congregational churches doing? there are four answers.

First, that in the local churches, *i. e.* worship, preaching and teaching, and that which is done through guilds, Christian Endeavour Societies, etc.

Second, Foreign Missionary work, which is conducted in much the same way as in the American churches, by voluntary societies. Indeed, the points of resemblance are quite remarkable. The American Board of Commissioners for Foreign Missions was originally a union society in which various denominations co-operated. The same was true of the London Missionary Society. As the denominations in America have grown, one after another withdrew from the Board to carry on missionary work on denominational lines, until, in 1870, the reunion of the Old and New School Presbyterian churches occasioned the farther withdrawal of Presbyterians, and the Board, with a few individual exceptions, was left in Congregational hands. As the result of a similar process of self-elimination, the London Missionary Society has been left in the hands of the Congregationalists of England.

Third, the Home Missionary work. The organisation which aids feeble churches, plants new churches, and employs evangelists is called "The Church Aid and Home Missionary Society," and is a confederation of all the County Associations. At present

The Church Aid and Home Missionary Society is under the able and honoured leadership of its Secretary, Rev. W. F. Clarkson, but the principal work is done by the County Secretaries and Committees. Chapel Building is another important department of the general work. Much is also accomplished in the same direction by individual churches in London and the Provinces, of which The Church Aid and Home Missionary Society takes no account. Important churches usually have their mission chapels or schools, and often one or more evangelists. The English system of missionary work in almost all departments is the same as in this country,—carried on by means of local churches and voluntary associations of churches in each county and district.

But, *Fourth*, the distinguishing feature of the missionary activity of English churches is to be found in the great cities. The world offers no better illustration of what it is possible for Christians to do for the cities than is seen in the London Congregational Union, or Association, whose Secretary is Rev. Andrew Mearns, author of "The Bitter Cry of Outcast London." This Union is similar to other County Associations, and is confederated with them in the Church Aid Society. "The Forward Movement" had its origin in the publication of "The Bitter Cry," by Mr. Mearns, which is not remarkable for anything except its name and its fidelity in the narration of facts. The London Union faces the largest city missionary problem in the world, and "The Bitter Cry of Outcast London" was its first great appeal to the English people. The work of the Union is manifold, and probably more efficient for the relief of the "submerged tenth" than that of any other single agency, except possibly, the Salvation Army. Its headquarters are in the Memorial Hall, and in his management Mr. Mearns displays rare consecration and the qualities of a really exceptional leader. In London, in 1891, there were under the care of this society 180 mission-rooms and preaching stations, and 259 regularly constituted churches. This Union, while not neglecting East London, devotes its chief attention to the South, which the recent investigations of Mr. Charles Booth have shown to be even more degraded than the East. The centre of its operations is what is known as the "Mint District," in a hall called "Collier's Rents." In this work of the London Union there are many departments, *e. g.:* Poor Relief; Intelligence Offices—by which those out of service are helped to secure positions; a Committee by which those who have made a mistake in coming to the city are sent back to their rural homes; the Boot and Shoe Brigade—which provides children with boots and shoes in the winter, so that they may attend the public schools; the Penny Dinner department, through which those children who would otherwise suffer from hunger are furnished nutritious meals at cost price; the various Labour departments, in which Mr. Mearns anticipated General Booth; the Sunday Morning Breakfasts, to recruit which the streets are explored by intelligent and cultured gentlemen after midnight on Saturdays; and, most important of all, the distinctively missionary and evangelistic agencies. The various activities of the Congregational Union of London are even more worthy of study by those seeking light on social problems than Toynbee Hall, which is much more widely known.

The surging tides of vice and crime, the overcrowding in the great cities, the land problem, the ever present "Cry of the Children," the awful fact that millions on that one little island are living in conditions which almost touch the borders of abject degradation and starvation, make it all but impossible for the average Christian worker to devote much time to theological speculation; and, therefore, while among the ministers there is no lack of interest in theological questions, the chief and most persistent inquiries are, What may be done for men in this life? How may the poor be fed and the sick nursed? How may the Church and the State be saved from the attacks of vice, ignorance and crime? Consequently, schemes of missionary effort, and systems of speculative thought, are all coloured by the social condition of the people.

There is now much more earnest attention given to questions distinctly theological than there was a few years ago, but speculation in England almost always has relation to life. Few English pastors have much interest in the old controversies in theology; they are so busy with the social problems of to-day that they have little patience with those who preach of the Jews of ancient times, or dream of what may be in some far-off future.

In the days of the Commonwealth the Independents were strict Calvinists. In the present day Calvinism in its ancient forms is almost a curiosity in England. What has wrought this change? English theologians have not *thought* themselves away from the Calvinistic system. They have not very generally reached their present position as the result of critical study of the Scriptures. They hold their views concerning "the larger hope," and "life in Christ," chiefly because they are unable to believe in a God who would allow such conditions of misery as they see around them, and then sweep into a common gulf of everlasting perdition millions. born with tendencies to vice and crime too strong to be resisted.* I am not arguing

---

* The steps in the change in the doctrinal position of English Congregationalists may perhaps be traced as follows: (1) a process of reasoning; (2) the influence of Wesleyanism; (3) more extensive culture; (4) more sympathy with their fellowmen; (5) a consideration of life on the human rather than on the Divine side; (6) more stress on the fatherly love than on the sovereign majesty of God.

concerning the correctness or incorrectness of the theological opinions commonly held in the English churches, but rather calling attention to the fact that the misery of the multitude moulds and colours the thinking of both ministry and laity.

The present City Mission work of the Congregational churches in London, and the other great cities of England, is fearfully inadequate, and yet nothing more inspiring in that line can be found in the world. Hugh Price Hughes recently said: "It is insignificant in comparison with what is needed; it is magnificent when studied by itself."

The work of Church Aid and Chapel Building is retarded by obstacles inherent in the English social system. The "Bitter Cry" of the minister in the small towns and hamlets of England is just now becoming distinctly audible. It is the terribly bitter cry of poverty and social barrenness, and the English Free Churches have a serious responsibility on their hands in attempting to remedy these evils in the country districts, which have at last found a voice. That such circumstances exist is not to be charged to carelessness in the past, or lack of consecration in the present, but rather to the undue emphasis which has been placed upon the idea of "independency." The following are among the forces which have been the most potent in producing the present unfortunate condition: the lack of union and co-operation—each church too exclusively seeking its own prosperity;

the immense growth of the cities within the last fifty years; the depletion of the small towns and villages; the increase of activity and social ostracism in the dominant church. English Congregational ministers in the cities are not over-paid, and the churches are not extravagantly managed. The wail from the villages is the echo of the cry of poverty in the cities. The appeal should be answered not by large churches adopting different and more economical methods; not by curtailing the salaries of city ministers, but by more co-operation and new consecration on the part of the laity, in whose hands is the wealth.

Any study of Christian service in England which did not recognise Home and Foreign Missionary work, as distinct from what is being done for the great cities, would be inadequate. Home Missions are conducted by the County Associations confederated in the Congregational Church Aid and Home Missionary Society. The objects of this Society are officially stated as follows:

"1. To call forth the resources of the churches for wise and systematic use in Home Mission work.

"2. To assist churches which are unable to meet their financial requirements.

"3. To provide for a more adequate remuneration of ministers who are doing good work in necessitous districts.

"4. To enlist lay agencies for the preaching of

the Gospel in villages and remote places, and the establishment and maintenance of Sunday-schools.

"5. To form district auxiliaries for gathering information and administering aid.

"6. To increase the influence of Free Church principles."

At the best, statistics furnish a very inadequate idea of what is accomplished by any man or institution, and yet on statistics we are largely dependent for information. The amount of money expended in 1891 in grants for Home Missions was £23,298; 677 churches and 381 mission stations received financial aid. The churches under the care of this Society provide accommodations for about 210,000 hearers, and the mission stations for about 20,000.

The cause of Church Erection is in the hands of the Congregational Chapel Building Society,—and of other more local societies, as those (1) in Lancashire and Cheshire; (2) in Liverpool; (3) in Yorkshire, and (4) The London Congregational Union, or Association.

The London Missionary Society, which corresponds with our American Board, is now nearly one hundred years old, having been founded in 1795. Its sole object is to provide for the preaching of Christ in foreign lands. It sustains missions in China, India, South and Central Africa, Madagascar, the West Indies, Polynesia and New Guinea. The aim of the Society, adopted in 1796, is stated as follows:

"As the union of Christians of various denominations, in carrying out this great work, is a most desirable object, so to prevent, if possible, any cause of future dissension, it is declared to be a *fundamental principle* of the Missionary Society that its design is not to send forth Presbyterianism, Independency, Episcopacy, or any other form of Church order and government (about which there may be difference of opinion among serious persons), but the glorious Gospel of the blessed God, to the heathen; and that it shall be left (as it ought to be left) to the minds of the persons whom God may call into the fellowship of His Son from among them, to assume for themselves such form of Church government as to them shall appear most agreeable to the Word of God."

The income of this Society is not far from £121,455 per annum. It supports about two hundred English missionaries, and about twelve hundred native missionaries and pastors. In addition to these it reports about 4,200 native preachers, 69,000 church members, and 270,000 native adherents. But figures faintly indicate the work of such an organization. When we remember the men whom the London Missionary Society has sent forth—Medhurst, John Williams, Livingstone, Moffat, Gilmour, etc., and that it now numbers among its missionaries such men as Griffiths John, in China, and W. G. Lawes, in New Guinea, both heroes and scholars of great ability and lofty manhood, and that these are only types of scores of others, we realise that the English churches are not altogether occupied with social problems at home, and that among them no supposed laxity in theology "cuts the nerve of missions." In the autumn of 1892 the society sent out at one time thirty new missionaries, two or three of them pastors with a distinguished record at home, and these were but the first fruits of a great Foreign Missionary revival. During the past two years there has been a forward movement in Foreign Missions quite as notable as that for the relief of England's poor. Hand in hand these two movements have advanced, and those who have been most active in inspiring in the hearts of the English people a consciousness of their responsibility and privilege at home are foremost in their appeals in behalf of the unevangelised abroad.

In England, local churches are organised in substantially the same way as in the United States. The theory of the Church is the same. There is not, however, so much emphasis placed upon the fellowship of churches as in America. Councils are unknown, either for the recognition of churches, or for the ordination or installation of ministers. The Christians in a community who intend to unite in the formation of a church call for such aid as they desire, but that call goes to individuals as individuals, and not as representatives of churches. Until within about fifty years strong emphasis was placed upon the independence of the local church.

During the first quarter of the present century two tendencies in Congregationalism were plainly discernible,—the Conservative and the Progressive. The Conservative emphasised independence; the Progressive reached toward fellowship. For a long time all attempts to bring the churches into anything like systematic co-operation for aggressive work were looked upon with suspicion. Freedom had been won by long and bitter struggles, and the descendants of the heroes of Cromwell's time did not propose to receive into their camp any "Trojan horse" in which might be concealed enemies who would overthrow liberties so dearly bought. But the old dread of fellowship has almost disappeared. One hundred years ago anything like the late International Council would have been regarded as a strategem of the Papacy. As the days of conflict have receded, the difference between fellowship and authority has been more clearly defined and understood, and now but few churches insist on absolute independence. The English churches are not more isolated than the American, but they are more jealous of encroachments on their liberty. Local churches are constituted by Christians in the community. They do not feel called upon, as a condition of their coming into being, to secure official recognition from other churches. They fear to do so, lest they should seem to acknowledge some authority other than that which inheres in the body itself, and which comes direct from the only Lord of the Church, and the Conscience.

The methods of entering the ministry in England differ from those in the United States. An educated ministry has not been so generally insisted on in England as in America, but careful training has always been favoured, and so far as possible, secured. An interesting discussion concerning qualifications for the ministry was carried on in the denominational papers during the year 1892 by Rev. Thomas Green, late Chairman of the Union of England and Wales, and Rev. S. B. Handley. Mr. Green argued with the greatest tenacity that each church should choose its own pastor for itself, and that no other church or minister has the right to question the education, or fitness for the work of the ministry, of the person thus chosen so long as the church calling him is satisfied that he is the proper man for its pastorate. The fact that the Universities were exclusively in the hands of the Established Church made an educated ministry among Dissenters harder to secure, but the many Congregational colleges founded in recent years have greatly obviated that difficulty. The present method of entering the ministry has been described to me by a competent authority substantially as follows: *

---

* Rev P. T. Forsyth, of Leicester.

The churches usually send inquiries to the colleges, or when there is a vacancy in a church the President of a College recommends a student. The only examination in theology is college examinations. No further test of doctrinal orthodoxy is applied. No Council of ministers decides concerning the fitness of a candidate. The colleges have great power in this regard, whereas the churches have little control of the colleges, which are to a great extent endowed bodies, and independent. At an Ordination Service a young minister usually makes a voluntary statement * of his religious beliefs and experience, but this is commonly brief and of a most vague and general character. It is made to the church calling him, rather than to representatives of neighbouring churches. The old custom of asking questions of the candidate after he has presented his statement has almost entirely died out. In the United States the church calling a pastor, whom it desires to have ordained, summons an Ecclesiastical Council, and commits to it the responsibility of determining whether the man called is worthy of confidence, and of the confidence of the churches. In England the local church keeps the reins in its own hands. While, as already stated, there are no examinations beyond the college examinations, such neighbouring ministers as are present

---

* Rev. Bryan Dale, commenting on this fact says, "It has been so only within the last twenty years, and is not so generally."

assist in the exercises as individuals, and not as representatives of churches.

On leaving one charge for another a minister is received by a Recognition Service. Here again the independence of the local church is conspicuous, for this Recognition Service is not conducted by representatives of neighbouring churches, but by the individual church alone. The invitations to this service go out from the church to such ministers as it chooses to ask, and a pulpit announcement is sent to the neighbouring churches, but no formal invitation is extended to them to appoint delegates. Invitations are also occasionally sent to ministers of other denominations. Neither the ministers nor the other churches of a community have any voice concerning the settling of a new pastor in any one of the churches. The only protection, that neighbouring ministers and churches have, is to decline to invite an objectionable person to become a member of the Ministers' Fraternal Union, or to refuse to receive him into the County Union. These expedients are sometimes resorted to, but not very frequently, because they are so extreme that they could hardly be used without libel, particularly in the case of the County Union.

One naturally asks next as to how ministerial standing is certified. It is by a transfer from one County Union to another. The organisation of the County Union will be explained later. Except in extraordinary cases no Union refuses this transfer to a man it has not ejected. The student is received on certificate from his college. If a man comes from another denomination, which declines to give him a transfer, the recommendation of one or two known ministers of the Congregational body is accepted, if they are in a position to give it with intelligence.* If a church calls a minister without college training, or without a previous pastorate, there may be required for membership in the Union, besides the election of the church, a certificate from a minister well known in the denomination; but that seldom happens. A correspondent writes me as follows: "If an American were to come over and settle here, and was not a celebrity, we should need a recommendation from some well-known names, either on that side of the water or this. Indeed, it is possible that he would not be received on a recommendation with signatures from this side of the water only."

We come now to the Basis of Union between the churches. That is very difficult of definition. Theologically only a tacit understanding prevents a man who is a Unitarian from honourably remaining in the Congregational body; and yet, as a matter of fact, the line of separation between Congregationalists and Unitarians is far more clearly drawn

---

* In such cases some County Associations require a personal interview, and that an "Inquiry Committee" (of permanent standing) be satisfied.

in England than in America.* Sentiment is strong where rules are weak. A doctrinal basis was adopted by the Congregational Union of England and Wales in 1833, and that is published in the Year Book. It is distinctly orthodox and Calvinistic, but the greatest care is taken to indicate that it is only a testimony as to the views held at that time, and not to be regarded as authoritative.

In the organisation of a church the largest liberty is allowed. In the fellowship of the churches there are nominally but two steps, although actually there are three. First: the local churches; then, the County Association; and, finally, the Union of England and Wales. Many *towns* have a Ministers' and Deacons' Association, which is only for discussion and friendly intercourse and is not a part of the fellowship of the churches.

An important point to notice is that there is no real connection between the County Unions and The Congregational Union of England and Wales. There is what geologists would call a "fault." The Congregational Union is not an organisation of the County Unions, but of single churches; a few Congregational churches are neither in a County Union nor the Congregational Union. The various County

---

* Most of the Trust Deeds, transmitting property for the use of these churches, are Calvinistic; and cases have occurred of ministers being ejected for not preaching in accordance therewith, but such cases are rare,

Unions, or Associations, are united only in the Church Aid and Home Missionary Society for helping the poor churches, planting new churches, and starting evangelistic work. How, then, is admission to the Congregational Union regulated? By the County Unions being called upon to act as sponsors. The names of only such ministers and churches are printed in the Year Book as are sent up by the County Unions. A County Union could send up the name of a minister, and even of a church, who preferred not to belong to it, if the officers of that Union were satisfied as to their Congregationalism. The Congregational Union of England and Wales consists of such ministers of subscribing churches as have been vouched for by the local Unions, and of delegates from those churches, but it is not an organisation of the local Unions. Many of the leaders in English Congregationalism feel that this is an unsatisfactory condition, and efforts will probably be made to make the Congregational Union more nearly an organisation of County Unions by amalgamating it with the Church Aid and Home Missionary Society.

There is thus a noticeable contrast between the Congregational Union of England and Wales and the National Council of the United States.

The National Council is composed of delegates from the State Associations, local Associations and Conferences. In all but one or two States the State Association is composed of delegates from the individual churches. There is an orderly progression in our system, and, while neither the local Association, nor the State Association, nor yet the National Council, has any authority, still all are continuously connected representative bodies.

The Congregational Union of England and Wales, on the other hand, recognises three kinds of members—Representative, Honorary, and Associate:—

" Representative members are appointed by any church connected with the County Union, or recommended by it, provided that church contributes not less than ten shillings annually to the fund of the Union. If it makes such contribution it may elect delegates in the proportion of one to every fifty members, but no church may appoint more than four delegates. Any church known as a Union Church, that is, one in which neither church membership, nor tenure of office, is dependent on opinions regarding the subjects or form of baptism, may appoint delegates on the same terms as other Congregational churches. The committee of any college or society recognized as a Congregational college or society, and which subscribes not less than ten shillings annually, may elect two delegates. The pastor of any church which contributes to the fund according to the preceding rules is *ex officio* a representative member.

"Honorary members. Retired pastors of Congregational Churches who, on the recommendation of the Committee of the Union shall be elected by open vote of an Annual or Autumnal Assembly, shall be Honorary members, and have all the privileges of Representative members. Missionaries of the London Missionary Society during their residence in England may under this rule become Honorary members.

"Associate Members. The members of any church competent to appoint delegates according to the foregoing Rules, and the pastors and members of any church which does not contribute to the funds of the Union, but is otherwise competent to appoint delegates, may become Associates on the payment of an annual subscription of five shillings. Accredited pastors of Congregational churches in the British Colonies shall, when residing in the United Kingdom, be eligible as Associates." *

The basis of union between the churches in England, while somewhat resembling that in the United States, in important respects is quite different. In England there is nothing corresponding to our Councils. A new church is started by the action of individuals, or local churches, or at the suggestion and by the aid of the County Union. If a colony goes off from an old church, circumstances determine the recognition it receives. Often a church is planted as a mission station by the efforts of some existing church which takes charge of the enterprise. From a "mission" it becomes a "branch" church, not independent, controlled by the initiating church, yet with meetings and sacraments of its own. Then, in due time, it is cut adrift as an "independent" church, and the pecuniary help it needs is furnished not by the parent church, but by the County Union through the Church Aid Society, as for other weak churches.

In the reception of members the English usage differs in some minor respects from that in the United

---

* Condensed from the Year Book, Congregational Union of England and Wales.

States. In the American churches candidates are asked to appear either before a church meeting or before the Standing Committee of the church, and submit to an examination. In England a church usually designates one or two of its members to confer with candidates, and ascertain whether they possess spiritual life, and then the membership acts on the information which these brethren present. In the United States—though the custom is by no means universal, and is rapidly disappearing—candidates are received on their acceptance of Articles of Faith and a Covenant. In England, after a vote is taken, they are usually received by the pastor giving to them the right hand of fellowship, which act is accompanied by a brief address and prayer.* Some churches receive members in a separate or private meeting; others take the vote of such a meeting, and then publicly admit, or recognise the new members at the Lord's Table. Other churches transact such business in an open meeting, to which all persons who feel inclined may come, it being taken for granted that only such will be present as are in sympathy with the proceeding. No doctrinal tests are required as conditions of membership, and yet if a person wished to unite with a Congregational church, and should either openly avow, or give good reason for the suspicion, that he was out of harmony with the views entertained by the church which he pro-

---

* "Manual for Ministers and Deacons," p. 4.

posed to join, he would be advised to go elsewhere. The difference between the English usage and the American is, that the former reasonably presumes that those who desire to become church-members will not prefer the request unless there is sufficient agreement between their own views and those of the church concerning vital Christian doctrine to make their membership desirable, while the latter tends to require demonstration of this. The sole condition of membership in the Independent churches of England is credible evidence of a personal Christian experience. In the Congregational churches of America, on the other hand, assent to a series of formulated doctrines and a covenant is usually required before candidates are received into fellowship.

There is little difference between the English and American usage in matters of discipline. One fact, however, is worthy of special mention, and that is, that English churches recognise that a person may resign his membership in the local church.* In America the theoretical contention has usually been that the only way out of church-membership is by death or discipline, although the quite frequent practice, in cases of abandonment of the communion, has been the dropping of the names of such members from the roll of the church and withdrawal of fellowship from them.

We have thus outlined the organisation, and

---

* "Manual for Ministers and Deacons," p. 40.

what may be called the machinery, of English Congregationalism. The English churches emphasise spirit and life, rather than government and authority. They believe in continuous inspiration; that the humblest and poorest, if his heart is open and pure, may expect the guidance of the Spirit. We place much dependence on machinery; of that they are careless. An illustration of the same principle is found in the monetary system of the British kingdom. England alone among European nations has thus far declined to adopt a decimal currency. She uses pounds, shillings and pence, and all business with her has to be transacted according to that currency. The English speak of guineas, as well as of pounds, though such a coin as a guinea is not now issued and has not been since 1813. Yet trade flows to their shores in continuous streams, and merchants are more careful about getting business than about conforming their commercial methods to those of the rest of the world. The Congregational system of England is much like that of her currency. It works well because spirit is more than form, and life than mechanism.

It has been observed before, in this lecture, that the English churches put comparatively little emphasis on Creeds and Confessions, and yet there is one curiosity closely akin to these which still survives, and plays an important part in their ecclesiastical system. The reference is to "Doctrinal Schedules in Trust Deeds." The name explains the thing. When a church, or institution, is founded, it has been customary to insert in the deed of the property certain conditions, according to which it is to be held and by which its use is to be determined. And so there is the strange anomaly of churches declining to be bound by a written Creed, and yet having in the deeds of their property that which is practically a creed of the strictest kind. This "dead hand" rests on many English churches and institutions. Such deeds were more common in the past than at present. One of the papers at the International Council was by Dr. Thomas Green, of Ashton-under-Lyne. Dr. Green is one of the most interesting figures in contemporary Congregationalism, and his paper was a scathing denunciation of the system of which we are speaking. He described these Trust Deeds as follows: "The objects we are to speak of are frequently regarded with great veneration. They are theological miniatures which are intended to represent in microscopic form what certain persons, who have subscribed some money, take to be the principal features of the Christian faith. They are made by skilful professional people employed by the subscribers; and both the artificers and the donors are most frankly to be credited with the greatest sincerity and with the very best intentions. They believe that they believe all they say; and feeling its value they very much desire that other people not at present born should also believe it, and they construct the little portrait as a means for bringing about this important end."

On the other hand, it must be granted that Dr. Green has not presented the whole subject, and there is another side, as will be seen from the following suggestions by Rev. Bryan Dale, Secretary of the Yorkshire Union: "Consider (1), that these Schedules were not intended to limit the truth of God, or prevent men from thinking for themselves; (2), but to determine the use of property in certain directions, for which it was devoted; (3), and that they have been largely the result of the experience of its being diverted from the use intended. The oldest Trust Deeds were simply for 'the Worship of God'; and in a great many instances ministers and elders who became Unitarians retained the endowments connected with the building, as well as the building itself, while the evangelicals had to go forth and erect other places of worship. (4), If the building has no Trust Deed determining its use, but is left with the majority of the congregation, such a majority may be manipulated, quarrels are likely to ensue, and where are the rights of the minority? The question is not a simple one."

The Trust Deeds of the English churches differ very little, if any, from the conditions which are attached to many gifts in the United States, as for instance, the endowments and the creed of Andover Theological Seminary. The fallacy which lies at the basis of such gifts, and which makes them often a hinderance to the Kingdom of God rather than a help, is the fact that many men imagine that they have the right to determine how the money of which they are stewards for a little while shall be used for all time, and that they, in the period in which they live, have full light on the universe of truth. These two parts of one great fallacy have caused infinite trouble on both sides of the water; and yet the question is entirely pertinent, What form of trust deed would not have caused trouble? We are coming to realise, slowly and through sad experiences, that wealth belongs to the race and to God. The individual is allowed its possession while he lives; he ought not to be allowed to determine how it shall be used in all the future. A man's right to what he calls his wealth is not an eternal right. Furthermore, the self-righteousness of those who, living in a narrow world and having but little light, imagine that they know what will be best for all the centuries will not much longer be tolerated. Such persons have made trouble enough already. The English churches, and the American as well, are coming to understand that quite as much confidence should be placed in living men as in dead men, and that no one age is characterised by omniscience.

The English Trust Deed will probably be greatly

modified, but it is not likely soon to disappear. The Chapel Building Society has a model deed, which is of as much value as such documents usually are, and which is commonly adopted by churches to which it gives assistance. In the not distant future let us hope that the Spirit of God will be trusted to guard against the misuse of money, and to lead God's people into all the truth He wishes them to know.

The English Independents believed in an educated ministry, even when it was well-nigh impossible to get a liberal education without going abroad ; and when the doors of the Universities were closed against them one of their first acts was to found academies.* These academies were primarily designed for the training of ministers, and yet in time they came also to do a great work in the training of the people. They were to Nonconformity what the Universities were to the Establishment. Later many of them developed into colleges. The Universities which were so long closed against Dissenters were opened in 1870, and as a result there is now going on a process of adjustment to new educational conditions which is causing material changes in the constitution of the Nonconformist colleges. The Universities are the glory of the nation, and most young Englishmen ambitious of learning wish to take their degrees either at Oxford or Cambridge. As a result, the Congrega-

---

* Encyclopædia Britannica, "Independents."

tional colleges are devoting themselves more exclusively to theological training. The process is not yet fully completed, for in several of the colleges there are courses in arts—" the humanities," as well as courses in theology—" divinity."

In the old days, before railroads had brought all districts of England near together, such institutions arose in different parts of the Kingdom. When the Universities were opened to Nonconformists, some of the colleges ceased to be needed; in one or two instances combinations have been made; but there are still too many schools of theology. In London there are nominally two, but practically three, (for Cheshunt, while belonging to the Countess of Huntingdon's denomination, is chiefly Congregational), all doing practically the same work, when one would be quite sufficient. Indeed, it may be questioned whether the London institutions might not with the greatest benefit all be merged in Mansfield College, at Oxford. In the North there are Lancashire College at Manchester and the United College at Bradford. They are only about an hour apart by railway. They are doing the same kind of work, and each naturally clings to its own existence, though the churches would be benefited if the two were united.* This process of combining the smaller colleges involves

---

* "On the other hand consider : (1), Much depends upon the students being kept in touch with the actual life of the churches ;

much difficulty, and will require tact and wisdom, and yet the best interests of the Independent churches seem imperatively to demand such a course. Oxford is very central. Mansfield College is already firmly established in that ancient seat of learning. While it has its perils, and defects no doubt, it offers to students opportunities of culture which no other college can offer. And yet it is only partially endowed, and is still poorly equipped—if any college with Dr. Fairbairn at its head may be so characterised. It should have many more professors, and it would have them immediately if some of the smaller institutions would merge their endowments in those of the college which is sure to be the most influential and helpful of all in the Kingdom. When we remember that England is hardly larger than the State of New York, and that its Congregational churches have six or eight institutions, all doing the work of the widely scattered theological seminaries in the United States, and that none of them are fully equipped as to their professors, while all have expensive buildings and grounds, it is easy to see that there is an unwarranted waste both of men and of means. We may confidently expect that in the not distant

---

(2), The colleges largely depend on the contributions of the churches; (3), The churches are aided by the preaching of the students; (4), Any advantage gained by amalgamation is more than counteracted by other disadvantages."—REV. BRYAN DALE.

future the problem will be solved, and instead of six or eight poorly-equipped colleges there will be two or three strong, well-manned, and wisely located theological seminaries.

Much has been written during the last few years concerning the strength and weakness of Independency. The champions of the Establishment are strangely interested in the vitality of Congregationalism, and hardly a month passes that some enterprising reviewer does not devote himself to this subject. The *Nineteenth Century Review* has recently published two noteworthy articles on the subject.* According to the confession of its friends the weakness of English Congregationalism is largely in the following conditions :

1. *The prevalence of the commercial spirit.* The churches are influenced too much by their surroundings, and are not positive enough in making a new and better environment. The questions uppermost in the minds of the people are said to be financial rather than spiritual, and all Nonconformists are declared to be under the pressure of ambition to be as "respectable" as the Establishment. "They build costly churches and employ costly agencies, and then devote themselves to raising money rather than to the salvation of souls." But the financial difficulty is not peculiar to English Congregationalism. It faces all Christian workers, especially where there

---

* The *Nineteenth Century Review*, vol. for 1890, pp. 628-639.

are no endowments. The Establishment, in a measure, is free from such perplexities, because its older churches have been built by the wealth of the nation; and yet it is not entirely free, for their "restoration" has required strenuous efforts and often real sacrifice. On the other hand the Free Churches have to provide for the erection of their edifices, for the support of the services of the sanctuary, and for carrying on missionary enterprises. These burdens are often heavy, and it is not surprising if questions of ways and means are sometimes given what seem to be places of undue prominence.

2. *The under-education of the ministry.* But that is disappearing under the influence of Mansfield College, New College, Lancashire College, and other institutions which will be mentioned more at length in a later lecture.

3. *The absence of a central organisation*, or, possibly, the absence of local organisations. This difficulty is one which faces all Free Churches. Where each church is independent many churches will often be without ministers, and many ministers without pastorates.

These difficulties, when contrasted with the supposed advantages of an episcopal system simply lead to a balancing of advantages and disadvantages. A Bishop and central organisation undoubtedly facilitate the administration of affairs. But, on the other hand, Independency has its own peculiar elements of strength. In England, and all densely populated regions where many people are very poor, endowed churches are almost a necessity. Whatever our theories as to what ought to be, the fact is that the well-to-do classes of society usually, as soon as they are able, move away from the densely populated districts of large cities. Consequently the suburban churches are strong, while those are weak where the population is more numerous and poverty is the most pinching. The Establishment has a great advantage in its endowments, which enable it to continue its work undiminished in localities from which the wealthier classes have migrated. Undoubtedly endowments have their evils, but we are at present concerned only with their benefits.

Yet, how to evangelise the great cities is only one factor in the world-wide problem; and the fact is that even with their endowments, which give them a real advantage, the Established churches do no better work than the Free Churches.

4. Another source of weakness is the almost universal custom among Nonconformists of having *but one minister for a church.* Mr. T. Herbert Darlow says:* "This Congregational fondness for middle-class respectability is at once a cause and an effect of the undue importance we attach to preaching as compared with pastoral work. For the shep-

---

* *Nineteenth Century Review,* Oct. 1890.

herd's true mission lies among the scattered, and not the folded sheep. But the minister who is primarily a private chaplain to his pew-holders has scant energy to spare for souls without. The truth is that a large congregation cannot be properly worked by only one minister. Hardly any other Christian denomination attempts such an impossibility. It is rare, indeed, to find a vicar with £500 a year or upwards in a busy town who has not, as a matter of course, one or more curates to help him. But it is almost equally rare to find a similarly situated Congregational minister who is not single-handed at his task. We need not discuss the secret of this not quite creditable result—whether a congregation gathered, as it so often is, by personal attractions, prefers to wear out its favourite preacher rather than appoint him a deputy; or whether the preacher be sometimes unwilling to share his income, even when it is large, with an assistant. The fact remains that twice one are more than two; and I believe that Congregational church work would be far more efficient if curacies were as much the rule as they are now the exception." The position taken by Mr. Darlow is sound, and the Free Churches on both sides of the water must find some better plan than a "one man ministry," or they will lag far behind the Roman and Episcopal churches in the "forward movement."

The difficulties most to be dreaded by the English

dissenting churches are: the commercial spirit; the desire on the part of the middle-class people when they have acquired a competence to secure the social recognition which can usually be found only in the Established Church; and the tendency to rely too much in new times and new conditions upon principles and methods which were best in other times and different conditions, but which have long since ceased to be vital.

Turning from the weakness of English Congregationalism we note a few of the elements of its strength:

It possesses a denominational *esprit de corps* not commonly found on our side of the water. The difference may be easily explained. Persecution develops strength, and unites those whom it oppresses. From earliest times the members of the Congregational churches in the United States have been distinguished for culture, social position and influence. Their leaders have been men of education and recognised quality and character. In the New England Colonies, as in the New England States, these churches were predominant. In England, on the contrary, the Congregationalists, in common with other Nonconformists, have had to win for themselves from reluctant opponents every advantage which they have gained. If they have not been knit together by common interests they have been united in the face of common dangers. The very opposition which they have received has developed in them a rugged and dauntless strength. There is a sturdiness in the fibre of the English Nonconformists seldom found in more favorable circumstances. We pride ourselves on our lack of denominational enthusiasm; they emphasise their loyalty to their ecclesiastical principles.

The Congregational Union of England and Wales in its spring and autumnal meetings exerts a much wider and deeper influence than our National Council. The programmes for the meetings of the former body are more carefully prepared, and the subjects for discussion have more vital relations to the advancement of the Kingdom of God. We fritter away, with senseless business, time which they devote to the consideration of fundamental principles. The Moderator of our National Council is only a respectable figure-head, whose duties end with the Council over which he is elected to preside. He makes no deliverance to which the churches are expected to listen. On the other hand, the Chairman of the Union of England and Wales is chosen because he is a representative man, whose best thoughts the people are anxious to hear, and his two addresses—one at the spring, the other at the autumnal meeting—are the most important utterances to Congregationalists during the whole year. The subjects for address from the Chair of the Union always deal with living questions. For instance, Baldwin Brown in 1879 spoke on "Our Theology in Relation to the Intellectual Movements of our Times," and his second address was on " The Perfect Law of Liberty." Dr. Parker, in 1884, gave two great orations, one of them on " The Larger Ministry," and the other on "Orthodoxy of Heart." Dr. Mackennal, in 1887, spoke on " The Witness of Congregationalism " and " The Life of the Spirit"; and Dr. John Brown, 1891, spoke on "The Historic Episcopate" and "The Historic Christian People." These addresses were published in full in the denominational papers and went into nearly all the households of the churches. The Chairman of the Union for the year is the recognised leader of the Congregational army in England; we in America have no such leader. Not until we exalt our National Council, making it entirely different from a shadow of the Presbyterian General Assembly, and its Moderator something more than a man set to turn the crank of the wheels which grinds out mere routine business, will the chief convocation of the American churches compare in importance and value with the Union of England and Wales.

The English churches as a rule are more perfectly organised for work than the American. The diaconate has larger honour, and in many churches the deacons are more distinctly leaders in the church than with us. There, as here, rotation in the office is gradually becoming more common. The Sunday services receive no less emphasis than with us, but that the church edifice is intended for wide and varied activity as well as for preaching on the Lord's Day is more clearly and generally recognised. Their " Chapels " are hives of industry. I can imagine no better training in pastoral theology than a careful study of such hand-books as the manuals issued by the Chorlton Road Church in Manchester, where Dr. Goodrich is now pastor, and Dr. Macfadyan was formerly; by the Union Chapel in Islington, Dr. Allon's ; and by the Queen Street Church in Wolverhampton, of which Charles A. Berry is pastor. The idea of " the larger parish," which we have neglected, is more firmly grasped in England. That implies that the Church is the centre and home of the ecclesiastical household, while clustered about it are numerous smaller institutions—" chapels," " branches," " missions," etc., in which are preaching services, Sunday-schools, and whatever forms of Christian work may be required by the community in which they are located. The " one-minister " idea is beginning to disappear from most of their large churches, and those who are practically curates are assisting Nonconformist pastors as those assistant pastors help vicars in "the Church."

The English churches teach one lesson which may well be studied by all who fear that the growing disinclination to make doctrinal conditions of church-membership will result in a diminished spiritual life. In England no church with which I am acquainted insists upon the acceptance of a Creed as a condition of membership: and yet the spirituality of the people; their devotion to their work; their loyalty to the Bible, the Church and the sacraments, and to all that belongs to the worship of God, and to the great principles of evangelical doctrine—especially the Deity of Christ and the Doctrine of the Cross—are quite as intense as with us, and even more pronounced.

Another fact characteristic of Congregationalists in England is the tendency to change their emphasis from Independency to Fellowship. The regulative principle of their polity in the past has been the absolute independence of the local church. On that their emphasis has been placed. Anything which looked like the faintest encroachment of authority has been instantly and strenuously resisted. In former days there was reason for vigilance, and the independence of the local church was the citadel of its strength: but in course of time that happened which often happens,—loyalty to a principle led to the abuse of that principle; consequently the English churches were formerly without that consciousness of unity which was needed in order that they might be helpful to each other, and that the best work for Christ and His Kingdom might be accomplished. The formation of County Associations began soon after the year 1800. During the last quarter of a century independency has very generally been giving place to fellowship. The Union of England and Wales has stimulated this movement, but not so much as have the County Associations. The pressure of social problems has also helped to develop the rapidly growing consciousness of solidarity. While here and there churches still preserve their old independence, most of them have ceased to be sensitive lest fellowship may be the first step toward authority. All that is implied in the name "Independent" has been won, and won forever, and by no possibility can be lost; and now the movement is "from liberty to unity." The growth of the County Associations, the place occupied by the Union of England and Wales, the influence of the most prominent men, and, we may add, the influence of American Congregationalism, have all contributed something toward the change which is evidently in progress.

This change is significantly indicated by the fact that, whereas, a few years ago the English churches were usually called "Independent," they are now almost universally called "Congregational." The Congregational idea indicates fellowship. The *esprit de corps*, to which reference has already been made, in so far as it has existed in the past, was developed by loyalty to the principle of independency, and by the pressure of the circumstances in which the people lived. Those who realise that great forces are banded against them instinctively draw together. In these later days a more gracious temper is manifesting itself, and those who have the spiritual life, as if drawn by unseen attractions, are coming into fuller and more helpful association. The movement which has various names, but of which the English papers for the past two or three years have been full—called now "Federated Independency," and now "The One Church in One Town Movement"—is an illustration of the growth of fellowship. "Federated Independency" means local churches uniting in a common work, and the "One-Church-in-One-Town" does not mean one building in one city, but the organisation of all Congregationalists of a single municipality in one body for the advancement of the cause in which all are engaged, and as a step toward the larger organisation of all Christians, for which so many are already praying and some even confidently expecting.

These are some of the more salient features which present themselves in a study of contemporary English Congregationalism. No denomination in the world is more intensely alive to the importance of social questions, which have been truly called the questions of our time. As Baldwin Brown put it in 1879, "The kingdom of man is at hand, and the English churches, English scholars and English ministers are devoting themselves to these questions with unsurpassed earnestness." If a great London pulpit is to be filled there is quite as much eagerness to know the candidate's views concerning sociology as concerning theology. Is he loyal to humanity? Is he ready to work heart and soul for uplifting the millions from vice and crime? The Parable of the Good Samaritan seems to have gotten into the blood of the Nonconformists of England. The emphasis of the churches has been on independency, but that is now giving place to the fellowship of independent Christian communities united in the service of man, and thus in the worship of God. In the missionary enterprise of the local church, in their enthusiasm and equipment for work, the descendants of the Pilgrims in England are unsurpassed among Christian communions.

The points of contrast in ecclesiastical organisation between the English and American churches are many and striking, and yet no more than would be expected from the differing circumstances in which the people have lived and do live. It is always difficult for those who dwell in one land fully to appreciate the work of those whose homes are in other lands, and therefore in this lecture I have tried to expound rather than to criticise. Doubtless there are many elements of weakness in English Congregationalism—as there are in all other forms of polity; doubtless many of its tendencies if imported into the freer air of America would cause disturbance. The task of the expositor however is far more agreeable, and in this instance far more profitable, than that of the critic. Among the grand divisions of the Christian host which is steadily moving toward the conquest of the world for Christ with fidelity to the essential truth of the Christian revelation, in absolute loyalty to the Master himself, none are more faithful than the descendants of these Pilgrims who remained in Old England; none are working more patiently for the triumph of the principles for which the fathers died; none are more consecrated to the service of God and man, and none are facing the future with more confident and glad anticipation.

As these words are penned a great shadow comes from across the Atlantic. All who are interested in the struggle for ecclesiastical liberty in our times, and a still larger number in many lands by whom Christian manhood is more highly prized than denominational affiliation, are pained by the sad news that Henry Allon, the accomplished pastor of Union Chapel, Islington, and a great and honoured leader among English Nonconformists, has been called from the earth. He was a superb example of what modern English Dissent is, and of the quality of men which it makes. Others in various departments of our ecclesiastical life have been greater than he, but no man in recent times has more rarely combined lofty devotion to principle, finished and beautiful culture, high and fine spirituality, with all those qualities of "sweetness and light" which Matthew Arnold would have been slow to believe could be found in a Nonconformist. For nearly fifty years he ministered in one of the largest churches in London. His influence has been felt in all departments of English thought and service. He was the editor of the "British Quarterly Review," a friend of Dean Stanley and Gladstone, twice chairman of the Congregational Union of England and Wales, a literary and musical critic of acknowledged eminence. An urbane gentleman, a delightful companion, a sympathetic friend who won his way into all sorrow and suffering as instinctively as the sun shines in the darkness, a broad and liberal theologian, one who insisted on his right to do his own thinking, and defended others in their right to do the same; the pastor of a church composed of the wealthy and cultured in which the element of worship was carried to its finest development, and yet where the poor and the outcast were never forgotten,—his name will long be honoured, not only among Nonconformists but also among all who have known anything of the development of spiritual and social life in England in the nineteenth century. No more just or well-deserved tribute can be paid to the vitality and power of English Congregationalism than to say that while he lived Henry Allon was a true representative of its spirit and its working, and now that he has gone others remain worthy to wear his mantle and to take up his ministry.

V.
CREEDS.

"In the first place, such symbols have seldom carried the unanimous assent of those adopting them. Even the Cambridge Platform was avowedly held, as to some points, in the beginning, and still more decidedly in the generation after, only 'for substance of doctrine.' In the second place, no one generation of churches can possibly have any authority to impose any creed or polity, however dear to itself, upon the churches of another generation—to whom God may be pleased to give a clearer understanding of His will."

—Dr. Henry M. Dexter.

"Because on some special scientific path I can proceed no farther than to this particular point, does that imply that the road ends there?"—Rothe.

"No chemist has prospered in the attempt to crystallise a religion. It is endogenous, like the skin, and other vital organs. A new statement every day. The Prophet and Apostle knew this, and the Nonconformist confutes the Conformists by quoting the texts they must allow. It is the condition of a religion to require religion for its expositor."—Emerson.

V.

CREEDS.*

THE Congregational theory of ecclesiastical polity admits of no general creed for all the churches. There is no Congregational denomination: what is called by that name is in reality a congeries of local churches; and no movement toward fellowship on either side of the Atlantic has yet limited, in the slightest degree, their autonomy. Independent ecclesiastical societies are of necessity independent in the matter of creeds, as well as in other things which concern their life and government. Consequently, there are Confessions of Faith which are supposed to represent the theological belief of the churches in various localities, but there is no one which is authoritative for others than those who choose to make it binding. In the nature of things, if a commission were appointed for the purpose of devising a General Confession, to which all the

---

*The Theological Outlook among the English Congregational Churches is treated in another chapter of this book, and is therefore only casually touched on in this.

churches should be expected to conform, its work would be a failure; for, the moment it was framed and an attempt was made to impose it upon the churches, the intrusion would be resented, or the constitution of the churches themselves would be changed. They might become Presbyterian or Episcopalian, but such a document could never govern the action of Congregational churches unless by a distinct vote each local church chose to adopt it; and even then the churches would be at liberty to modify it whenever they might choose, without consultation with their neighbours. The Congregational usage in England and America has been for local churches to formulate their own confessions of faith, if they desire, and then for the question of the substantial orthodoxy of those documents to be determined by the churches whose fellowship is sought.

The English churches are more independent than the American, and hitherto the question of fellowship has occupied their attention but little. Many churches have no formal articles of faith. A substitute much resorted to in the past has been the Trust Deed with its "Doctrinal Schedule."

The Baptist churches are as distinctively "Congregational" as those which bear the name. They are the children of the Independents, and in them is seen the natural development of the principles for the assertion of which the Free Churches exist. Very few, if any, Baptist churches have doctrinal symbols. Among them there is a general consensus of doctrine; and their churches are more generally Calvinistic than those of any other denomination, but they have been kept so by tradition and by a kind of spiritual attraction, rather than by uniformity in creedal requirement. We search in vain for any distinctive confession of faith which is representative of the Baptist churches. There have been individual or local pronunciamentos in England, as that of 1688, and two or three in the United States, like the New Hampshire Confession of 1833; but none have authority; all are of limited influence; and when a Baptist is asked concerning his creed he usually replies "The Bible is our creed."

The history of English Congregationalism indicates that there has been a gradual escape from the traditions of Presbyterianism concerning the importance of doctrine as a test of the spiritual life. During the early years of the Puritan Revolution the preëminent spiritual force came from Scotland, which was universally Presbyterian. In England also there were many who followed the teachings of Thomas Cartwright, who, like John Knox, received them direct from Calvin. The Puritan Revolution in the first instance was a revolt of Presbyterian theology, and Presbyterian theories concerning the Church and worship, against the ceremonies which prevailed in the Established Church. It was a revolution of Presbyterianism against Episcopalianism.

At first those who represented the Parliament, and who were not Presbyterians, placed little emphasis upon the religious element in the controversy. The Scotch and the Presbyterians in England were united in seeking the emancipation of the Church from Episcopal control. They were opposed to the King, not because they objected to the interference of the State in religious matters, but because the King represented the Episcopal theory of the Church. On the other hand, John Pym, Sir Harry Vane and John Hampden were fighting for the freedom of the English State against royalty. With them it was Parliament against the King; with the Scotch it was Presbyterianism versus Papacy and prelacy. At first the forces opposed to the King coalesced with great difficulty. The Parliamentary Army was a host of antagonisms. The Scottish Presbyterians were in favor of "a covenant"; the English party were in favor of "a league." At length a compromise was made, by which, as Dr. Stoughton finely says, "It was determined that the Scotch bond should be a *league* for civil purposes, and a *covenant* for religious ones." By the "Scotch bond" he means the treaty which bound the English and the Scotch together in their opposition to the King. The Scotch were narrow and bigoted; the English were tolerant and mystical. In the objects at which they aimed the two parties were far apart, as events subsequently proved. One was for a Presbyterian State, with its creeds, and rules of binding authority on all the citizens; the other advocated separation between Church and State, the first step of which was to get rid of the King.

When the Revolution was well under way "the Puritan clergy, in the December of 1641, asked that ecclesiastical matters" (which were the subject of controversy) " might be referred to a Free Synod, differing in constitution from the old Convocation of clergy. In October, 1642, a Bill was introduced for that purpose, and it is noteworthy that two significant resolutions in connection with it passed the Committee of the Commons: namely, that the vote against bishops should be appended to the Bill, thus foreclosing attempts for the revival of Episcopacy; and, that Parliament did not intend to abrogate the Prayer Book, thus leaving a door open for the use of a revised liturgy."* This Bill was introduced on the 15th of October, and before the month ended war broke out at Edgehill. "Before the Assembly met, in July, 1643, Lord Brooke had been killed at the siege of Lichfield in the month of March; John Hampden had been shot on Chalgrove Field in the month of June . . . Literally, a life and death struggle was going on; and the grave men in Genevan gowns or plain doublets, who marched through the Dean's Yard to take their places in the now world-renowned Council Chamber,

---

* Stoughton " Jubilee Lectures," p. 142.

had then and afterwards not only to contend for truth but to struggle for existence." *

In the midst of this conflict, when Presbyterian ideas as to the Church were strongly predominant, the Westminister Assembly was convened,—the same which formulated the Westminster Confession of Faith. Its original object was the revision of the Thirty-nine Articles of the Church of England; later came an order commanding it to take in hand the Liturgy, and the subject of ecclesiastical discipline. A study of the proportion of parties in that Assembly will give a somewhat clear idea of the influences which were at work among English Nonconformists. A few moderate Episcopalians were appointed to the Assembly: among them four Bishops; but only one of these attended, and he was present but once, while the other Episcopalians soon dropped off. The majority of the members were Presbyterians, and altogether there were not over ten or eleven Independents. Sixty-nine in all answered to the roll-call of the first meeting. In the end the Revolution was won by the Independents, who differed from the Presbyterians not so much concerning theological doctrine as concerning ecclesiastical polity. Of the Independents who helped to form the Westminster Confession five were among the most distinguished members of the Assembly: Philip Nye, a veritable Martin Luther

---

* Stoughton "Jubilee Lectures," p. 143.

in spirit; Jeremiah Burroughs, who has been likened to Melancthon; William Bridge, an encyclopedic scholar; Sidrach Simpson, "who was first ejected by Archbishop Laud and afterwards disciplined by the Assembly"; and, last of the group, Thomas Goodwin, one of the ablest and most distinguished orators and thinkers of his time, a man who has been called the "Atlas of English Independency." These were all sturdy Calvinists, and however much they may have differed from their brethren concerning ecclesiastical affairs they were in profound sympathy with them in matters of doctrine. Consequently, when the Westminster Confession was formed its doctrinal statements were approved by the Independents, and accepted by them with the same loyalty as by the Presbyterians; and a few years later when the Savoy Confession was adopted, it was in doctrine almost identical with that of Westminster, the most important modifications being those which concerned church government and discipline.

The Westminster Assembly met in London in 1643; the Savoy Assembly met in the Savoy palace on the Strand, in London, in October, 1658. The times were such as to test the fidelity of the most stalwart spirits. The Savoy had been convened with the consent of Cromwell, but only twenty-six days before its first meeting the great Protector had passed away. Unrest and uncertainty were in the air, and yet at that time there seems to have been little doubt but that the State, as Cromwell had established it, would be permanent. About two hundred delegates from one hundred and twenty congregations constituted this Assembly. It completed its work in eleven days. Among its most prominent members were Goodwin, Nye, Bridge, Caryll, Greenhill and John Owen, all but the last of whom had been in the Westminster Assembly. The advocates of the Calvinistic system of theology were predominant in the Savoy as in the Westminster Assembly. While the Presbyterians sought to compel uniformity of religious belief, the Independents, or Separatists, as represented by Sir Harry Vane and Cromwell, were relatively tolerant of theological differences. The tolerance of the latter was the result of their independency. They claimed the right to think and act for themselves, and what they asked they were also ready to give. While, therefore, they differed from their Presbyterian brethren as to polity, they agreed with them as to doctrine, as a comparison of the Savoy with the Westminster Confession makes plain. Thus it came to pass that the English Congregational churches confessed their faith by means of the same standards as the Presbyterians, and both held to the system called Calvinistic.

But the reaction of Independency against the rigid doctrinalism of Scotland began about the year

1700, as is seen in the example of Isaac Watts, and gradually there grew a wide divergence from the older Calvinism. Without doubt there are still living in England many elderly Independents who were trained in the Westminster Catechism, and who can give correct answers to all its questions, but the number is fast diminishing. These Confessions have been practically laid aside, although from the period of the Commonwealth to the early years of the present century they were generally accepted as true exponents of the theological thought of English Independents.

The only other doctrinal statement which can make the slightest claim to being called an official utterance of Congregationalists in England is the Declaration of the Congregational Union of England and Wales which was adopted in May, 1833, and which is printed annually in the Year Book of the Union. That document ought always to be read in connection with the Preliminary Notes, which are as follows:

" 1. It is not designed, in the following summary, to do more than to state the leading doctrines of faith and order maintained by Congregational Churches in general.

" 2. It is not proposed to offer any proofs, reasons, or arguments, in support of the doctrines herein stated, but simply to declare what the Denomination believes to be taught by the pen of inspiration.

" 3. It is not intended to present a scholastic or critical confession of faith, but merely such a statement as any intelligent member of the body might offer, as containing its leading principles.

"4. It is not intended that the following statement should be put forth with any authority, or as a standard to which assent should be required.

"5. Disallowing the utility of creeds and articles of religion as a bond of union, and protesting against subscription to any human formularies as a term of communion, Congregationalists are yet willing to declare, for general information, what is commonly believed among them, reserving to every one the most perfect liberty of conscience.

"6. Upon some minor points of doctrine and practice, they, differing among themselves, allow to each other the right to form an unbiassed judgment of the Word of God.

"7. They wish it to be observed, that, notwithstanding their jealousy of subscription to creeds and articles, and their disapproval of the imposition of any human standard, whether of faith or discipline, they are far more agreed in their doctrines and practices than any church which enjoins subscription and enforces a human standard of orthodoxy: and they believe that there is no minister and no church among them that would deny the substance of any one of the following doctrines of religion, though each might prefer to state his sentiments in his own way."

These two confessions, the Savoy and that published in the Year Book, are the only English Congregational creeds of more than local significance. Neither of them has any authority, and neither has wide acceptance at the present time, although, when adopted, probably both fairly represented the doctrinal position of the ministers and the churches.

The second may be called moderately Calvinistic—whatever that very convenient term may signify. It affirms that the Congregational churches believe the Scriptures of the Old and New Testament to be divinely inspired, and of supreme authority. The doctrine of The Trinity is not stated with Calvinistic clearness. It is as follows: " They believe that God is revealed in the Scriptures as the Father, the Son, and the Holy Spirit, and that to each are attributable the same divine properties and perfections. The doctrine of the Divine existence, as above stated, they cordially believe, without attempting fully to explain." What is commonly called "Original Sin" is described as "a fatal inclination to moral evil." The teaching concerning the person of Christ is that " He is equal with the Father, and 'the express image of His person;' that He revealed the whole mind of God for our salvation; and that by His obedience to the Divine law while He lived, and by His sufferings unto death, He meritoriously 'obtained eternal redemption for us,' having thereby vindicated and illustrated Divine justice, 'magnified the law,' and 'brought in everlasting righteousness.'" Concerning Eschatology the teaching is that the process of sanctification is completed on the earth, and that at death the souls of the righteous, freed from all evil, are received immediately into the presence of Christ; while the wicked will go away into everlasting punishment.

These are some of the salient features of this Creed, which is short, and as good as such mechanisms usually are. It contains no utterance concerning the questions of criticism now in dispute; nothing concerning the errancy or inerrancy of "the original autographs"; nothing about theories of the Atonement; and not a word as to whether those who have not known Christ in this world will have an opportunity to accept or reject Him in the future.

This Congregational Union Creed is a kind of patchwork, a makeshift—something which has little of the horizon of modern thought. It would not have been strong enough for the sterner thinkers of earlier times, and is not broad enough for those who dwell in the full light of modern investigation. The old theology as embodied in the Westminster and Savoy Confessions had a grasp and grandeur of suggestion and expression which is wanting in most modern creeds. While those men of the Puritan Revolution attempted more than was possible for human powers to express they at least recognised the vastness of their task; consequently, there is in their composition a loftiness of ideal, a dignity of language, a largeness of suggestion, and a certain rhythmic quality which is wanting in such a confession as that of the Union, and equally in most which have been issued among the American churches. Doctrinal mechanisms get cheaper and more tawdry the more frequently they are manufactured. Not one in modern times for grandeur of thought and splendor of diction equals the ancient creeds of the Church. Creed-making is a "lost art." The old theology, whatever defects it may have had, can never be charged with having belittled the high themes of which it treated. The most that can be said for the second of the English Creeds is that it is a respectable composition, which at the time of its writing did not misrepresent the attitude of the English Congregational churches. It is published year after year not because it is revered or loved, but either because it would be too much trouble to vote it away, or because it is thought worthy of preservation as a way-mark on the road along which English theological thought has moved. It contains no emphatic mention of the Fatherhood of God, no reference to the brotherhood of man, no recognition of any duties to the State or to society, and no mention of duties of any kind which do not relate distinctly to what is technically called religious teaching, or religious observance. In these respects it is not exceptional, but rather typical. It is no longer of value as a standard, and has not for many years been truly representative of English Congregationalism.

The Savoy Confession is the most important general statement of doctrine ever issued in the name of English Congregationalism, and should be studied by all who desire to understand the influences which have moulded theological thinking in England. It was prepared by a Committee all but one of whom had been members of the Westminster Assembly. It contains a lengthy Preface (fourteen pages); the Westminster Confession of Faith with sundry changes (twenty-two pages); and a Platform of Church Polity (five pages).

The doctrinal part of this Declaration, with the exception of those passages which concern church polity, is distinctly a mere modification of the Westminster Confession, and the modifications themselves are insignificant. The Preface, however, is somewhat remarkable as indicating the character of the Independents in the time of the Commonwealth. They were not only stalwart in their doctrinal opinions, but also tolerant of the opinions of others, as is clearly indicated in the following statement of the Preface. After speaking of the duty of confession it says:*

"And accordingly such a transaction is to be looked upon but as a meet or fit *medium* or *means* whereby to express that their *common faith and salvation* are no way to be made use of as an *imposition* upon any: Whatever is of force or constraint in matters of this nature causeth them to degenerate from the *name* and *nature* of *Confessions*, and turns them from being *Confessions of Faith*

---

* The italics are in the Preface.

into *exactions* and *Impositions of Faith*." * Another utterance worthy of more than passing notice is the following: "Let this be added to give full weight and measure, even to running over, that we have all along this season held forth (though quarrelled with for it by our brethren) this great principle of these times, *That amongst all Christian States and Churches there ought to be vouchsafed a forbearance and mutual indulgence unto Saints of all persuasions, that keep unto, and hold fast the necessary foundations of faith and holiness, in all other matters extra fundamental, whether of Faith or Order.*" †

The Preface then proceeds to show that while Independents are tolerant toward others they are not lax in their own views, and on this point contains some statements which merit attention. Observe the following: "We have and do contend for this, That *in the concrete*, the persons of all such gracious Saints, they and their errors, as they are in them, when they are but such errors as do and may stand with communion with Christ, though they should not repent of them, as not being convinced of them to the end of their days; that those, with their errors (that are purely spiritual, and intrench and overthrow not civil societies), as *concrete with their persons*, should for Christ's sake be borne withal by all Christians in the world; and they notwithstand-

---

* Schaff, "Creeds of Christendom," Vol. III., p. 708.
† *Ibid*, p. 170.

ing be permitted to enjoy all Ordinances and spiritual Privileges according to their light, as freely as any other of their brethren that pretend to the greatest Orthodoxy ; as having as equal, and as fair a right in and unto Christ, and all the holy things of Christ, that any other can challenge to themselves." *

That so many persons, in so short a time, were able to come to agreement in their statements of such truths is surely a phenomenal fact, and worthy of the emphasis which it has received. The harmony of the Savoy Assembly to this day is unparalleled. The sessions lasted but eleven days; a large part of the time was spent in prayer and consulting, and in the end there was perfect unanimity. This result, furthermore, was reached without previous correspondence or consultation. The Preface says, quaintly and beautifully, that their churches had been like ships sailing apart and alone on "the vast ocean of those tumultuous times"; and yet while in the articles of the Declaration the people confessed to their shame that they had neglected one another, they acknowledged "that God had so ordered things that their neglect had redounded to His glory, in that when they came together they found that they were in perfect unity." They recognised that there were serious divisions in the Christian world, and boldly affirmed that

---

* Schaff, "Creeds of Christendom," Vol, III., p. 710.

those divisions would have been less if there had been greater liberty. This confidence of the Savoy divines in liberty is most surprising when the narrowness and bigotry of many of their beliefs are considered.

Concerning the doctrinal position of the Savoy Assembly the Preface says that they agree for substance with that Confession prepared by the Westminster Assembly: "To which Confession, for the substance of it, we fully assent, as do our brethren of New England and the churches also of Scotland, as each in their General Synods have testified." * They declare, however, that only those things were put into their Confession which may properly be called matters of faith: "what is of Church-order we dispose in certain Propositions by itself." Observe the following: "We say further, it being our utmost end in this (as it is indeed of a Confession), humbly to give an account what we hold and assert in these matters." †

The difference between what was done at Savoy and at Westminster is now evident. The Savoy divines attempted simply to give an account of the doctrinal views of those whom they represented, and not to formulate a standard for the churches. The Westminster divines, on the other hand, prepared a creed which was in the nature of a doctrinal test, to which religious teachers, and officers in the

---

* Schaff, "Creeds of Christendom," Vol. III., p. 714.
† *Ibid*, p. 715

church, were expected to subscribe. Naturally, this usage affected more or less the Independents who accepted the same doctrines, and it has taken a long time for Congregationalists to put into practice the teaching of the Preface of the Savoy Confession, and to regard that Confession as a testimony rather than a test. Some men think that what they believe with intensity all others ought to accept with equal positiveness. Against that fiction English Independency utters its strong protest.

The subject of Church Order, about which there was much controversy in those times, is now treated with a notable absence of narrowness, and with the same emphasis on the obligation of tolerance that has usually characterised the treatment of questions in theology. At this point I venture to copy a long letter from the Rev. Dr. John Stoughton to the Rev. Dr. Philip Schaff, and by the latter inserted in his valuable work on "The Creeds of Christendom." Dr. Stoughton, more than any other writer, may be called the historian of English Independency; his books on this subject are many, and are among the best authorities we possess. It is therefore better for me to borrow this important passage verbatim from Dr. Schaff,* than to refer to other authors. It should be said that in the years that have elapsed since Dr. Stoughton's letter was written there have been marked changes in theological

---
* Vol I. p. 834.

thinking, but it was no doubt entirely accurate a score of years ago. Dr. Stoughton writes:

"Looking at the principles of Congregationalism, which involve the repudiation of all human authority in matters of religion, it is impossible to believe that persons holding those principles can consistently regard any ecclesiastical creed or symbol in the same way in which Catholics, whether Roman or Anglican, regard the creeds of the ancient Church. There is a strong feeling among English Congregationalists against the use of such documents for the purpose of defining the limits of religious communion, or for the purpose of checking the exercise of sober, free inquiry; and there is also a widely spread conviction that it is impossible to reduce the expression of Christian belief to a series of logical propositions, so as to preserve and represent the full spirit of gospel truth. No doubt there may be heard in some circles a great deal of loose conversation seeming to indicate such a repugnance to the employment of creeds as would imply a dislike to any formal definition of Christian doctrine whatever; but I apprehend that the prevailing sentiment relative to this subject among our ministers and churches does not go beyond the point just indicated. Many consider that while creeds are objectionable as tests and imperfect as confessions, yet they may have a certain value as manifestoes of conviction on the part of religious communities.

"The Westminster Assembly's Catechism never had the authority in Congregational churches which from the beginning it possessed in the Presbyterian Church of Scotland, and its use in schools and families for educational purposes, once very common, has diminished of late years to a very low degree. The Savoy Declaration, which perhaps never had much weight with Congregationalists, is a document now little known, except by historical students. The Declaration of 1833 was prepared by a committee of the Congregational Union, of which the Rev.

Dr. Redford, of Worcester, was a member. He, I believe, drew up the Articles, and it was only in accordance with his well-known character as a zealous antagonist of human authority in religion that he introduced the following passages in the preliminary notes: [See pages 187–188 of this lecture.]

"It would be well to insert a statement made to me by one who from his official position has the best means of ascertaining the state of opinion in our churches:

"'I do not believe that the Declaration of 1833 could now with success be submitted for adoption to an Assembly of the Congregational Union; in part, because not a few would dispute its position, and in part because many more—I believe the majority—without objecting on strictly doctrinal grounds, would object on grounds of policy.'

"I may add to this, in the words of the Dean of Westminster, who wrote them on the authority of 'a respected Congregational minister,' that, beyond care in the matter of ordination, 'no measures are adopted or felt to be either desirable or necessary for preserving uniformity of doctrine, excepting only that the trust-deeds of most of their places of worship contain a reference to leading points of doctrine to which the minister may be required to express his assent. In practice this is merely a provision against any decided departure from the faith as commonly received among us, the trustees of the property having it in their power to refuse the use of the building to any minister whose teaching may be contrary to the doctrines contained in the deed. Such cases, however, are extremely rare.'

"In some cases trust-deeds make reference to the Declaration of 1833, as containing the doctrines to be taught in substance within the places of worship secured by such deeds; but in most cases a brief schedule of doctrines is employed, of which the following is an example:

"'1. The divine and special inspiration of the holy Scriptures of the Old and New Testament, and their supreme authority in faith and practice.

"'2. The unity of God. The Deity of the Father, of the Son, and of the Holy Ghost.

"'3. The depravity of man, and the absolute necessity of the Holy Spirit's agency in man's regeneration and sanctification.

"'4. The incarnation of the Son of God, in the person of the Lord Jesus Christ; the universal sufficiency of the atonement by His death; and the free justification of sinners by faith alone in Him.

"'5. Salvation by grace, and the duty of all who hear the gospel to believe in Christ.

"'6. The resurrection of the dead and the final judgment, when the wicked "shall go away into everlasting punishment, but the righteous into life eternal."'

"The Secretary of our Chapel Building Society informs me that 'one reason for the disuse of the Declaration may be its length, and the circumstance that, to put it beyond question what document is meant, it has been thought it would be needful to embody it in the deed, which would add to the cost.'

"It has been remarked, on the authority of one already cited, 'that, notwithstanding the absence of tests, there is among Independents a marked uniformity of opinion on all important points.' Perhaps this statement, still true on the whole, would require more qualification than it did some years ago. There are among us a few men of mental vigour who have departed very considerably from the published creeds of Congregationalism. There may be a larger number whose opinions are of an Arminian cast; but, again to use language supplied by a friend, in whom I place confidence as to this subject : 'It would still be fair, I think, to describe our ministry as moderately Calvinistic. An immense majority of the ministers are so. An impression to the contrary has, I am aware, become prevalent; but that is owing, I believe, to the fact that the greater number of the men who have departed from the Calvinistic type hold prominent positions, and have "the habit of the pen."' It is a difficult and delicate task to report the state of large religious communities among whose members there exist some diversities of opinion. One person biassed by his own predilections will give one account, and another person under an influence of the same kind will give another.

"In what I have said I have endeavoured to be as impartial as possible; and, to give the more weight to my statements, I have sought the assistance of official brethren who have wider means of information than I possess, and who may look at things from points of view not exactly identical with my own."

An understanding of the doctrinal attitude of early English Congregationalists necessitates careful study of the Westminster Confession, but nothing gives a truer insight into the ecclesiastical and spiritual temper of their leaders than the Preface of the Savoy Confession. Those Pilgrims of Old England were worthy brethren of the Pilgrims who laid the foundations of religious liberty on Plymouth Rock. In various periods of the Pilgrim history different theological systems have been in the ascendant. First an austere type of Calvinism won almost universal acceptance. In time that gave place to a rationalising tendency, which in the eighteenth century was followed by a general decadence of spiritual life. Then came the Evangelical Revival led by the Wesleys and Whitefield, which made itself felt in the Congregational churches quite as much as in the Establishment and which resulted in strengthening the hold of professing Christians on the fundamental truths of the Christian religion, quite as distinctly as in awakening the dormant spiritual life; but those truths had no longer the same Calvinistic colouring.

In later years, in consequence of the influence of the Evangelical Revival, the advancement of science, a better understanding of the universe, a more intelligent reading of the Scriptures, and of the immense pressure of the terrible social conditions, there has been a change in the thinking of Christian scholars in England amounting almost to a revolution. Now, the Immanence of God is emphasised rather than the Transcendence; now, Fatherhood has taken the place of Sovereignty, except with those thinkers who are wise enough to see that in any adequate system of theology there must be a synthesis of both ideas, (for the King is Father, and the Father is King); now, positive declarations concerning Eschatology are no longer made, and a larger number both of ministers and laymen believe either in Conditional Immortality or in Ultimate Restoration.

In the old day, the duty of man to man, and of brotherhood as founded on Fatherhood, had no place in the creeds, but if confessions were now written the doctrine of human brotherhood would have a conspicuous place. In earlier times the Bible was received as the Word of God, though without the light which has fallen upon it by modern investigations; but now criticism has largely modified the doctrine concerning Holy Scripture, although it has not weakened its authority.

In the midst of the storm and stress of theological controversy, one doctrine alone remains unchanged, and that concerns the person of our Lord. In the Savoy Confession, in the Creed published in the Year Book, and in the hearts of almost all who bear the Congregational name in Old England, belief in the absolute Deity of Christ is fundamental. In the light which He, God manifest in the flesh, sheds upon humanity and eternity all problems are studied, with unsurpassed reverence and consecration. Both ministers and churches make the first article of their creed, and the faith which regulates their lives, the opening words of the Gospel according to St. John:—"In the beginning was the Word, and the Word was with God, and the Word was God."

Let us now turn from Old England to New England. The first Confession of Faith which had any relation to the fellowship of churches was adopted at Burial Hill in 1865, and that is called a "creed" by a misuse of language, for it is really a simple declaration never intended for confessional purposes. But, before that, various councils, more or less representative, had reaffirmed the faith of the churches as expressed in the Confessions of Westminster and Savoy. This was repeated several times during the first two hundred years after the landing of the Pilgrims. Consequently while there always was intense theological activity on this side of the sea, and while the Congregationalists of New England have probably made more statements of faith, representing local churches, than were ever before made, no new declaration was issued in the name of *all* the churches. The Westminster Standard of Doctrine, "with the exception of the sections relating to synodical church government," were accepted in the New World, and "formerly the Assembly's Shorter Catechism was taught in all the schools of New England."* The Cambridge Platform deals, almost exclusively, with questions of polity. It was adopted in a meeting of "The Elders and Messengers of the Churches assembled in the Synod at Cambridge, in New England, in June, 1648." It approved the Westminster Confession one year after its publication in the following minute; "This Synod having perused and considered with much gladness of heart, and thankfulness to God, the Confession of Faith published of late by the reverend Assembly in England, do judge it to be very holy, orthodox, and judicious in all matters of faith ; and do therefore freely and fully consent thereunto, for the substance thereof. Only in those things which have respect to church government and discipline we refer ourselves to the

---

*Schaff's " Creeds of Christendom," Vol I., p. 835.

Platform of Church Discipline agreed upon by this present assembly; and do therefore think it meet that this Confession of Faith should be commended to the churches of Christ among us, and to the honoured court, as worthy of their consideration and acceptance. Howbeit, we may not conceal that the doctrine of *vocation* passed not without some debate. Yet considering that the term of *vocation* and others by which it is described are capable of a large or more strict sense or use, and that it is not intended to bind apprehensions precisely in point of order or method, there hath been a general condescendency thereunto. Now by this our professed consent and free concurrence with them in all the doctrinals of religion, we hope it may appear to the world that as we are a remnant of the people of the same nation with them, so we are professors of the same common faith, and fellow-heirs of the same common salvation."*

It is worthy of notice that the date of the American Cambridge Synod preceded that of the English Savoy Assembly by ten years.

The next utterance of the churches of New England concerning doctrine was made by the Synod of Boston in May, 1680. It adopted and published "the Savoy Recension of the Westminster Assembly, together with the Cambridge Platform." The following is from the Preface to its Declaration:

---

* Schaff's "Creeds of Christendom," Vol I., p. 836.

"That which was consented to by the Elders and Messengers of the Congregational Churches in England, who met at the Savoy (being for the most part, some small variations excepted, the same with that which was agreed upon first by the Assembly at Westminster, and was approved by the Synod at Cambridge in New England, *anno* 1648, as also by a General Assembly in Scotland), was twice publicly read, examined and approved of; that little variation which we have made from the one, in compliance with the other, may be seen by those who please to compare them. But we have (for the main) chosen to express ourselves in the words of those reverend Assemblies, that so we might not only with one heart, but with one mouth, glorify God and our Lord Jesus Christ." *

The churches of New England had not yet emerged from the conflict which culminated in the Puritan Revolution in England. They gave little attention to questions of doctrine. Staunch Calvinists they were, indeed almost to a man, but their Calvinism had not yet worked itself to its logical conclusions—for Calvinism must always end in liberty, both of thought and person. If God is the Sovereign, and Jesus Christ the one and only Mediator, democracy in State and Church are inevitable. The fathers of New England were so busy getting possession of, and confirming, the rights of personal

---

* Schaff's "Creeds of Christendom," Vol. I., p. 837.

liberty that they did not, at first, see to what ends they would logically be carried by the principles which they had adopted. Ecclesiastical questions occupied attention almost exclusively until about 1740, the time of "The Great Awakening." When the leaven of Calvinism had reached far enough the doctrinal problems which have filled the minds of New England theologians for two centuries began to push themselves into prominence. At first the question, Have we the right to think for ourselves? engrossed attention; later that was followed by another inquiry, What shall we think?

The Synod of Saybrook, which convened in September, 1708, would never have been held except for a dispute which arose concerning questions of ecclesiastical procedure. It is not surprising therefore that the body which gave to the State of Connecticut the strangest, most absurd, most illogical, and now most obstructive ecclesiastical expedient known to American Congregationalism, namely, "The Consociation," which is a cross between Presbyterianism and Independency, should have made very little reference to doctrine. That Synod agreed to accept the deliverance of the Synod of Boston, which had reaffirmed the Savoy Confession. It " also accepted 'the Heads of Agreement assented to [in 1692] by the united ministers [of England], formerly called Presbyterian and Congregational,' and so virtually gave indorsement to three creeds as essentially teaching the same system,—the doctrinal part of the Articles of the Church of England, the Westminster Confession or Catechisms, and the Confession agreed on at the Savoy."*

After the Civil War (1865) the churches in various parts of the United States felt that there was especial need for consultation and co-operation, in view of the various problems which faced the American Churches and the American State as the result of that war, and of the emancipation of the slaves. That conviction, which was first publicly voiced in the Convention of the Congregational Churches of the Northwest meeting in Chicago, finally led to the fourth General Council of American Congregationalism, which met in Boston in June, 1865. A Committee had been informally appointed to prepare a doctrinal Declaration of Faith for presentation at that Council. The Committee consisted of the late Rev. Joseph P. Thompson, D. D., of New York, one of the ablest and most scholarly ministers of the American pulpit; Rev. E. A. Lawrence, D. D., a professor at East Windsor (Conn.) Theological Seminary; and Rev. George P. Fisher, D. D., of Yale Theological Seminary, New Haven. The report presented by this Committee was referred to a Committee constituted as follows: Rev. J. O. Fiske, D.D., of Maine; Prof. Daniel J. Noyes, D. D., New Hampshire; Rev. Nahum Gale, D. D., Massachu-

---
* Schaff's " Creeds of Christendom," Vol. I., p. 837.

setts; Rev. Leonard Swain, D. D., Rhode Island; Dr. Albert G. Bristol, New York; Rev. John C. Hart, Ohio; Dea. Sherman S. Barnard, Michigan; Rev. George S. F. Savage, Illinois. The Committee was subsequently enlarged by the addition of the following Theological Professors: Samuel Harris, of Bangor; Edwards A. Park, of Andover; Edward A. Lawrence, of East Windsor; Noah Porter, Jr., of New Haven; James H. Fairchild, of Oberlin; Joseph Haven, of Chicago. This new Committee brought in a new report, which was not rejected, but which was laid over for consideration.

In the meantime a great excursion to Plymouth had been arranged, and, on a glorious day in June, one thousand and forty-seven persons went to that town, to stand together in the cemetery on Burial Hill, among the graves of their Pilgrim ancestors, whose heroic achievements they celebrated. The place and its memories were full of inspiration. When the Assembly had reconvened at Plymouth and the report of the Committee was again called for, an entirely new document was presented. The sentiments of the first report were all there, but they were expressed in a vigorous and resonant rhetoric, which they had before lacked and which caught the ear and enchained the attention at once. Its effect on the audience was instantaneous, and favourable. Some opposed its immediate adoption, arguing that action so important should be preceded by longer time for consideration; others thought that the report was too vague—a form of words intended to evade a more positive utterance. But at last, with great solemnity and an electric enthusiasm, the report was adopted " for substance," and without an opposing vote. The following is a copy of the now historic document:

"BURIAL HILL CONFESSION.

" Standing by the rock where the Pilgrims set foot upon these shores, upon the spot where they worshipped God, and among the graves of the early generations, we, Elders and Messengers of the Congregational Churches of the United States in National Council assembled—like them acknowledging no rule of faith but the Word of God—do now declare our adherence to the faith and order of the apostolic and primitive churches held by our fathers, and substantially as embodied in the confessions and platforms which our Synods of 1648 and 1680 set forth or reaffirmed. We declare that the experience of the nearly two and a half centuries which have elapsed since the memorable day when our sires founded here a Christian Commonwealth, with all the development of new forms of error since their times, has only deepened our confidence in the faith and polity of those fathers. We bless God for the inheritance of these doctrines. We invoke the help of the Divine Redeemer, that through the presence of the promised Comforter, He will enable us to transmit them in purity to our children.

" In the times that are before us as a nation, times at once of duty and of danger, we rest all our hope in the gospel of the Son of God. It was the grand peculiarity of our Puritan fathers that they held this gospel, not merely as the ground of their personal salvation, but as declaring the worth of man by the incarnation and sacrifice of the Son of God, and therefore applied its principles to elevate society, to regulate education, to civilise humanity, to purify law, to reform the Church and the State, and to assert and defend liberty; in short, to mould and redeem, by its all-transforming energy, everything that belongs to man in his individual and social relations.

"It was the faith of our fathers that gave us this free land in which we dwell. It is by this faith only that we can transmit to our children a free and happy, because a Christian, commonwealth.

"We hold it to be a distinctive excellence of our Congregational system that it exalts that which is more above that which is less important, and by the simplicity of its organisation facilitates, in communities where the population is limited, the union of all true believers in one Christian Church, and that the division of such communities into several weak and jealous societies, holding the same common faith, is a sin against the unity of the body of Christ, and at once the shame and scandal of Christendom.

"We rejoice that, through the influence of our free system of apostolic order, we can hold fellowship with all who acknowledge Christ, and act efficiently in the work of restoring unity to the divided Church, and of bringing back harmony and peace among all 'who love our Lord Jesus Christ in sincerity.'

"Thus recognising the unity of the Church of Christ in all the world, and knowing that we are but one branch of Christ's people, while adhering to our peculiar faith and order, we extend to all believers the hand of Christian fellowship upon the basis of those great fundamental truths in which all Christians should agree.

"With them we confess our faith in God, the Father, the Son, and the Holy Ghost [the only living and true God];* in

---

* The words in brackets were inadvertently omitted in the volume of Proceedings, but inserted in the text of the Manual. See

Jesus Christ, the incarnate Word, who is exalted to be our Redeemer and King; and in the Holy Comforter, who is present in the Church to regenerate and sanctify the soul.

"With the whole Church, we confess the common sinfulness and ruin of our race, and acknowledge that it is only through the work accomplished by the life and expiatory death of Christ that believers in Him are justified before God, receive the remission of sins, and through the presence and grace of the Holy Comforter are delivered from the power of sin and perfected in holiness.

"We believe also in the organised and visible Church, in the ministry of the Word, in the sacraments of Baptism and the Lord's Supper, in the resurrection of the body, and in the final judgment, the issues of which are eternal life and everlasting punishment.

"We receive these truths on the testimony of God, given through prophets and apostles, and in the life, the miracles, the death, the resurrection of His Son, our Divine Redeemer—a testimony preserved for the Church in the Scriptures of the Old and New Testaments, which were composed by holy men, as they were moved by the Holy Ghost.

"Affirming now our belief that those who thus hold 'one faith, one Lord, one baptism,' together constitute the one Catholic Church, the several households of which, though called by different names, are the one body of Christ, and that these members of His body are sacredly bound to keep 'the unity of the Spirit in the bond of peace,' we declare that we will co-operate with all who hold these truths. With them we will carry the gospel into every part of this land, and with them we will go into all the world, and 'preach the gospel to every

---

Congregational Quarterly, Vol. X., p. 377, where Dr. Quint shows that they belong to the original MS.—Shaff, "Creeds of Christendom," Vol, III., p. 735.

creature.' May He to whom 'all power is given in heaven and earth' fulfil the promise which is all our hope : ' Lo, I am with you alway, even to the end of the World.' *Amen*."

The presentation of the Declaration which was adopted on Burial Hill was characterised as follows by Dr. John P. Gulliver, now a professor in Andover Seminary, but then a pastor in Connecticut: " It was an audacious proceeding which no one but a soldier, a Democrat, and an old-school man—all in one—could possibly have attained to." * The Burial Hill Declaration is not a creed, and was not intended to be binding on the churches, but rather to express what was believed to be the common faith of Congregationalists at that time. Its composition was a happy inspiration. It has been used by many churches for purposes for which it was never designed, and for a score of years has had a place in numerous Confessions of Faith. That it was not entirely satisfactory, however, is evident from the following leaflet, which is copied from the original publication now in the Congregational Library, Boston, entitled, " The Surprise Party of Yesterday: Fraternal Complaints : " †

"(1) It was not currently understood in the coun-

---

* The New York *Independent*, July 6, 1865. The reference here is to Rev. Alonzo H. Quint, D. D., then of New Bedford, Mass., who gave to the report its final form.

† Said to have been written by the Rev. E. F. Burr, D. D., of Connecticut.

cil that the subject of a Declaration of Faith was to be brought forward for settlement at Plymouth.

"(2) The circumstances of the place were such as in their very nature to preclude a fair expression of opinion, and among large numbers, even a competent knowledge of what was passing.

"(3) The document passed upon was not that legitimately under the consideration of the Council —but that document mutilated, deranged, *crazed*.

"(4) The immense promptitude and precipitation of the excellent Vice-Moderator were contrary to the genius and usage of our Ecclesiastical Bodies, especially in dealing with matters of the highest religious moment.

"(5) As matters are now left, it may be plausibly charged that the Declaration adopted at Plymouth was not the deliverance of the National Council.

"Gentlemen of the Council! Shall the Hereafter say as the Present already does, that the Declaration of 1865 was passed by a *Pious Fraud!*

"All of which is respectfully submitted by friends of the Report of the Committee of Reference."

On November 17, 1871, the Triennial National Council, organised to provide some regularly recurring general assembly of representatives of the local churches, not for general authority but for mutual conference, held its first session at Oberlin, Ohio.

That Council was wise enough in adopting its Constitution to attempt to formulate no new creed. It made, however, a brief declaration concerning a doctrinal basis which was of the most general character, and practically left to the local bodies represented in the Council the responsibility of determining whether they had a right to membership.

The messengers of the churches at Oberlin little understood the importance of their action. From the time of that Council the name of Calvin, as an authority to whom the descendants of the Pilgrims owe superior deference, disappears, and the broader name "evangelical" takes its place. Prior to that, Calvinism had been the distinguishing characteristic of Congregational theology; and those who were no longer Calvinists in the old sense tried to delude themselves and the public with such phrases as "consistent Calvinism," "moderate Calvinism," and "modern Calvinism." At Oberlin the representatives of the churches frankly assumed the catholic position. They denounced no sacred symbol; they supplanted no old standard with a new one; they simply allowed Calvin to take his place among the prophets and sages of all the Christian centuries, while they brought into clear relief the exact truth, that some of our churches are Calvinistic, some Arminian, (more of them neither, consciously), and all of them evangelical.

The Oberlin Declaration is as follows:

"The Congregational churches of the United States, by elders and messengers assembled, do now associate themselves in National Council:

" To express and foster their substantial unity in doctrine, polity, and work; and

" To consult upon the common interests of all the churches, their duties in the work of evangelisation, the united development of their resources, and their relations to all parts of the kingdom of Christ.

" They agree in belief that the Holy Scriptures are the sufficient and only infallible rule of religious faith and practice; their interpretation thereof being in substantial accordance with the great doctrines of the Christian faith, commonly called Evangelical, held in our churches from the early times, and sufficiently set forth by former General Councils.

" They agree in belief that the right of government resides in local churches, or congregations of believers, who are responsible directly to the Lord Jesus Christ, the One Head of the Church universal and of all particular churches; but that all churches, being in communion one with another as parts of Christ's catholic Church, have mutual duties subsisting in the obligations of fellowship.

" The churches, therefore, while establishing this National Council for the furtherance of the common interests and work of all the churches, do maintain the Scriptural and inalienable right of each church to self-government and administration; and this National Council shall never exercise legislative or judicial authority, nor consent to act as a council of reference."

This first convention of the triennial National Council was hardly completed before the feeling began to be manifest that the new body ought to justify its existence by the formulation of a new creed. The meeting at Oberlin in 1871 had been its beginning. For two or three years previous to its meeting at St. Louis in 1880 the denominational papers had discussed the subject of the new creed, and when the Council convened in that city that question was uppermost in the minds of the delegates. Without much discussion, and with no acrimony, it was voted that the time had come for a statement of doctrine which should fairly represent the theological beliefs of our American churches. The National Council Commission accordingly was constituted and instructed to prepare a document which should in its opinion fairly represent the faith of the churches, and also be a statement of doctrine which could be used by new churches which wished to be in the Congregational fellowship, but which contained no members inspired to write a creed. All who read that " Creed of 1883 " must be impressed with its wisdom, catholicity and general fairness. It has little of the liturgical quality of the Apostles' and Nicene Creeds; it has none of the abstruse metaphysics of the Creeds of Nicæa or Chalcedon; but it is a clear, strong, manly utterance concerning the doctrines believed in the American churches. Prof. George P. Fisher, the most distinguished theologian on the Commission says:

" The 'Creed Commission' was instituted by the National Council held at St. Louis in 1880. It was instructed to prepare ' a simple, clear and comprehensive exposition ' of the truths of the Gospel 'for the instruction and edification of our churches.' A brief account of the sessions of the Commission and of their prolonged labours may be found in an editorial in the *Congregationalist* of March 27th, 1884. The Creed was published early in March of that year. It appeared in the *Independent* of March 6th. It was signed and recommended by twenty-two of the Commissioners, *viz.:* by Drs. Julius H. Seelye, Charles M. Mead, Henry M. Dexter, Alexander Mackenzie, James G. Johnson, George P. Fisher, George L. Walker, George T. Ladd, Samuel P. Leeds, David B. Coe, William M. Taylor, Lyman Abbott, Augustus F. Beard, William W. Patton, James H. Fairchild, Israel W. Andrews, Zachary Eddy, James T. Hyde, Alden B. Robbins, Constans L. Goodell, Richard Cordley and George Mooar. Dr. Goodwin had not attended the meetings of the Commission, and had resigned his place as a member. The two members whose names are not appended to the Creed were Dr. Karr and Dr. Alden.

"Immediately on its publication the Creed was received with expressions of approbation on all sides. The *Independent* in an editorial said: 'There is not a Creed of its length put forth by any other denomination which so exactly represents its faith. It is vastly nearer to the belief of the Congregational churches than the Westminister Confession is to that of the Presbyterian Church, or the Augsburg Confession to that of the Lutheran Church, or the Heidelburg to that of the Reformed Church. . . It represents the living, actual faith that is held in the last decades of this century. . . It is an admirable statement of the Church's faith.' It was added that nothing in it is 'loose or evasive.' 'Notice especially the admirable language of the last article, and its sufficient and careful eschatology.' The following sentences respecting the Commission, from the *Advance* of March 6th, reiterate the warmth of its commendation: 'Their work speaks for itself. We believe it will give almost universal satisfaction. . . It is Congregational, Catholic, Christian. . .

We think they have voiced well the consensus of the churches. . . Will the churches generally accept the Creed? We think they will.' Under date of March 7th, Dr. Mark Hopkins, President of Williams College and then President of the American Board [of Commissioners for Foreign Missions] wrote: 'The Commission deserves the thanks of the churches, and I have no doubt their work will be generally accepted. . . The Creed will be of great service as something that can be accepted for substance of doctrine.' (*Christian Union*, March 31st, 1884.) Dr. R. S. Storrs of Brooklyn, and successor to Dr. Hopkins as President of the American Board, wrote, under date of March 14th: 'This Creed seems to me fairly to represent the general convictions of the Congregational Churches, so far as I know them, and to be well adapted for use in the organisation of such churches, and in their subsequent religious instruction.' (*Christian Union*, March 20th, 1884.)"

These selections from memoranda by Prof. George P. Fisher show that beyond the most sanguine anticipations of its most ardent advocates the new creed met the approval of the churches and of the Christian community. It is called a Creed, and yet in reality is only a Declaration of *their opinion* concerning what was believed in the American Congregational churches, appointed for that purpose by the National Council. It was never approved by any General Council, and never offered to one for its approval. And just here appears a peculiarity of all the so-called Creeds of the Pilgrim churches. No one has had the least authority—all have been "declarations" concerning what *is accepted* rather than standards of what *should be be-*

lieved. In this respect the doctrinal utterances of Congregationalists, from that of Savoy to that of the National Council of 1883, differ from those issued by other churches. Most other Creeds are standards to be accepted, or tests offered, sometimes to all who seek membership in given denominations, and sometimes only to those who are set apart to rule and to teach: the Pilgrim Creeds are statements of what *is* supposed to be the belief of the Pilgrim churches. That part of the National Council Creed which is in the nature of a Declaration of Faith is as follows:

THE REPORT OF THE COMMISSION.

The Commission appointed, under the direction of the National Council of the Congregational churches of the United States, "to prepare, in the form of a Creed or Catechism, or both, a simple, clear, and comprehensive exposition of the truths of the glorious gospel of the blessed God, for the instruction and edification of our churches," herewith submit to those churches the following

STATEMENT OF DOCTRINE:

I. We believe in one God, the Father Almighty, Maker of heaven and earth, and of all things visible and invisible;

And in Jesus Christ, His only Son, our Lord, who is of one substance with the Father; by whom all things were made;

And in the Holy Spirit, the Lord and Giver of life, who is sent from the Father and Son, and who together with the Father and Son is worshipped and glorified.

II. We believe that the Providence of God, by which He executes His eternal purposes in the government of the world, is in and over all events; yet so that the freedom and responsibility of man are not impaired, and sin is the act of the creature alone.

III. We believe that man was made in the image of God, that he might know, love, and obey God, and enjoy Him forever; that our first parents by disobedience fell under the righteous condemnation of God; and that all men are so alienated from God that there is no salvation from the guilt and power of sin except through God's redeeming grace.

IV. We believe that God would have all men return to Him; that to this end He has made Himself known, not only through the works of nature, the course of His providence, and the consciences of men, but also through supernatural revelations made especially to a chosen people, and above all, when the fulness of time was come, through Jesus Christ His Son.

V. We believe that the Scriptures of the Old and New Testaments are the record of God's revelation of Himself in the work of redemption; that they were written by men under the special guidance of the Holy Spirit; that they are able to make wise unto salvation; and that they constitute the authoritative standard by which religious teaching and human conduct are to be regulated and judged.

VI. We believe that the love of God to sinful men has found its highest expression in the redemptive work of His Son; who became man, uniting His divine nature with our human nature in one person; who was tempted like other men, yet without sin; who, by His humiliation, His holy obedience, His sufferings, His death on the cross, and His resurrection, became a perfect Redeemer; whose sacrifice of Himself for the sins of the world declares the righteousness of God, and is the sole and sufficient ground of forgiveness and of reconciliation with Him.

VII. We believe that Jesus Christ, after He had risen from the dead, ascended into heaven, where, as the one Mediator between God and man, He carries forward His work of saving men; that He sends the Holy Spirit to convict them of sin, and to lead them to repentance and faith; and that those who through renewing grace turn to righteousness, and trust in Jesus Christ as their Redeemer, receive for His sake the forgiveness of their sins, and are made the children of God.

VIII. We believe that those who are thus regenerated and justified, grow in sanctified character through fellowship with Christ, the indwelling of the Holy Spirit, and obedience to the truth; that a holy life is the fruit and evidence of saving faith; and that the believer's hope of continuance in such a life is in the preserving grace of God.

IX. We believe that Jesus Christ came to establish among men the kingdom of God, the reign of truth and love, righteousness and peace; that to Jesus Christ, the Head of this kingdom, Christians are directly responsible in faith and conduct; and that to Him all have immediate access without mediatorial or priestly intervention.

X. We believe that the Church of Christ, invisible and spiritual, comprises all true believers, whose duty it is to associate themselves in churches, for the maintenance of worship, for the promotion of spiritual growth and fellowship, and for the conversion of men; that these churches, under the guidance of the Holy Scriptures and in fellowship with one another, may determine—each for itself—their organisation, statements of belief, and forms of worship; may appoint and set apart their own ministers, and should co-operate in the work which Christ has committed to them for the furtherance of the gospel throughout the world.

XI. We believe in the observance of the Lord's Day, as a day of holy rest and worship; in the ministry of the Word; and in the two Sacraments, which Christ has appointed for His church: Baptism, to be administered to believers and their children, as the sign of cleansing from sin, of union to Christ, and of the impartation of the Holy Spirit; and the Lord's

Supper as a symbol of His atoning death, a seal of its efficacy, and a means whereby He confirms and strengthens the spiritual union and communion of believers with Himself.

XII. We believe in the ultimate prevalence of the kingdom of Christ over all the earth; in the glorious appearing of the great God and our Saviour Jesus Christ; in the resurrection of the dead; and in a final judgment, the issues of which are everlasting punishment and everlasting life.

Thus as clearly as possible we have tried to present the salient facts concerning the creeds of the Congregational churches of the English-speaking world, so far as they are entitled to be called representative. The Congregational churches of England have few creeds, except as their "Doctrinal Schedules" in Trust Deeds may be called by that name. In the sense that the Westminster Confession is a creed, neither the English nor the American Congregational Churches have ever formulated any. At the Savoy, at Burial Hill, and at Oberlin, "declarations" were made, and at St. Louis a Committee of honoured and able ministers was appointed to prepare a "statement" of what was commonly believed by the American churches. Although their work was directed to be in the form of a creed or catechism or both, it has only so much authority as it contains truth. On the other hand a large proportion of the Congregational churches in America have such documents, which are peculiarly their own and binding on their membership.

It may therefore be said when representative creeds are considered that the Congregational *fellowship* makes less of such standards than any other denomination, except the Baptists; while judged by their local usage, the Congregational *churches*, particularly in America, have put a more constant and imperative emphasis on the importance of creeds than has any other branch of the Christian Church.

VI.
DOCTRINAL CONDITIONS OF CHURCH MEMBERSHIP.

"We no longer recite the old Creeds of Athanasius or Arius, of Calvin or Hopkins. The forms are flexible, but the uses not less real.... Truth is simple, and will not be antique; is ever present, and insists on being of this age and of this moment. Here is thought, and love, and truth and duty, new as the first day of Adam and of Angelo."—RALPH WALDO EMERSON.

"I say that the noblest opportunity God gives to men is that of testifying, with lips which He himself has touched, to the glory of His character, to the majestic grace of His plans, to the work which men of a consecrated spirit may do for Him in the world."
—RICHARD S. STORRS.

"The whole expression 'Christian Truth' is greatly wanting in clearness. What is '*Christian*' truth? Knowledge in the light of the historical fact 'Christ,'—a light which is to be conceived of as in continual growth."—RICHARD ROTHE.

"The contents of the Christian revelation are richer and more varied to-day than they were in any past age. We have fellowship with Christ in revealing God.... To have fellowship with Christ in His work, the life of Christ must be ours."
—ROBERT W. DALE.

VI.

DOCTRINAL CONDITIONS OF CHURCH MEMBERSHIP.*

SHOULD those who desire to become members of Christ's visible Church, and thereby to testify their devotion to Him and the ends which He sought to realise, be required to assent to statements of doctrine of any form whatever; and if so, what form?

We have nothing to do at this time with the question whether the doctrinal formulæ should be presented for acceptance to religious teachers or to those called to positions of administration. The first step toward an intelligible answer to the inquiry is to learn what is the existing usage concerning admission of members to local churches. To obtain this information two courses were open to us: one to take the utterances of recognised representatives of the churches, and the other to make investigation among the churches themselves. Both methods have been adopted, with the following results.

---

* The Substance of this Chapter was read before the International Council of Congregational Churches, London, England, July 15, 1891.

In Great Britain and throughout the world there is no higher authority on Congregational usage than the honoured and accomplished President of the International Council.* He may be taken as a competent witness concerning English Congregationalism. He says: "Nor is it consistent with Congregational principles for a particular church to draw up a creed, and require its acceptance by candidates for membership. A Christian church is not a private society whose regulations can be modified by its members at their pleasure, but a society founded by Christ Himself, and intended by Him to be the home of all Christians. Nothing, therefore, should be required of an applicant for membership but personal faith in Christ; this may exist, and there may be decisive evidence of its existence, in persons who have no clear intellectual apprehension of many of the great truths of the Christian Gospel: it may exist, and there may be decisive evidence of its existence, in persons by whom some of these truths are rejected. Men come into the Church not because they have already mastered the contents of the Christian revelation, but to be taught them."† The author says that doubtless many have been kept out of the Church because of their religious opinions, and adds: "But in England the Congregational tradition has been sufficiently

---

* Rev. R. W. Dale, D. D.
† "Manual of Congregationalism," p. 186.

strong, even where Congregational principles have not been clearly understood, to prevent Congregational churches from drawing up a formal creed, and enforcing its acceptance as a condition of communion. When such a creed has been once adopted and enforced .... the Church is no longer under the immediate control of the living Christ. Its freedom and its independence are lost. It is governed not indeed by the decrees of an external council, but by the decrees of the dead. ... It is not by enforcing a theological test as a condition of communion that a church can protect itself from heresy. Its only protection is the presence of Christ, and the illumination of the Holy Ghost."*

In order that there might be no doubt concerning the usage in England, letters were addressed to a number of representative ministers asking the following questions: "Does your church make acceptance of Articles of Faith a condition of church membership?" "If you do not condition church membership on the acceptance of certain doctrines, what are your requirements?"

Robert F. Horton, Joseph Parker, A. Goodrich, Henry Allon, Samuel Pearson, Robert W. Dale, and Charles A. Berry responded, all saying that their churches made no doctrinal test for membership. These seven eminent and honoured pastors are fairly representative of Great Britain. The

---

* "Manual of Congregationalism," pp. 187, 188.

right of a church to require the assent of those uniting with it to a formula of doctrine is not recognised among English Congregationalists.

In the United States usage is largely different. Dr. Dexter says: "The public admission of members who have been received by vote, usually takes place just before the Communion Service, when the new members give their public assent to the Articles of Faith and Covenant, as they are read by the pastor . . . . The signature of every new member to the Articles of Faith and Covenant in the book kept for that purpose should follow, at the first convenient moment." *

That this passage does not exactly voice the sentiment in the United States at present will be evident when the responses to the above questions from eminent American ministers are examined. The following report that assent to Articles of Faith is required by the churches of which they are pastors: E. P. Goodwin, First Church, Chicago; A. F. Sherrill, First Church, Atlanta; C. F. Thwing, Plymouth Church, Minneapolis; W. H. Davis, First Church, Detroit; F. A. Noble, Union Park Church, Chicago; W. M. Taylor, Broadway Tabernacle Church, New York; and David Gregg, late pastor of the Park Street Church, Boston.

The following ministers report "Yes," with qualifications, such as "in substance," or "conditionally,"

---
* "Congregationalism, what it is, etc." p. 185.

or "practically," which in all cases means as their letters show, that while a formal acceptance may be asked it is distinctly understood to be only formal: S. H. Virgin, Pilgrim Church, New York; C. H. Richards, Central Church, Philadelphia; R. S. Storrs, Church of the Pilgrims, Brooklyn; R. R. Meredith, Tompkins Avenue Church, Brooklyn; F. T. Bailey, State Street Church, Portland, Maine; J. B. Thrall, First Church, Salt Lake City; George L. Walker, Centre Church, Hartford, T. E. Clapp, First Church, Portland, Oregon; T. T. Munger, United Church, New Haven; Alexander McKenzie, Sheppard Memorial Church, Cambridge.

A closer inspection of these letters shows that of those who make a doctrinal condition, Drs. Virgin, Richards, Walker and Clapp explain that rigid acceptance is not required, but only "for substance"—which may mean much or nothing; while the churches in Salt Lake City, Plymouth in Minneapolis, First in Detroit, Union Park in Chicago, United in New Haven, Sheppard Memorial in Cambridge, Tompkins Avenue in Brooklyn, all receive members by the Apostle's Creed. The Church of the Pilgrims, Brooklyn, does not require assent to the Articles of Faith when new members are received, and yet all are asked if they have examined them and propose to abide by them. They are read by individuals, and not read to them and interpreted for them.

Those who responded, "No," are: H. A. Stimson, Pilgrim Church, St. Louis; A. H. Heath, First Church, St. Paul; J. G. Vose, Beneficent Church, Providence; A. J. F. Behrends, Central Church, Brooklyn; E. A. Lawrence, First Church, Baltimore; H. M. Ladd, Euclid Avenue Church, Cleveland.

Probably the majority of the churches in the United States require formal acceptance of statements of doctrines; but many of the most prominent do not. Of those that do, many present only the Apostles' Creed, and the number is rapidly increasing of those who ask only assent to the Covenant, which embodies always something like the early confessional symbol—faith in the Father, in Jesus Christ His Son, and in the Holy Spirit. The formula for the reception of members proposed by the National Council Commission contains little besides the Apostles' Creed, and that formula may be presumed to indicate the tendency in the churches of the United States.

The following is the summary of the usage of evangelical churches generally, concerning doctrinal tests for the admission of church members:

The Presbyterian Church of the United States requires acceptance of such conditions from its ministers and officers, but not from its members.

The Baptist churches of the world receive members who give credible evidence of having experienced the new birth.

The Episcopal Church in England and America requires of all whether they were born within the church or not assent to the Apostles' Creed.

The Methodist Church on both sides the Atlantic receives members on credible evidence of a change of heart.*

The Congregational churches of England make no doctrinal test, but assume that those who they have reason to believe are honest will not seek church membership unless they are Christians.

A majority of the Congregational churches in the United States require assent to doctrinal symbols from those wishing to enter their membership. The reason for the usage in the American churches is not difficult to find. The custom appeared soon after the beginning of the present century,—about the time of the Unitarian controversy. Originally no doctrinal tests were required in New England. The most authoritative witness on this point is Cotton Mather, and he says: "The churches of New England make only vital piety the terms of communion; *and they all* with delight see godly Congregationalists, Presbyterians, Episcopalians, Antipedo-Baptists and Lutherans, *all members of the same churches*, and all sitting together without offence at the same holy table." †

Again: "To the relation of [the candidate's]

---

* More than this is nominally, but not often actually required.

† Cotton Mather, *Ratio Disciplinæ Intr.*, p. 4.

own religious experience is added either a confession of faith of his own composing or a briefer intimation of what publicly received confession he chooses to adhere to."*

Again: "It is the design of these churches to make the terms of communion run as parallel as may be with the terms of salvation. A charitable consideration of nothing but true piety in admitting to evangelical privileges is a glory which the churches of New England would claim to." †

The earliest church that I have found to require public assent to its Articles of Faith was that in Fitchburg, Mass., in 1808. Even concerning that, the pastor, Dr. Worcester, wrote; "It was never designed to exclude any from our Communion who appear to be made really subjects of experimental religion." ‡

Park Street Church, Boston, was organised in 1809 with a strict creed to which subscription was required from those desirous of entering its membership. In the years immediately following, nearly all the churches which did not become Unitarian raised doctrinal fortifications around their doors, which it was fondly believed would be sufficiently strong to resist the invasions of heresy.

From Apostolic times there have been confessional

---

* Cotton Mather, *Rat. Dis. Intr.*, p. 99.
† *Ibid*, p. 88.
‡ Life of Samuel Worcester, p. 279.

symbols expressing faith in Father, Son and Holy Ghost, but doctrinal conditions of admission to the churches are an innovation, having been, as above stated, introduced in the early years of the present century, as a result of what is known as the Unitarian Controversy. "After their vineyard was plundered and trampled they put up the bars. And they put up the wrong bars! There are impenitent sinners who can adopt with perfect sincerity the most tremendous tests that can be desired of orthodoxy in opinion. What was wanted was a rigid enforcement of the old rule that 'no person ought to make a profession of religion and join the church without experiencing a change of heart, and the church ought not to receive any person into their fellowship, whether he has been a professor or not, unless they are satisfied in a judgment of charity that he has been born again.'" *

Turning from history to the Scriptures we find them silent concerning the whole subject. On the day when three thousand were added to the Church no confessions were in existence. What is said in the Scriptures concerning the duty of confessing Christ has no relation to membership in a visible society. Paul's reply to the jailer at Philippi told the inquirer how to be saved, not how to get into the church. When the rite of baptism was administered, candidates confessed faith in Jesus Christ,

---
* Wolcott Calkins, D. D., *Andover Review*, March, 1890.

but that was all. Later, the symbol was extended to include faith in the Father and the Holy Ghost. The only examples of discipline mentioned in the Scriptures are for immorality. The confessions of the early Church were simple and vital. A convert was never expected to accept a formula of doctrine distilled from the Scriptures by a process of speculation supposed to possess all the virtue of inspiration without the name.

Two arguments are urged in favour of doctrinal conditions of church membership:

(1) They preserve soundness of doctrine. This has usually meant "sound" according to Calvinistic standards; but the Presbyterian and Baptist churches, which never required creedal assent from individual members, have been more successful in retaining their Calvinism than the Congregational churches. Indeed, the Oberlin Council explicitly substituted for the name "Calvinistic" that of "Evangelical." The Baptist churches have creeds neither for ministers nor for laymen, and they are the most intensely Calvinistic of all the denominations. The machinery which was devised to protect Calvinistic orthodoxy is driving it from the churches.

(2) Again, it is said that because all members have a voice in the government of Congregational churches therefore they should be kept homogeneous by a common creed. Once more the weak-

ness of machinery appears. The Baptist churches, without a creed for minister or layman, have been united by the mighty spirit of evangelism which makes their history read like that of an almost continuous revival, and they are if possible more loosely organised than Congregational churches.

The only arguments that have ever been advanced in favour of doctrinal conditions for church membership prove exactly the reverse of what they are supposed to prove. "It is not by enforcing a theological test as the condition of communion that a church can protect itself from heresy. Its only protection is the presence of Christ and the illumination of the Holy Spirit."*

Are such conditions desirable? The answer is in the negative, and for the following reasons:

(1) The custom of making doctrinal conditions for admission to the church is a violation of the spirit and letter of Scripture. St. Paul says that those who are "weak in the faith" are to be received. Our Lord Himself said, "This is life eternal, that they might know Thee." A doctrinal barrier at the church door violates the Christian ideal of a church, which is that it is composed of those who are born of God. St. John said the test of the new birth is love:—" Whosoever loveth is born of God." Jesus said the same:—" By this shall all men know that ye are my disciples, if ye have love one toward

---

* "Manual of Congregational Principles," R. W. Dale, p. 188.

another." But certain American churches say, "By this shall all men know that ye are Christ's disciples, if your intellectual opinions concerning the Trinity, Atonement, Decrees and Future Punishment are according to traditional interpretations."

It is said: "We make a distinction between *our* church and the Church Universal; we do not claim that acceptance of our views is necessary in order that men may be saved, but only that they may be in our denomination." That presents the sadder spectacle of a few people separating from the universal Church on purely human grounds. If the Church is divine, it is one; if it is human, it has no more sanctity than any other society or club. Societies which claim the right of separation from the body of believers in Christ can be called "churches" only by courtesy.

(2) To compel those who desire to confess Christ to assent to a confession of faith is to bind them by "the decrees of the dead," to forbid that they shall be led by the living Christ, and to make progress in knowledge and growth in spiritual life impossible. A man becomes a Christian under the influence of the living Spirit; is convicted of sin by the same Spirit; regenerated by the same Spirit; is to be sanctified by the same Spirit: but he is told that unless he can bend his mind so as to make it accept certain theological dogmas which were written by men long since dead, and, when living, mak-

ing no claim to such inspiration as moved the writers of the Holy Scriptures, he cannot enter Christ's Church. The "dead hand" in the State is terrible enough; the "dead hand" in the Church stifles progress and life itself.

(3) If Christ founded the Church then He has determined the conditions by which it is to be entered. Therefore we are reduced to this dilemma: either there is no Divine Church, or there should be nothing conditioning membership in it which does not condition entrance to the ."Kingdom of God." In the teaching of our Lord the Church and the Kingdom are practically identical. He made entrance to the Kingdom to depend on the new birth. The door into the Church and into the Kingdom are one and the same, and the society which closes doors which the Master left open, by that act separates itself from the Divine order.

(4) Doctrinal conditions of Church membership should not be required for admission to the Church because knowledge of the truth needed to intelligently assent to them is the fruit of the Christian life. To ask a new-born Christian to subscribe to articles of doctrine is as absurd as to expect an infant to tell the history of his parents, the motives which determine their action, and why they love him, before he can be recognised as a member of the family. We do not undervalue doctrine or creeds; but we do maintain that any intelligent con-

ception of doctrine, more than the consciousness of sonship, must result from growth in the Divine life. Little life means little knowledge of truth ; large life and a rich experience necessitate a large, generous and vital creed. Doctrinal statements, if worth anything, are packed with the results of the long investigation of mature Christians. Moreover, the profoundest truth cannot be put into hard and fast language; its expression will be as varied as the natures of those by whom it is voiced and to whom it is addressed. "Whosoever loveth, knoweth God." There is a knowledge of truth discernible only by the loving spirit. In the spiritual sphere those who love most know most. The clearest visions of truth are reserved for the *pure*, who shall *see God*, and the *loving*, who *know Him*. Divine revelations can never be congealed into dogmatic forms. This principle is forgotten and violated when a series of doctrines are presented, and their acceptance demanded as a condition of church membership from those whose love has already proved their union with Christ. Dr. Dale says: "Men come into the Church, not because they have already mastered the contents of the Christian revelation, but to be taught them."

(5) Requiring assent to doctrinal statements cultivates dishonesty. Even if the creeds presented be unmixed with error, those who subscribe to them say that they believe in statements which are the result of the patient thought of the best minds of

all the Christian centuries; and that they cannot say truthfully until they have been taught those truths by the Spirit and the experiences of life. The infinities and eternities are explored every time a new creed is composed. Moreover, the most emphasis in doctrinal formulæ is never on the practical and easily comprehended duties, such as love and service, but on what is to be done in Eternity and what is determined in the counsels of God. "These truths do you solemnly profess and believe?" The candidate is expected to say, "Yes." Now what does that mean? It means that at the door of the Church one has been asked to tell an untruth, because only by a process of casuistry utterly unlike the sincerity which becomes a child of God can he convince himself that it is right to say he believes. He should say "I do not know." Thus by the Church a Christian is given a lesson in insincerity. If he may profess what he does not actually believe, why may he not do what he is not sure is right?

Being induced to assent to what one is not sure that he approves is fraught with vast peril to a young life. "Do you love God?" "Do you love to read your Bible?" These and similar questions are pressed, then emptied of their contents, then evaded; then a formula of doctrine is treated in the same way; and at last when this jugglery is ended, a man is reminded of the solemnity of the obligation which he has taken, and that he has made a vow which can never be withdrawn. A more cunning system for promoting intellectual dishonesty could hardly be devised.

(6) Doctrinal conditions for church membership misrepresent Christianity. The Master said He came that the people "might have life, and that they might have it more abundantly"; and the evidence of life is always something vital,—St. Paul calls it fruit; but the doctrinal test makes ability to accept the results of the intellectual processes of others the essence of the Christian religion. At that point difficulty begins. Intellectual belief cannot be compelled. It is a result of life. Thought is coloured by hereditary bias and training. To expect those who are Arminians by nature to subscribe to a Calvinistic creed is to ask an impossibility, and to demand it is to require falsehood. If doctrinal formulæ are essential, and opinions are not a matter of choice, then there is a great gulf which can never be crossed between multitudes and true religion. Such unscriptural claims have hindered the progress of the Kingdom more than almost anything else, because when men have looked for the living Christ they have seen only a form of words meaningless to them. Such documents misrepresent our Lord, who came to thrill humanity with divine life, and not to teach a new system of theology. His pathetic reproach to the Jews was

not that they refused his doctrines, but "Ye will not come unto me that ye might have life."

(7) Doctrinal tests of church membership are not desirable because they bar from the sacraments and other means of grace, many who most need them, and who give the best evidence of the Christian life. The Sacraments surely have more than a formal efficacy. Those who partake of the Holy Communion in the right spirit are brought into vital union with Christ. In all ages Christians, whether they have celebrated the Lord's death in the spirit or by use of the bread and wine, have realised that the Supper satisfied a real hunger of the soul. Those who have been sealed to God in Baptism, especially after they have reached maturity, seldom escape the influence of that holy rite. The sacraments, however, are so administered that the world thinks of them as the property of the Church, and in many, if not most, churches they are openly declared to be reserved for church members. Many persons truly realise their sinfulness, and trust in Christ as the Saviour, who would like to be in fellowship with all of the same faith. In all that is vital to salvation they believe, but in particular theories of Inspiration, or the Trinity, or the Atonement, they may not believe, while they show by every Scriptural evidence that they have been born of the Spirit. Because they are not Calvinistic or Arminian, because they hold to a moral influence

rather than a substitutionary theory of the work of Christ, they are denied the benefit of the sacraments, and the protection and inspiration which always attends association with those who are truly His followers. Our Lord's exhortation about causing the little ones to stumble is as much in need of emphasis in these days as when first spoken. It is painful to acknowledge that many not now in our churches would be members in good standing if they were a little less honest. Thousands, not unwilling either to obey God or to follow Jesus Christ, have been denied admission to the churches solely because the Spirit has led them to conclusions concerning speculative questions differing from the ones reached by those who wrote the Standards. To presume to deny the privileges of the Church and sacraments to those who, having the spirit of Christ, are not able to assent to certain human interpretations of truth, is to assume responsibilities which were never authorised by our Master, and from which the humble surely would shrink.

The Church of Christ is the body of Christ. It is a living body. Connection with a living organism can never be realised by a mechanical contrivance. When life interfuses life the two become one. Doctrinal statements, however true, are only human mechanisms. They have no ability to generate life. A machine in coöperation with a man may fashion another machine, but without the living man it can do nothing. All who accept the living Christ are transformed into His likeness; and who has a right to dictate to any one, in whom Christ dwells, what he shall believe or do? Did not St. John say: " Ye have an unction from the Holy One, and need not that any man should teach you"? If he, the Beloved Disciple, made an obedient spirit the only condition of discipleship, what right have men removed by thousands of years from the living presence of the Founder to raise other conditions?

Questions of doctrine have always been causes of contention and division; and the more inscrutable the mysteries the more positive have been those who have felt that they were divinely called to protect Providence from the speculations of his creatures. Christendom is divided into sects chiefly because men differ about what they think God does in infinity and eternity. Most creeds are the expression of those thoughts, and simply mechanisms, —that is, artificial combinations constructed for a purpose; not natural growths. Life unifies. Christ is the vine; Christians the branches. Imagine a branch saying to a bud: " Before you presume to grow another inch answer certain questions. Do you believe that this tree is an oak or a maple? Was it planted ten years ago or twelve? Did some one decide on its planting a century ago, or did it grow from seed which had fallen by the way?" The newborn bud makes no answer, but simply grows where the life pushes it. To ask questions about doctrine, of those in whom Christ dwells, is little less than an impertinence. If the life is there it will make its own forms, and develop according to its own laws. The important thing is to be sure that the heart is given to God, and that the mind and will are under the guidance of His Spirit. All else may be left, nay, must be left, to the Spirit, who in His own time and way will lead into all truth.

Let us now briefly recapitulate:—1. Doctrinal statements are not required by the Congregational churches of England; only the Apostles' Creed is required by the Episcopalians of the Old World and New; the Presbyterian, Methodist and Baptist churches make no doctrinal tests; such conditions were not demanded by the Congregational churches of the United States until the Unitarian defection about the beginning of the present century; they are required now by a majority of those churches, but less and less rigidly insisted on, while many of the American churches make no doctrinal tests at all.

11. There is no basis for such requirement in Scripture, and no warrant in early usage. The most that was asked in the Apostolic times is indicated by early baptismal symbols, which never demanded statements of belief concerning the Bible, the "plan of salvation," the purposes of the Almighty, or eschatology.

111. Such tests at the door of Christ's church:
Violate the idea of the church;
Assume that fallible men are wiser than the Founder of the Church;
Assume that babes are competent to understand mysteries that angels have desired to look into;
Cultivate dishonesty;
Obscure the teaching of Christ concerning the nature of the spiritual life;
And bar from the Sacraments and other means of grace those whom the Saviour accepts as His followers.

Doctrinal conditions for church membership are in process of passing away, and must entirely disappear before the Spirit of God can do His perfect work, the truth of Christ be clearly understood, and the life of Christ have full power on all for whom the Saviour died.

No clearer expression of the Scriptural teaching on this subject has been given in recent times than the following from one of our oldest and most honoured Theological Seminaries:* "The aim of every creed for admission to church membership should be 'to make the terms of communion run as parallel as may be with the terms of salvation.' The baptismal covenant is first of all a personal one. The baptismal creed should be in the first person.

---
* *Andover Review*, Vol. 11 p. 71.

If we duly consider the Apostle's 'word' on which the first church was organised we see that any person who can say, intelligently and sincerely, 'I accept Jesus Christ as Saviour and Lord,' has a creed long enough and full enough for membership in Christ's church. The door of the church ought to swing wide open to every one who can say this. There are other and better ways of preserving the purity, order and discipline of Christ's church than the one of excluding Christians."

VII.
THE PULPIT.

"I know of nothing which can do human life so much real and lasting good as the religion of Jesus Christ; therefore I preach it with the energy of conviction, not unmingled, I trust, with the joy of experience. As a minister of Christ, I feel that the message with which I am entrusted is a message to the whole world, seasonable through all time, at home in all lands, an infinite message, which so grows upon the mind as to leave the impression that it can never be all delivered."—DR. JOSEPH PARKER.

"The Word did not speak once for all (unless we take the letter for the Word); the Word speaks without ceasing, and the letter of the Gospel is only the necessary means through which this Word speaks to all. This is the only just idea of the institution of the ministry. The minister is a minister of the Word of God. Christianity, a religion of thought, should be spoken."

—DR. A. VINET.

"A preacher is in some degree a reproduction of the truth in personal form. The truth must exist in him as a living experience, a glowing enthusiasm, an intense reality. The Word of God in the Book is a dead letter. It is paper, type, and ink. In the preacher that Word becomes again as it was when first spoken by prophet, priest, or apostle."—HENRY WARD BEECHER.

"Perhaps preaching is altogether a mistake now-a-days. If so, let it be abandoned; but as long as we have it, and as long as we desire to have it good and telling, we cannot despise intellect in any ministry, but must try to secure it by all reasonable means."

—J. P. MAHAFFY.

"The open secret of the world is the art of subliming a private soul with inspirations from the great and public and divine Soul from which he lives."—RALPH WALDO EMERSON.

VII.

THE PULPIT.

THE history of the Christian pulpit for the last eighteen hundred years, if properly written, would be the history of the civilised world. Pulpits have had quite as much to do with the progress of events as thrones; preachers and missionaries, as much as statesmen and soldiers. It would be difficult to trace the evolution of the pulpit. Dr. Hatch has shown that the philosophers and rhetoricians of the ancient times occupied a position similar to that of Christian preachers;* and it is well known that heathen religions have a place for something akin to the modern sermon. In all ages the living man has exerted a more potent and vital influence than letters and books. It was not the Epistles of St. Paul which carried the gospel into many lands, but the Apostle himself. People were first impressed with the magic of his spoken words, and thus prepared for the reception of written messages. Most of the early Fathers were preachers. Chrysostom

---
* " The Hibbert Lectures," 1888, p. 113.

could not have reached his place of power, and thrilled the world by his almost unexampled eloquence, had he not been one of a long line of Christian orators. Luther was a masterful preacher; so were John Wycliffe, John Knox, and the fathers of the Puritan Revolution and of modern Protestantism. While it has been the policy of the Roman Church to exalt the Mass, and by means of a splendid ceremonial to appeal to the sensuous rather than to the intellectual, she has also given to the world some of the noblest preachers of all time. From Chrysostom to Ambrose and St. Bernard, to Massillon and Lacordaire, the line has been unbroken. But while the emphasis of the Roman Church has been on its ritual rather than on its pulpit, Protestantism has made the pulpit the throne of its power. The Reformation was begun, and continued, by preaching. The history of Protestantism could easily be traced in the sermons of its preachers.

Professor Mahaffy of Dublin, in his supercilious way, has said: "As regards the future of preaching I confess that among the better classes, and with educated congregations, I think its day has gone by." * That sentence shows little knowledge of human nature. The Professor forgets that, in modern, as in ancient times, the greatest assemblies that regularly gather are attracted by the preaching of the Gospel, and that they are composed of cul-

---
* "Modern Preaching," p. 155.

tured people many times and, largely, of men. If the future may be judged by the past the day is far distant in which the pulpit will cease to influence thought and conduct.

To attempt a survey of the whole field of modern preaching would be outside the proprieties of this lecture, and yet any study of English Congregationalism would be incomplete which did not devote a large place to its pulpit. While they have emphasised the responsibilities and privileges of the whole Christian community, Congregationalists have demanded and received from their pastors and teachers services which have been unsurpassed in the history of the Church. We approach the subject which now commands our attention with a deep conviction of the essential greatness of our pulpit-ancestors, and also with the belief that the importance of a study of the best models of the homiletic art has not been duly appreciated in recent years. Really great preachers have always gladly acknowledged their obligation to the masters who have preceded them. Almost every conspicuous pulpit orator has tarried long under the spell of the splendid eloquence of Chrysostom and Bernard. The style of Jeremy Taylor has been reproduced in many a modern Anglican and American Episcopalian. Henry Ward Beecher generously confessed his obligation to Barrowe and South; and the most casual reader of Mr. Spurgeon's sermons must have observed that his thought and speech were saturated with the literature of the Puritan preachers. There is however a growing feeling that the study of pulpit models is unworthy of the ministerial profession, and consequently a noble and essential part of the preacher's preparation has been unduly discredited. The abuse of helps, and the plagiarism which has crept into the ministrations of many churches of one denomination, are no doubt largely the cause of this unfortunate mistake. Lawyers rejoice in the traditions of the bar; artists learn from the old masters the secrets of colour and form; musicians fill their souls with the harmonies of Beethoven and Mozart until new harmonies rise and demand expression; soldiers never weary of reading the records of those who have planned campaigns and fought fiercely-contested battles in other times; and preachers can find no more valuable help toward making their sermons effective than a wise study of the methods and achievements of the pulpit in other lands and times. The sermons of McLeod and Guthrie, Robertson, Kingsley and Maurice, Bethune and Bushnell, Beecher and Spurgeon, Newman and Brooks are an unfailing inspiration, and cannot be too reverently and carefully read. The object of this lecture is to introduce to the acquaintance of students and young preachers a few of the master-spirits of the English Congregational pulpit, and thus to suggest studies which may be profitably pursued in the future. It will be best to follow a chronological order, and it will be impossible within these limits to do much more than mention a few of those great expounders of the Christian revelation who have influenced the thought and developed the life of the Nonconformist churches.

The three most conspicuous Dissenting preachers in the seventeenth century were John Robinson, John Howe and John Owen. If ministers may be judged by the influences which they start rather than by the sermons which they publish John Robinson, the Pilgrim pastor, was one of the greatest of preachers, and yet his sphere of service was a narrow one. A graduate of Cambridge, a profound thinker, an essayist whose writings have something of the grasp of thought and condensation of expression which characterised Lord Bacon, it is hard to think of him as preaching to that little group of people gathered in William Brewster's Manor House in Scrooby, and afterwards as leading a company of dissentients into exile. Such men usually cling to the Universities and are seldom foremost in action. Robinson's work as a preacher was at Scrooby, where he was the teacher and Clifton the pastor; and afterwards at Leyden, where he became the pastor of the little church of Separatists, a part of whom became the Pilgrim Fathers. Robinson was a man of distinguished intellectual gifts. While in Holland he became a member of the University of Leyden.

His week days were devoted to his duties in the University, to the oversight of his people, and to the discussions which arose between the Calvinists and their opponents. No man in the University but Robinson was considered equal to the task of controverting Episcopius, the champion of lax views in theology ; and the chroniclers of the time tell us that he met and confounded his opponent, to the delight of all who had chosen him their representative. Robinson, I believe, has left no sermons behind him. His published writings are chiefly essays, from which it may be supposed that he usually preached without writing. But if the style of the essays gives a hint of his style as a preacher that little church at Leyden was not fed on milk. When the Pilgrims sailed for the New World their pastor remained behind, intending to follow, but his life was cut short (1625), and he never joined his people at Plymouth. Little is known of him as a preacher, yet he must ever be regarded, on both sides of the sea, as the father of modern Congregationalism. Doctrinally he was a High Calvinist, a man of liberal spirit, not afraid of investigation, and always open to the light.

John Howe was perhaps the most prominent preacher of the Cromwellian period. In the midst of the intellectual desolation of the Puritan Revolution he represented the highest and finest scholarship, and in 1657, after Cromwell came into power, was made the Private Chaplain of the Protector. Robinson's literary legacy consists of a few essays; Howe has left numerous volumes of sermons, many of which to this day must be regarded as noble examples of pulpit eloquence. He was neither so learned as John Owen, nor so keen a controversialist as Richard Baxter, but he seems to have had a finer spirit and a more spiritual intellect than either of his great compeers. After the death of Oliver and the abdication of Richard Cromwell, Howe retired from office, and until his death in 1705, spent the remainder of his life in comparative obscurity. To that obscurity we owe some of his profoundest teaching. All who love earnest thinking, nobly expressed, and infused with supreme reverence, even after two hundred and fifty years have passed, may well linger long with John Howe's "Living Temple," his "Principles of the Oracles of God," and with some of his sermons, like that on "Charity in Reference to Other Men's Sins," "The Vanity of a Formal Profession of Religion," or "The Love of God and our Brother." Howe can hardly be recommended as a model for the pulpit of to-day; indeed it is hard to understand how his hearers were patient enough to sit through discourses so long a those which he preached. They were not popular in the modern sense. They were addressed to the intellect rather than to the heart. They contain few illustrations, and are more like great treatises on theology and ethics than like direct addresses to living men in the midst of the storm and stress of every-day life; and yet they are glorious examples of their own peculiar style of pulpit oratory.

John Owen (1616-1683) was a tower of strength to early Nonconformity, his career really beginning in resistance to Archbishop Laud's regulations. He also belonged to the period of the Commonwealth. At first his sympathies were largely with the Presbyterian party, but his Separatist principles gradually becoming pronounced, he upheld the Independent form of church government, and thenceforward he was a leader in the cause of liberty, being summoned several times to preach before Parliament— once, the day after the execution of Charles I.; an appointment, however, which he did not fulfil. Owen was a great favourite with Cromwell, and when the Protectorate was established he was made Dean of Christ Church at Oxford. In 1663 he was invited to a pastorate in America but declined to leave England. He was a voluminous author, a scholar of encyclopedic information, a controversialist equal to Richard Baxter, and yet he was as tolerant of the views of others as he was positive in his own convictions. Without compromising himself he was able to hold and advocate his own principles so as to retain the personal confidence of Kings Charles II. and James II., who often conferred with him concerning the welfare of their Dissenting subjects.

In the year 1670, he was invited to the presidency of Harvard College in the Massachusetts Colony, and was also invited to similar duties in Dutch Universities. These calls he declined. Owen passed his life in publicity, and his works, which are very verbose in style, should be read with this fact in mind. He was like the old prophets in the range of what he was called to do. He nobly performed the tasks imposed upon him by Providence, and his name will live with that of Robinson, Howe, and even with that of Cromwell himself.

In the eighteenth century we find two men who were great spiritual forces and who exerted a formative influence in early English Independency. Their names rise like mountain peaks from a level of comparative barrenness in religion. Living in the generation preceding the Evangelical Revival under Wesley and Whitefield, they were in some respects its forerunners. It is easy to go farther and assert that Watts and Doddridge were the necessary precursors of the Wesleys and Whitefield. They were very different men. Watts and Doddridge preached to select congregations; Wesley and Whitefield appealed to the masses outside the churches. Watts is remembered chiefly as a writer of hymns, of which some are unsurpassed in any language, while many others have become a burden to our hymn-books and the despair of those who desire to introduce into our hymnology not only noble thoughts but also appropriate literary expression.

In his time Isaac Watts was the most eminent of English preachers, and one of the most voluminous and versatile of English authors. He was prominent both in letters and philosophy. He was born in Southampton in July, 1674, and died in London November 25th, 1748. At twenty-seven years of age he became pastor of Mark Lane Chapel, London. Although throughout all his long and brilliant career a victim of disease, often compelled to preach when suffering unutterable pain, he continued his work with unabated zeal and fidelity, and remains to this day one of the most justly honoured of all those men who have had a part in shaping our polity. The characteristics of his pulpit oratory were the clearness of his logical processes, the almost crystalline beauty of his style, and his constant appeal to Scripture. His rhetoric was fine, but not florid. He was possessed of a musical voice, and of elocution the nearest perfection among the public speakers of his time. His sermons in print, however, lack magnetism. They have a mechanical quality, a suggestion of Blair's Rhetoric, a kind of writing which belongs to a society where men are more intent on style than on results; they show little of that fine spiritual suggestion which is so common in Robertson and Bushnell, and nothing of that fervour and glow which illuminate the pages of Brooks and Beecher. His sermon on "The Love of God," which is the introduction to the series on "The Influence of the Love of God on the Passions," is clear and strong, but does not take hold of the reader and compel his attention. His exquisite elocution and earnestness of manner, however, probably compensated for lack of magnetism in composition. Many of his hymns have exactly the quality which is most missed in his sermons. His prose contains nothing so uplifting, and eloquent, as the hymn whose first stanza is:

> " Eternal Wisdom, Thee we praise;
> Thee the creation sings:
> With Thy loud name rocks, hills and seas
> And heaven's high palace rings."

Watts was a philosopher as well as a preacher, and although he, who by many was regarded as the equal of John Locke in speculative thought, could not be expected to have the fire of a popular orator; yet he was the most popular preacher of his time. In his later life his doctrinal views underwent a serious change. While he never became Unitarian he approached Arianism. Of him Dr. Johnson has said: "He was one of the first authors that taught the Dissenters to court attention by the graces of language. Whatever they had among them before, whether of learning or acuteness, was commonly obscured and blunted by coarseness and inelegance of style. He showed them that zeal and purity might be expressed and enforced by polished diction."* Dr. Vicesimus Knox, in his "Christian Philosophy," has thus characterised Watts: "For my own part I cannot but think that this good man approached as nearly to Christian perfection as any mortal ever did in this sublunary state... And be it ever remembered that Dr. Watts was a man who studied the abstrusest sciences, and was as well qualified to become a verbal critic or a logical disputant on the Scriptures, as the most learned among the Doctors of the Sorbonne or the greatest professors in polemical divinity." And of his preaching Dr. Southey has said: "His sermons had all the advantages that could be given them by an impressive elocution and a manner of delivery which with curious felicity seems to have been at the same time elaborately studied yet earnestly sincere."† Eminent as a scholar, a preacher, a poet; a man of rare spirituality, who had the faculty for presenting truth so as to make it credible to the thoughtful; the herald of the new day which was to break on English Christianity through Wesley and Whitefield; the first minister to declare and formally to defend anti-State principles, Isaac Watts must ever be remembered as one of the most vital forces in the development of Christian thought and Independent ecclesiastical polity in Great Britain.

When Sir Humphrey Davy was asked what he

---
* Life of Watts, Harsha, p. 44.
† *Idem.*

considered his greatest discovery, he replied, "Michael Faraday." It would not be true to say that Isaac Watts was the discoverer of Philip Doddridge, but the names of Watts and Doddridge are associated in much the same way as those of Davy and Faraday. Doddridge died only three years after Watts, yet it may almost be said that Watts was the Elijah and Doddridge the Elisha of the Nonconformity of the eighteenth century. Watts was a theologian as well as a preacher, and Doddridge was, perhaps, the chief theological instructor of his generation. Watts was the first great English hymnologist, and Doddridge was the second. Watts lived to be seventy-five years old, in feeble health most of the time; three years later (1751) Doddridge died, at fifty years of age, his last years having been passed in much pain and anguish of spirit. Doddridge looked to Watts as his master and leader, and yet Doddridge seems to me decidedly the more interesting character. There is something strangely beautiful in the history of that man, for twenty-one years pastor of the church at Northampton, working among those who were intellectually inferior to him, inspiring them by the simplicity and beauty of his character, and, at the same time that he was preaching to the common people, conducting a theological seminary, in which he combined in his own person a complete theological faculty. Like Watts he is known chiefly by his hymns. If the Reformation under Wesley sung its place into the hearts of the English people, Watts and Doddridge had as much to do with that almost preternatural revival as the Wesleys and Whitefield. Charles Wesley's hymns were unwritten when those of Watts and Doddridge were in the hearts of the people. Doddridge possessed a nature of exquisite spirituality. He is best known by his books, "The Rise and Progress of Religion in the Soul," and "The Family Expositor"—which contains a version and paraphrase of the New Testament, with critical notes and comments. Of his hymns there need be mentioned only those beginning, "Let Zion's watchmen all awake," "My God, Thy service well demands," and "Awake my soul to meet the day." Many of his hymns were written as perorations to his sermons. He was accustomed to condense argument and application into a few verses at the close of a sermon, and thus some of the richest and most beautiful hymns in our language came into being. The chief object of Dr. Doddridge as a theological instructor was to make his students experimental preachers, and he encouraged them to think, write and speak much on subjects connected with vital religion. He had large hospitality for all that is fine and beautiful in literature, and trained his students to scholarly habits. The University of Aberdeen conferred on him the degree of Doctor of Divinity. His sermons are far more natural and inspiring, sympathetic and vitalising, than those of Watts; and yet his chief and most enduring work was not as pastor at Northampton, but as the founder of institutions for theological education in Great Britain, and as a hymnologist. As the names of Robinson, Howe and Owen rise above those of all other Independent preachers in the seventeenth century, so the names of Watts and Doddridge are equally prominent in the eighteenth. Men of such culture, whose sermons were widely read, whose books were recognised as among the best helps to the spiritual life; whose hymns were the finest expression of devout aspiration in the language, could not fail to win something of favour and toleration for the people among whom they worked, and to whose service they had given their lives. The study of ecclesiastical history in England in the eighteenth century is by no means inspiring. The people were turned to evil ways; infidelity and a cruel and cheerless Deism absorbed the thoughts of multitudes of men; but no time should be called barren which can point to such thinkers, teachers, authors, preachers and singers as Isaac Watts and Philip Doddridge. They were friends while they lived, and their names are indissolubly linked in the history of the Free Churches of England.

In the present century there have been many eminent and honoured, as well as eloquent and faithful, preachers in the English Congregational pulpit. At a public gathering in the United States a minister spoke substantially as follows : " I believe that the English Church is the greatest Church on the earth. It has given the world its greatest authors, its most eminent workers, and its noblest preachers." He was thinking of the Establishment, and he spoke not as an Anglican churchman, but as an American Congregationalist. His testimony is valuable, but it is sadly out of harmony with facts, —so far as concerns preachers. It is doubtful if any Church ever produced more brilliant and consecrated preachers than have occupied the Congregational pulpits of England since this century began. They have not filled a very large place in the world's thought because they have been " Dissenters "; but when their sermons are studied, the work which they did tested, and the quality of their ministry compared with that of others, those Independent ministers rise to an unquestioned equality with the best preachers and workers of their generation. Many of them are little known on this side of the water, but they cannot be long unknown to any who reach below the surface of society in Great Britain, and who would become acquainted with the influences which have there moulded thought and life. Among them are John Angell James of Birmingham, the predecessor of that preëminent Christian scholar and preacher, Robert W. Dale ; Robert S. McAll of Manchester, who in the intensity of his style reminds one of Robertson ; Dr. Richard Winter Hamilton of Leeds, an orator of impassioned eloquence; William Jay of Bath, whose "Morning and Evening Exercises" have been read around the world; Thomas Raffles of Liverpool, that genial Christian gentleman, that born Bishop, that preacher whose name is associated with almost all great movements in the recent history of Lancashire ; James Parsons of York, who resisted all appeals from larger cities, but whose splendid eloquence gave him a fame brighter than that of any Archbishop of York in former times; Samuel Martin of Westminster Chapel in London, to whom with rare unanimity was applied the epithet of "saintly"; James Baldwin Brown of Brixton, who did more than any man in recent times to liberalise Nonconformist theology, who seems to have united in one almost unique personality the spirit of a cavalier and of a Puritan, to whom John Hunter has applied the phrase that Gladstone applied to Maurice—"the spiritual splendour of the world"; and last, and perhaps greatest of all, that impersonation of English Congregationalism, and noblest orator of modern English Nonconformity, the lion-visaged, lion-hearted Thomas Binney. I must not forget to add to these the names of James Sherman of Tottenham Court Road, Dr. John Harris of New College, London, Campbell and the Claytons, Collier and Dr. Vaughan, Enoch Mellor of Halifax, Dr. Andrew Reed, founder of

Ayslums for Idiots, Dr. Halley, Thomas Jones, the poet-preacher, A. J. Morris, Dr. Alex. Raleigh, George William Conder of Leeds, David Thomas of Bristol; and I might mention many others who exerted a powerful influence while they lived, and whose spirit is still vital in the churches to which they ministered.

A closer inspection of these names suggests many interesting facts. Most of these ministers had but one pastorate. John Angell James was for fifty-four years pastor of Carr's Lane Chapel in Birmingham; Andrew Reed was fifty years with Wycliffe Chapel, London; Thomas Binney for forty years was pastor of the Weigh House Chapel in London; James Parsons passed his whole ministry in York, and his father, Edward Parsons, was forty-eight years pastor of a church in Leeds; Samuel Martin spent nearly his whole ministerial life in Westminster Chapel, and Baldwin Brown tarried but two or three years in Bedford before he took up the work in Brixton which he laid down only with his life. There is something beautiful and inspiring in these long pastorates, and the memory of those ministers is enshrined in the history of the churches which they served, and rests upon them like a benediction. Those men must have been possessed of peculiar intellectual and spiritual gifts, for churches are quick to detect false notes in the lives of their leaders. And let it also be added that those are great churches which know how to keep their pastors.

To attempt to classify the men whose names have been mentioned is a more difficult task. John Angell James, as would be expected from his books, was not only a giant intellectually, but a man of evangelical spirit, more anxious concerning the upbuilding of his people in the spiritual life than the advancement of the cause of Disestablishment. Robert S. McAll, the peerless preacher of Manchester in his day, had that intensity of expression, combined with that intuitive faculty, which so often belongs to those who struggle with physical disease. His sermons, while they have a well-defined framework of Calvinism, impress me as preëminently spiritual. On the other hand, Samuel Martin, while he was not less spiritual, was in an almost unique fashion a Biblical preacher. Every lesson in his sermons seems to have been drawn from the Scriptures. His lecture on "Socialism" is a curious illustration of how a man of one book will find in it the inspiration of all his intellectual operations. In that lecture every thought concerning "the straits of pure Socialism" is drawn from some character or scene in the book of Genesis.

Those "great lights of Nonconformity" were immensely helped by the enthusiasm of their congregations. James preached to large audiences in Birmingham; McAll did not live to see his wishes for a large church realised, but his people inspired him with their sympathy; Samuel Martin's preaching was so effective that after the church which seated fifteen hundred had been filled to overflowing there was built for him in Westminster the now famous Chapel, which seats three thousand, and in that he ministered for ten years, until worn out with much service he passed from his "saintly" life on the earth to the general assembly of the saints above. James Parsons, or, as he was commonly called, "Parsons of York," was intensely evangelistic in spirit and manner, and his sermons, while not less Biblical than those of other preachers of his time, were perhaps more directly aimed at the conversion of individual sinners. Parsons and McAll, and most of the others whose names have been mentioned, as was common in the early years of the present century, emphasised the severer sides of Scripture teaching, and yet the love of God as the prime motive in the spiritual life was never long out of sight. The phrase "knowing the terror of the Lord" had a different meaning fifty years ago from what it has to-day. Even such preachers as Mr. Spurgeon and others of the literalistic school, seldom refer in late years to the punishment of sin in the realistic way that formerly was almost universal among Calvinistic divines.

Paxton Hood has likened Thomas Binney to Lacordaire, and in one of his vivid lectures the names of the great French Benedictine and the English Independent are united as the subject of the lecture. Binney was unquestionably the leader of Nonconformity in his time, the one who did more than any other to bring into prominence, and keep before the public, the essential evil of the Establishment as a hindrance to the Kingdom of God. His figure was tall and commanding; his face when in repose was like that of a sleeping lion, and when he was thrilled by some great theme he towered above common men like a king. It was often said that if Thomas Binney had not been one of the most prominent of English preachers he would have been one of the most eminent of English barristers. Those who differed from him most were the first to acknowledge the preëminence of his intellect, the intensity of his spirit, and the courage of his heart. His audience probably contained as many educated men as any other congregation in London. His style was usually thoughtful and calm, but when fired by some great occasion he rose to magnificent eloquence. There is much in the descriptions of Binney as a preacher which remind an American both of Henry Ward Beecher and Dr. Richard S. Storrs. He had that flaming eloquence and endless variety of mood which characterised Beecher, and something of the dignity of manner and splendour of diction which distinguish Dr. Storrs. An utterance said to have been made by him at the laying of the corner-stone of his church, which he never made in the form in which it was reported, namely, that "The Church of England had destroyed more souls than it had saved," fell like a spark on tinder, and instantly Binney was the most abused man in all Great Britain. But he was not easily daunted, and did not shrink from the controversy. Although he seemed to have been made for war he was a man of great sympathy, especially for those who were troubled with doubts concerning Christianity. Consequently he had much influence with young men. The name of no leader of the past generation of English Independents is so frequently heard on the lips of those now living as that of Thomas Binney. He left strict injunctions against the publication of a biography; nevertheless, Dr. Allon, in introducing a volume of his sermons, has ventured to give an interesting sketch of his life; and Paxton Hood has written most helpfully concerning this prince of English preachers.

Of the men of this generation the one who did more than any other Independent to modify the theology of his day was James Baldwin Brown. He died early in 1884, but his memory is as fragrant in the Independent Church at Brixton, and among the people whom he loved, as on the day of his death. He was the son of an English barrister. He was intended by his father for the law, but, finally, under the influence of the Spirit, became a

Christian, and a minister. For many years after coming to London he was regarded with suspicion by both the churches and his brethren in the ministry because of his somewhat attenuated orthodoxy. An intensely earnest, chivalric, honest spirit, he could endure no sham, and would rather be misunderstood than utter one word not absolutely true. He has been called "the Maurice of English Congregationalism." Baldwin Brown was a far greater preacher than Maurice, though not so profound a thinker. Maurice had essentially the philosophical temper. He wrought in silence. He was a university professor. He saw things from the literary point of view. He has been called the Plato of modern theology, and well deserves that supreme praise. Baldwin Brown, on the other hand, reached intuitively the conclusions which Maurice reached by slower processes. All that Brown wrote bears the stamp of a man constantly dealing with the pressure of present problems. He was a scholar, but not scholastic. He never wrote as one outside the struggle of life but as one in the midst of its pain and suffering. There is an intensity in his style, an eager reaching, rushing toward conclusions, which distinguishes him as one sharing in the sufferings of those around him and a partner in their struggles. Among English Independents he was the first to give prominence to "the larger hope." The love of God was central and regulative in his theology. He had a unique power of interpreting to young men their own best thoughts, and leading them step by step out of intellectual and spiritual darkness. By his personality he preached quite as eloquently as by his words. For years he paid the penalty of being a suspect. But working on in silence, true to the truth as it was made known unto him, at length his splendid manhood superb intellectual gifts, and lofty spiritual character swept all before them, and in 1878 the Congregational Union of England and Wales honoured itself when it honoured him by calling him to be its Chairman. The addresses which he published that year are among the ablest which have ever been given from that Chair. The first one was entitled, "Our Theology in Relation to the Intellectual Movement of our Time"; and the second, "The Perfect Law of Liberty."

A passage near the end of his second address reads like a description of himself, so fully did he believe that the only solution of modern problems is to be found in a return to the simplicity of Christ. He says: " The fundamental principle of the Christian policy is, 'You leaders and people must first be reformed before you can reform society. Begin the work within.' That principle saved society from a bloody revolution when first the Gospel preached its doctrines of liberty to all classes of mankind; that principle lent to our great Revolution a lofty religious character which is unique in history; that principle, through the great evangelistic revival at the end of the last century, saved this country from the saturnalia of lust and blood which filled France with anguish; and that principle alone will save us in these days of tremendous social travail which are coming upon the world." *

Binney was the great Nonconformist leader of the first two-thirds of the nineteenth century; after him Baldwin Brown was until his death a foremost spiritual leader. I do not use the word theological, because with him theology manifested itself in spiritual rather than intellectual forms. He appreciated the peril of those who feel their faith slipping away from them, and it was the passion of his life to present Christianity in a way that would commend itself to the conscience and intellect of the people to whom he ministered;—in other words, he was more concerned about men than systems of thought, about spiritual life than theology. More than any other Congregationalist of recent years, except Dr. Dale, his books have been read by cultured Nonconformists—and indeed by Churchmen also.

The student will look in vain through the history of the Establishment, and through the history of all other religious bodies, for such a galaxy of preachers as those whose names have been mentioned as

* "Year Book," 1879, p. 100.

conspicuous in the early part and middle of the present century—the "Angel" James, the "Saintly" Martin, the genial, eloquent and impassioned Raffles, the intense and intuitive McAll, the evangelistic Parsons, the leonine Thomas Binney, and that great spiritual leader, Baldwin Brown. If English Congregationalism had done nothing for the world except to raise up men like these to sound the knell of decaying institutions and unworthy traditions, with their splendid eloquence and consecrated service, it would still have a history in which all who bear the Christian name might well rejoice.

But now the question arises, Have those men worthy successors, or have they left places which can never be filled? That inquiry is not difficult to answer. The same pulpits are not all occupied by men equally distinguished. Churches, as well as ministers have their peculiar work. Localities change. The old Weigh House Chapel in London, which years ago blazed with Binney's eloquence, was torn down in the interests of an underground railway. Westminster Chapel is surrounded by different people from those who were there in the days of Samuel Martin's beautiful ministry. Even Carr's Lane in Birmingham, the church of Angell James and Dr. Dale, is far downtown. In most places the churches which were prominent half a century ago are not equally prominent now. But who for a moment imagines that John Angell James in his palmiest days, in intellectual vigour or in spiritual fervour, ever surpassed him who succeeded to that ministry, and has continued it now for forty years, who was honoured by being made President of the first International Congregational Council— Robert W. Dale? Among the older men eminent in the English pulpit must be mentioned the able, the courtly and sweet-spirited Henry Allon of Union Chapel, Islington, who, if he had lived a few months longer would have celebrated the fiftieth anniversary of his pastorate of one church; Joshua Harrison, who was quite as long pastor of the Park Church in Camden Town; Edward White, who, after a long and honoured ministry in the pulpit, is devoting himself to literature; and J. Guinness Rogers of Clapham, who for forty years has been almost as great a force in the political as in the spiritual life of England. These ministers, and many others in London, as well as in the Provinces, bear witness that the Congregational pulpit in England is not losing its power.

When we turn from these men to those who are younger, and think of Fairbairn, Mackennal, George S. Barrett; and among the still younger men note the splendid earnestness of Robert F. Horton, the popular gifts of Charles A. Berry, the unquestioned power of John Hunter, and the brilliant oratory of C. Silvester Horne, we are sure that the race of great preachers is not extinct. Never were there abler men, more popular orators, more consecrated spirits, in the pulpits of England than those whose names have been enumerated, and there are many others who are worthy to be in the same fellowship.

Dr. Dale is easily the most eminent of living Congregationalists. His works are so well known that attention need be called only to the ethical element which pervades them, to the air of serious earnestness which is never absent, to a subtile sympathy which evades characterisation, yet which is inseparable from them, and to a certain richness of diction and chastened splendour of rhetoric which is never found except in those who have studied much and suffered much. In the list of those who read their sermons Dr. Dale is probably unequalled in the world.

The greatest genius in the English pulpit is undoubtedly Joseph Parker. He is a man of unique personality, one whose mannerisms often prevent the richness of his thought from finding the recognition which it deserves. To my own mind Parker is vastly more suggestive than Spurgeon ever was, and when he forgets himself and rises into the realm of the spirit, few in our time are his superiors. It is no little thing for so many years to have held a church in the heart of the business district of Old London, remote from all residential quarters, and that not only on Sabbath days but on week days.

If Joseph Parker had the perfect unconsciousness which Phillips Brooks wore like a garment, he would be the most remarkable of modern English preachers. He is a poet, an orator, a dreamer of dreams and a seer of visions, one whose greatness will be more appreciated by a later generation than by the present, because his infelicities of manner prevent many from discerning the splendid quality of his thought and the marvellous style of its phrasing.

Naturally the preachers of English Congregationalism are compared with those of the Establishment, and not until they are side by side do we realise how great the former really are. Considered simply as preachers not many would question that those whom we have named are worthy to be ranked in the very highest class of English pulpit orators. Few preachers in the Establishment, in recent days, have been so universally commended as Dr. Magee, Bishop of Peterborough; but when Dr. Magee is compared with Thomas Binney the contrast is surely not altogether in favour of the Churchman. Canon Liddon is the only Anglican of recent times who divides the first place in the pulpit with the Bishop of Peterborough, but when the sermons of Liddon are compared with the sermons of Dr. Dale they are found to be no more intellectual, no more finished, no more spiritual, and to lack that fine human sympathy which is never absent from the great Birmingham preacher, and which is seldom found in the sermons of the distinguished Oxford professor. As a platform speaker Liddon had little if any power, while Dale, in addition to his other eminent gifts, is one of the most powerful political orators of his time—the only man whom the people of his city were willing to hear after John Bright had finished. He is not only a great spiritual teacher but a vital force in English politics.

The name of Maurice instantly suggests that of Baldwin Brown. No doubt the first was the profounder thinker, but the second was the greater preacher. While Dr. Pusey was a distinguished professor according to the High Church standard, his sermons, so far as I am familiar with them, are surely inferior to those of Angell James, the author of " The Anxious Inquirer." Canon Farrar is one of the noblest of modern preachers. His spirit is Apostolic, his courage like that of the Hebrew prophets, but his style and his mannerisms are often a drag on his words. Naturally Farrar is compared with Parker, and few would question that as a pulpit orator the eccentric genius of the City Temple is far greater than the brilliant Archdeacon who ministers at St. Margaret's. Among the younger Bishops of the English Church none have developed more power in the pulpit than the Bishop of Ripon, Dr. Boyd Carpenter, a broadspirited, earnest, Christian man, of wide influence and great consecration. But few who have heard

Robert F. Horton of Hampstead would hesitate to place him side by side with the Bishop of Ripon, and accord to him still greater power in his ability so to present the gospel as to influence conscience and character

The genial Principal of Mansfield College, Oxford, Dr. A. M. Fairbairn, is the leader in theological education among English Congregationalists. Who in the Establishment can be placed beside him? Professors Sanday and Driver may be greater critical scholars, but who in the sphere of Systematic Theology or Comparative Religion deserves to be ranked with Principal Fairbairn? He is the preeminent theologian of Great Britain.

There still remains one name in modern Anglican and Roman Catholic history that seems to rise higher than any in English Protestantism, and especially in English Nonconformity. Is there any name to be ranked with that of Cardinal Newman? Newman's greatest work as a preacher was in the Anglican church. Candour compels the acknowledgment that no one can be placed side by side with him, and yet Newman's sermons were usually only for a select few. They were addressed to teachers and scholars; they read more like treatises on philosophy than messages from God to common men. In them there is nothing of that inspired spirituality which flames and burns in the Conferences of Lacordaire. The supremacy of his genius must be recognised. There has been no man of equal intellectual eminence in the English pulpit of the nineteenth century. And yet the genius of Newman did not get into his sermons; it was not a power to mould men. His utterances were the meditations of the cloister rather than the voice of one calling to repentance or seeking to persuade men to give their hearts unto God. He preached not as a prophet, but as a philosopher.

After a careful study of the subject I am persuaded that in the nineteenth century the Congregational pulpit of England has had the ablest, the most spiritual, and the most influential preachers of the British Kingdom. The only Nonconformist church which could compare with it is the one which has given to the world in recent years those princes of pulpit oratory, those almost matchless masters of the art of appeal and persuasion—Spurgeon and Maclaren.

After this outline study of the English pulpit, the question arises whether it has suggested any lessons of special value for those who are engaged in the same ministry in other lands. That pulpit has given new and peculiar emphasis to certain facts which are worthy of careful and constant recognition.

1. The ministry has a measure of responsibility for the moral life of the State. This has usually been recognised, but it is illustrated in the examples

of the men of whom we have been studying as perhaps nowhere else in Christian history. As the result of a vicious legacy the Christian Church about four centuries ago was in alliance with a corrupt and corrupting State. On the one hand were vast endowments and limitless power; on the other, were conscience and the teaching of Holy Scripture. The work which the early Nonconformists fronted was of great magnitude, and almost hopeless. In our land and time that condition of things cannot be appreciated. Then, religious liberty was only a name. Even after the Act of Toleration those who presumed to think for themselves suffered social ostracism, were harassed by the officers of State on the absurdest of pretexts, and the lofty morality which led them to go out of the Establishment for conscience' sake, was regarded by the authorities both of Church and State as even more obnoxious than open vice. A revolution in ecclesiastical affairs has been realised in Great Britain, and it is not too much to say that it is almost altogether due to the preaching of Nonconformists.

Not all has been the result of agitation on the part of the Congregationalists, for others, especially the Baptists, have been faithful in witnessing against a State Church. And Dr. Dale, in his sermon on "Christ and the State" before the Baptist Home Missionary Society, said "John Wesley and George Whitefield did more for the social redemption of England than all the politicians of this century and the last, whose names are associated with great reforms."* Their work, however, was largely indirect, since as a rule they have confined themselves more exclusively to church work, and given less attention to the political problem.

The Independents, on the other hand, have been directly and relentlessly attacking the citadel of the evil, and from the time of Watts to the time of Binney, from Doddridge to Dale, from Edward Miall—who was the greatest modern prophet of Disestablishment—to his worthy successor, Carvell Williams, from Dr. Raffles to Guinness Rogers, there have always been those who, braving political, social and ecclesiastical censure, have in the noblest way appealed to the people in behalf of national righteousness. Dr. Dale has well said: "If the social order is to be just, men must be just, if the social order is to be kind, men must be kind. We can hope for great and enduring changes for the better in the social order only as the result of great and enduring changes for the better in the spirit and character of the whole people. The ethical quality of the organisation of a State, politically, economically, socially, must I suppose be always more or less inferior to the general ethical life of the nation. Reforms which are far in advance of that life may be carried as the result of

---
* "Fellowship with Christ," p. 211.

transient enthusiasm, but they will not be effective and they will not endure." *

The example of English ministers in the contest for Disestablishment illustrates the possibilities of influence which are open to prophets of righteousness in all lands. The preacher occupies a unique position. His words will be heeded when speakers more likely to be prejudiced will attract little attention. Great evils threaten American life. Liberty is degenerating into license; democracy is becoming lawless. On our side of the water it is high time that the same fearless, prophetic spirit which has worked such a revolution on the other side was beginning to manifest itself in no uncertain way. The history of English Congregationalism proves that the ministers of the Church, without losing their spiritual influence, may also minister to the welfare of the State. No more saintly and successful pastors and preachers have lived in the present century than Drs. Allon and Dale, and for years they were trusted advisers of the great chiefs of the Liberal party. They were trusted because they were honest and wise, and dared to apply the principles of Christ to the life of the State. Christianity is working not only for the salvation of individuals; it aims also at bringing in better social and political institutions. The redemption of society has vital relations to the salvation of men. American

---
* " Fellowship with Christ," pp. 210-11.

preachers are yearly becoming more and more truly prophets of righteousness; they are realising that the ministry has relations to all the life of man, and they can have no better teachers or exemplars than the dauntless and unwearying Independents, who have fought the battles of religious liberty in England.

2. The pulpit in England has been one of the most positive forces in the amelioration of wrong social conditions, and its influence may be equally potent in the United States. Circumstances compel English preachers to devote more attention to the life that now is than to that which is to come. The tide of pauperism and crime is constantly rising; the overcrowding of the great cities has reached an enormity as yet unknown in the United States. The ministers are compelled to do the very same work that the Master did—heal the sick, clothe the naked, cast out devils, and preach the Gospel to the poor. Before they have time to ask men concerning the salvation of their souls they are forced to seek to improve their physical environment. As a consequence, charity and social reforms have a prominence in religious work not yet known here. Nonconformist ministers are at the head of many of the great movements for the social regeneration of England, and in some of the most difficult and perilous crises they have been the mediators between conflicting classes. What-

ever may be true of the dignitaries of the Establishment, there is no doubt that the average Nonconformist is in heartiest sympathy with those who are seeking to improve the life of men on the earth —and what is more, they are making that a department of church work. They have gotten hold of the fact that human beings cannot be studied simply as individuals. Each man is the product of long lines of ancestors; and his growth is moulded by his environment.

Appreciation of these truths may explain why in England in recent years there have been few great evangelists. Americans, like Moody and Sankey, have led in revivals which have had a temporary influence, but the English ministers as a rule are compelled to think of men more in the aggregate, not alone as single souls. If men are to be spiritual there must be conditions in which spiritual life may grow. Therefore English pastors go on the School Boards and Boards of Guardians of the Poor; they lead in the erection of improved tenement houses; and seek to make it possible for the children in the public schools to have sufficient food without thereby increasing pauperism. The English Congregational minister of the present time is quite as much a student of sociology as of theology; and well he may be, for the task before him is of appalling magnitude.

More swiftly than most Americans dream, the same social conditions are growing on this side of the water. The problem of the great cities is no longer peculiarly English or Continental. The absurdity of an attempt to promote a revival in such districts as Bleecker and Mulberry Streets, New York, is evident to all who have ever studied those localities. People sometimes get so low, so in the grasp of a vicious environment, that the Gospel must literally wash and feed them before it can cast out the more than a thousand devils which possess them. It has to prepare a soil in which its message can find lodgment. Patient effort to change the environment in which people live in order that there may be reasonable hope of the growth of the new life is as truly evangelistic as direct efforts to win men to personal loyalty to Jesus of Nazareth; and the practical appreciation of this fact is one potent cause of the success of the Salvation Army. The missionary societies of all denominations are making an immense mistake in not giving more attention to cities. No State and no Territory has so few churches or so few Christian influences in proportion to the population as there are in New York, Chicago and Boston. No course of study can be better fitted to make efficient ministers of the kind that are needed in our great cities, where men must be content to bury themselves and die unappreciated, than a study of the methods of the faithful but unknown pastors of the churches among the poor in Manchester, Birmingham and London.

One message from the English pulpit to the American, then, is that the present life has its claims, that they are quite as imperative as those of the future life, and that the task of saving men for eternity is absolutely hopeless if they are neglected in time.

3. There are no models of pulpit oratory in the Congregational churches of England which are distinguished above the great preachers of other branches of the Christian Church. He who seeks for the greatest preachers will find them here and there in all denominations, and in all lands. England has produced no greater pulpit orators than America. Her lessons to us are rather in the direction in which effort should move than in the manner in which truth should be presented. Great pulpit orators she has had, and so have the churches of the Continent; but great orators are not unknown in the American churches.

4. A study of the English pulpit makes it clear that the cry that the pulpit is losing its power is without basis in fact. There were never so many educated, attractive, eloquent and consecrated men preaching the Gospel as in these latter years of the nineteenth century. Commerce is making her demands, and science, with the other learned professions, is drawing large numbers of the choicest youth; but the clearer presentations of the truth of God as the only cure for the ills of human life, the

only satisfaction for human cravings, the only way in which manhood may be completed, is raising up an unsurpassed company of workers and preachers. And surely those who are well informed concerning what the English churches are doing, and the influence of the English ministers in political, social and educational circles, as well as in the pulpit itself, know that no class in modern society is exerting a more vital and beneficent influence.

No session of the Social Science Congress in 1884 was so well attended by members of that Association as the regular Sunday service in Carr's Lane Chapel, where Dr. Dale preached on " Social Science and the Christian Faith." * The subject of the sermon was not announced, but barristers, editors, business men, believers and unbelievers, when Sunday came, all by a common attraction were drawn toward that Nonconformist chapel, because they knew that from that pulpit a message would be issued worthy of their best thought, and which would be an inspiration to their highest life: nor were they disappointed, for no utterance of that Congress was more worthy of remembrance than the sermon to which they listened. What was true there is always true when those preach who possess spirituality, ability and common-sense, and who recognise that men have a right to demand that religion shall be proved credible before its acceptance is asked. The day

---
* The sermon is published in " Fellowship with Christ," p. 147.

for pious commonplaces, elaborate and rotund rhetoric, and sanctimonious "other worldliness" has gone by; but living men with a message which living men need will always find hearers, and never did such preachers receive more enthusiastic attention than in the very time when the press is supposed to have destroyed the power of the pulpit. If that power is ever lost it will be because the pulpit sets forth unworthy ideals of the Gospel, and of the nature of God and man. Those who have been trained to think for themselves will not endure platitudes, or the silly insinuation that they are to put chains on their reason and common-sense before they enter the sphere of religion. On the other hand, the eternal problems are pressing for solution with an intensity never before known. As science has enlarged the universe, as humanity has risen in dignity, the old questions come back and clamour with tenfold eagerness for an answer. Is there personality back of phenomena? Is there any infallible right? Is there any way in which he who has been wrong can get right? If a man die shall he live again? Any teacher in the pulpit, or elsewhere, who has answers for these questions will be sure of an audience. The great English preachers have not devoted themselves to commonplaces, to the tactics of dancing-masters, to the arts of milliners and dressmakers, but they have boldly faced and confidently answered the questions which the people, with deathless eagerness, have in all ages kept at the front. While preachers like Dale and Rogers, Mackennal and John Brown, Herber Evans, Goodrich and Pearson, Berry, Barrett and Horton, and teachers like Fairbairn, Simon, Cave, Reynolds, Scott and Duff continue their ministry, the power of the pulpit will increase, and its influence be a continual benediction, both in the individual and the corporate life.

And now I close this lecture on the English pulpit by quoting as an example of the very best pulpit eloquence a somewhat extended passage from the address of the President of the International Council of 1891, which combines as much of fundamental truth with reasonable and beautiful expression as can be found in the utterances of any of the great preachers among all denominations who have filled either English or American pulpits. While such a Gospel is preached in such a spirit, and with such sweetness and light, the work of the Kingdom will surely advance, and the "masses" and "classes" be attracted to the truth as it is in Jesus. The passage is as follows:

"To Judaising teachers, who insisted that heathen men could not share the blessedness of the Divine redemption and the Divine Kingdom unless in some sort they became Jews, I can imagine Paul saying, 'Ah, you are strangers to the real glory of Christ. When I stand up to preach in these great heathen cities—in Ephesus, in Corinth, in Rome, I see above me the same shining heavens that bend over Jerusalem—in Christ they were created, in Christ they endure; I see the same sun whose light falls on the temple in which our fathers worshipped —its fires were kindled by Christ, and apart from Christ those fires would die down and be extinguished. At night there shine the same stars that shine over the hills of Judea—it is in the power of Christ that through age after age their solemn movement is unbroken and their splendour undimmed. When I travel through heathen lands I see around me everywhere the manifestations of Christ's presence and power, and goodness; in mountains, and forests, and shining streams; in the vine and the fig-tree, and the ripening corn, in every flower that blossoms from the earth, in every bird that sings in the air. The winds are His, and the rain and the dew. In Christ were all things created; in Him they are held together; and separated from Him they would fall out of their order, and the whole universe would become a chaos.

"'But if the heavens which are stretched over these heathen men, and the earth beneath their feet, were created in Christ; and the wheat from which they make their bread, and the water which they drink, and whatever else sustains their life and adds to its comfort and delight; in whom were the heathen men themselves created? If it is only in Christ that these visible and material things endure, in whom is it that the men—men of every race and every tongue—endure? Have they an independent life? Does their existence rest on another foundation? Are they defended and sustained in being by some inferior Power? No; the men, like their country, were created in Christ. In Christ is the common root of the life of the race.'"*

* "Fellowship with Christ," pp. 351-352.

VIII.
THE OUTLOOK.

"It is certain that the Congregational scheme leads to toleration, as the national church scheme is adverse to it, for manifold reasons."
—HALLAM.

"We are now ere long to part asunder, and the Lord knoweth whether ever he should live to see our faces again: but whether the Lord had appointed it or not, he charged us before God and His blessed Angels, to follow him no further than he followed Christ. And if God should reveal anything to us by any other instrument of His, to be as ready to receive it, as ever we were to receive any truth by his Ministery: For he was very confident the Lord had more truth and light yet to break forth out of His holy Word."
—EDWARD WINSLOW, in "*Hypocrisie Vnmasked.*"

"It is getting to be a fashionable notion that toleration is the offspring of scepticism. If so, then Lord Herbert and Hobbes of Malmesbury ought to have been its apostles—but they were not; and the Baptists, the Independents, and the people called Quakers ought *not* to have been its early apostles—but they were."
—DR. J. STOUGHTON.

"The ideal perfection of the Church of Christ has been recognised by other communions as clearly as by our own; it was the signal merit of the Separatists of the sixteenth century that they affirmed the same law, the same life, the same inspiration for the invisible Church and the visible churches."—DR. ALEX. MACKENNAL.

"Among nations the head has at all times preceded the heart by centuries, as in the slave-trade; yes, by thousands of years, as will perhaps be the case in war."—JEAN PAUL FRIEDRICH RICHTER.

VIII.
THE OUTLOOK.

THE people of each generation think for themselves, and adjust themselves to the conditions in which they live. Times, as well as individuals, have their distinguishing characteristics, and these are manifested both in thought and life; consequently, changes in the expression of theological doctrine and in ecclesiastical organisation are inevitable. The truths which regulate thinking in one time differ from those which have influence in another, and yet there is a real unity in the life of the race, so that a change of conditions in one sphere causes changes in all other spheres of thought and action.

The evangelical doctrines have been formulated in different periods, and all bear evidence of the environment in which they assumed their present form. The doctrine of "The Trinity" crystallised the best theological thought of the time of the Council of Nicæa; "Justification by Faith," that of the era of the Protestant Reformation; "Inspiration" and "Last Things" are now in the crucible, and he understands little of what is going on around him who presumes to prophesy concerning their final expression. In political history the same correspondence between doctrine and life may be observed. In the time of Henry the Eighth the question of the supremacy of the crown against foreign interference was settled; during the Puritan Revolution the preëminent issue was whether the individual had a right to do his own thinking—whether freedom of conscience was possible. Cromwell went down, and the battle in favour of liberty seemed to have been lost; but the victory was complete, for, while the great Protector disappeared, the principles for which he contended were firmly established. The Puritan Revolution ended in the restoration of the monarchy; but the Puritan assertion of the right of each individual to think for himself, and to worship God according to his own conscience, is now recognised as axiomatic.

In the history of the Pilgrims and their descendants special truths have come into prominence when the times were ready for them. In the seventeenth and eighteenth centuries ministers and churches were rigidly Calvinistic in theology, and held firmly to the doctrines of the Westminster Confession. In that era the doctrine of Divine Sovereignty was needed as a basis for the ecclesiastical and political transformations which were to follow. The Separatists were Independents in the strictest sense, and had no more confidence in the Presbyterian system than in the Episcopal, but they were both Separatists and Independents because of their intense realisation of the Sovereignty of God. The rise of the social problem, far more than exhaustive study, has estranged the English Congregationalists of to-day from the severer type of Calvinism, and there are now few among their thinkers who do not repudiate the system. While the older forms of Genevan doctrine have become obsolete, and while the preachers and teachers most before the public have departed far from those interpretations of truth probably the majority of the churches, especially in the small towns and country districts, are still moderately Calvinistic. But the emphasis, as we have already pointed out, has passed from theology to sociology, and the inquiry now is not so much, What do you think of God? as, What will you do for man? In the stress of the conflict with Episcopacy, and with Presbyterian Scotland, alert and eager to introduce her ecclesiastical order into England, the churches were jealous of their independency; but now that they are strong and need fear no encroachments on their liberty they are beginning more keenly to appreciate the privileges of fellowship. Thus there are constant changes in English thought and life, and the dominant influences of this decade may be almost unknown in the next.

One of the most significant intellectual movements in England is the beginning of a revival of interest in the science of theology, at a time when social questions are absorbing the attention of all classes in the churches and out of them. It would be difficult to explain how, when the religious thought of England seemed almost entirely devoted to the consideration of humanitarian subjects, there could rise, as there is rising to-day, so intense an interest in criticism and theology. It is probably due to the influence of a few men. At the University of Oxford are three or four really great critical scholars. In Scotland there is a breaking away from the Calvinistic interpretations of truth, and the rise of a school of Biblical critics and constructive theologians of progressive spirit. Of course, long before the present leaders of the critical movement in Great Britain became known, others, not widely known, wrought in the same field, and German criticism was studied by a few; but it is the influences now dominant in the universities, which are reaching and transforming the thinking of all denominations. It has been said: "These men only touch the fringe of the churches, and a small portion of the ministry,—the youngest men." * That can hardly be correct, for others than the younger men are responding to the *Zeitgeist;* and yet the statement is largely true, and is an illustra-

---
* Rev. Bryan Dale.

tion of the fact already stated, that in England the churches are chiefly occupied with sociological questions, and are just beginning to show signs of a revival of interest in criticism and theology. The elevation of Marcus Dods to a theological chair in Scotland, the writings of Canons Driver and Cheyne at Oxford, the establishment of Mansfield College, the pre-eminence of Principal Fairbairn as a theologian, and perhaps also quite largely, the critical controversies in America, as reported in English papers, have stimulated interest in themes which only a decade ago were, to say the least, far less prominent than now. This revival of the study of theology is not yet widespread, and the devotion to social subjects is by no means diminished, but the one movement is coincident with the other. No questions have such attraction for thinking people as those which concern the supernatural, the spiritual life, and the problem of duty. If in England some of these have been relatively out of sight, it has been because other problems, for the time more imperiously demanding solution, have, by sheer force, pushed themselves to the front.

These two movements are now hand in hand: the one humanitarian, all-absorbing, almost universal; the other theological, attracting the attention of but few, and yet soon to occupy a large place in English thought.

Theological agitation in England is quite different

from what it is in the United States. Such a controversy as that over Professor Briggs would be impossible in any English denomination. The way the charges against Prof. W. T. Davison were received by his Wesleyan brethren, and those against Prof. Archibald Duff by Congregationalists, show that among the Wesleyans, who are theologically conservative, and Congregationalists, who are less so, there is large liberty. Congregationalists, Baptists, Presbyterians and Episcopalians, all have their eminent and honoured leaders who substantially agree with the New York professor. Mr. Spurgeon, some years before he died, raised his voice against the "down-grade" in theology. He had reference to many who were prominent in Baptist and Congregational churches, who were in sympathy with the higher critics, and, perhaps still more, who were humanising theology. He even withdrew from the Baptist Union, and no efforts at conciliation could induce him to return. But the great influence of Mr. Spurgeon utterly failed when he attempted to stem what he honestly believed to be the downward tendency in modern theological thought. When he uttered his cry of " down-grade," the majority of his more intelligent supporters, who honoured his fidelity, rejoiced in his eloquence, and were ready to co-operate with him in evangelistic efforts, simply smiled at his foolish attempt to invade a sphere which he was so poorly prepared to enter; and when he forgot himself and used stronger language than was kind, his course excited only pity. There is an unquestionable, if not yet a widespread revival of interest in theological themes, and there is no attempt of any magnitude to put shackles upon thinking. Freedom of thought in the Puritan churches has been bought at too dear a price to be easily relinquished. It would not be surprising if within a few years a new school of theology should arise in England, the centre of whose doctrine would be the Living Christ, a school whose thinking would begin with the need of man, rather than with speculations concerning God.*

The social environment in England will not materially change for a generation to come, and the pressure of poverty and misery is daily increasing. The great cities are growing larger, the struggle for existence intenser, the overcrowding more terrible, and its resultant evils more appalling. The author of "The Bitter Cry of Outcast London," declares that notwithstanding all the efforts of the churches and the State, the tide of vice, crime and social desolation is still rising. In the midst of such conditions one subject must well-nigh monopolise thought. On the other hand, the world-old and

---

* Since the above was written Principal Fairbairn's great work on "Christ in Modern Theology" has been published, and also that very suggestive series of essays entitled "Faith and Criticism," and both confirm our opinion that a new and vigorous school of Theologians is arising in England.

world-wide questions concerning God, duty, forgiveness and immortality are as imperative and persistent as ever, and, in the midst of the indescribable confusion of life, the answers to those questions must be different from what they would be if the thinkers could shut themselves in seclusion and evolve speculations from their inner consciousness. The Germans, in their philosophical and theological systems, have given the world results of pure thought and patient investigation. They have written, as only those can write who are removed from the storm and stress of the struggle for existence; but the English have not been able to separate themselves from their environment, and the Germans will not be able to do so much longer. Whatever the developments of theology, as distinguished from critical investigations, may be in England, there can be no doubt but that for years to come it will be written not in scholastic forms, but rather in terms of life. Criticism must be pursued in quiet, and expressed in scholastic language, but theology and preaching will be practical. The doctrines of God, human responsibility, immortal destiny, and even of Holy Scripture, will all be interpreted in the light of the miseries and sufferings of the people.

Thus far England has given the world few great speculative theologians, and even few eminent critics. In the department of criticism she has now some names of the highest rank, but, with the exception of Principal Fairbairn, it may be questioned if there is a single conspicuous English theologian. If we move backward, not only in the lines of the Congregational churches, but of all the churches, we look in vain for such names in theology as have been common in Germany and in America. Frederick Dennison Maurice has exerted a greater influence than any other modern teacher in the Established Church, but his work was suggestive, rather than constructive. Who is the English theologian to be compared with Schleiermacher, Dorner and Weiss; with Jonathan Edwards, Henry B. Smith and Professor Park? Surely Mozely, Wace or Ince would not be classed with them as original thinkers. There have been a few men among Congregationalists, like Pye Smith and Ralph Wardlaw, who have been more or less prominent; but theological instruction of the quality that has long prevailed in the schools of Germany and America, has until recently been almost unknown in England. Under the influence of the Germans on the one side, and of Americans on the other, a new race of theologians will probably arise, and their starting-point will be neither the Sovereignty of God, nor the Person of Christ, but the needs of humanity; and if their work is well done, as no doubt it will be, they will make valuable and original contributions to the science of theology,—such contributions as the life of no other nation than England makes possible.

There is a growing feeling that the gate into the ministry is too broad, and that, in some way, churches should be saved from narrowness, ignorance and weakness in the pulpits. The Independent theory is that a church may call to be its pastor whomsoever it chooses. If a local church wishes any man for its minister, whether he is trained in theology or not, it calls him. If he is to be ordained or installed, the church ordains him, asking such help as it may choose; not for the sake of advice concerning the call which has been issued, but simply to make the recognition services more attractive. As a result, many men in the English pulpits are without training, either in the Bible or in theology. Some of the most eminent preachers, like Joseph Parker and W. Hardy Harwood, have passed no time in theological schools, but they have compensated for this lack of early education by genius and industry. Such men are not to be confused with those who are without training. Many of the latter class, leaving their country for their country's good, have invaded our American churches; they come without credentials, often saying that these were lost at sea, until it has become almost a proverb that the harbour of Halifax is strewn with the testimonials of English ministers.

At different times in England attempts have been

made to remedy this evil, and yet strong and prominent Congregational leaders have insisted that any attempt in this direction would be an infringement of the liberty of the local church, and would do more harm than good. For instance, Rev. Dr. Thomas Green, ex-Chairman of the Congregational Union, says: "If an independent, well-reputed church invites, if a godly man accepts, that is enough for me, and I have yet to see that a committee's examination was a necessary testimonial to his full recognition. At present I see no reason for giving up the belief that the Spirit of God may call men to enter the ministry direct from the sheepfold, the plow, the fishing-nets, the tent-making, or even from the carpenter's-shop."* And commenting on Mr. Green's opinions Rev. Dr. Thomas, a prominent Welsh minister, says: "There is no other stand to be taken in Independency. I know that such freedom leads to tumult and irregularity at times, but if we wish to guard the privileges of our polity we must be willing to accept its drawbacks. The polity which unites the advantages of Independency and Presbyterianism without the disadvantages of either the one or the other has not yet been discovered." On the other hand, the Rev. S. B. Handley, Secretary of the Staffordshire Congregational Union, with equal urgency and more cogency, argues in favour of an educated ministry, and also

---

* See discussion in *The Independent*, London, 1891.

for safeguards by means of which the churches may be protected from designing and ignorant men. In America that safeguard is found in the council system, which has not hitherto had a place in English Congregationalism.

And yet, means for securing the purity and ability of the pulpit have not been neglected in the past; for, as this discussion has shown, the second Cheshire Congregational Union, formed in 1691, adopted the "Heads of Agreement by the United Ministers in and about London called Presbyterial and Congregational." From those "Heads" the following is an extract: "Of the Ministry. (1.) We agree that the ministerial office is instituted by Christ. . . . (2.) They who are called to this office ought to be endued with *competent learning and ministerial gifts*, as also with the grace of God; sound in judgment, not novices in the faith and knowledge of the Gospel. . . . (3.) That ordinarily none shall be ordained to the work of the ministry but such as are called and chosen thereunto by a particular church. (4.) That in so great and weighty a matter as the calling and choosing a pastor we judge it ordinarily requisite that every such church consult and advise with pastors of neighbouring churches. (5.) That after such advice the person consulted about, being chosen by the brotherhood of that particular church over which he is to be set, and he accepting, be duly ordained and set apart to his office over them; wherein 'tis ordinarily requisite that the pastors of neighbouring congregations concur with the presiding elder or elders, if such there be," etc.

Mansfield and several other colleges are now lifting the standard of theological education, for they insist on university training as a condition of the enjoyment of their privileges. To that previous preparation they add thorough instruction in theology. Before long most of the English colleges will make similar requirements, and the result will be a more thoroughly educated ministry than was possible when the Universities were closed to Nonconformists and education was difficult to obtain except by absence from the country. Yet it should be remembered that the theological training at Oxford and Cambridge, before they were open to Dissenters, was often surpassed by the local colleges —imperfect as those surely were. Until within little more than a decade there was no general system of education in England, and the population in country districts and in many of the towns were in comparative ignorance; but now schools are training the hearers, and they in turn are asking better training for the pulpit. The demand for an educated ministry is the voice of the people insisting that those who presume to lead shall be worthy to lead. Principal Fairbairn has well said that the perils of an uneducated ministry can hardly be exaggerated. This movement does not seek to limit

Christian workers, but to make Christian teachers and leaders competent for their mission.

During the last two years, and possibly stimulated by the International Council, there has been a great advance in the direction of Christian unity. The action of the Lambeth Conference in proposing four articles as a basis for such unity started the discussion in all parts of the world, and the propositions have been considered by different ecclesiastical bodies. But when the International Council was held the question was raised, Why were not all Congregationalists included in the invitation by which it was convened? When Dr. John Clifford, who with Dr. McLaren divides the intellectual primacy among English Baptists, made his address as delegate of the Baptist Union he asked, "Why are not we here? We are Congregationalists as well as you." And Dr. J. Monroe Gibson, Moderator of the Presbyterian General Assembly, suggested that there should be a Council of Denominations. The subject was in the air, and the International Council was hardly ended before its honoured Secretary, Rev. Alexander Mackennal, D. D., led in the effort to secure a Congress of Free Churches. (In England the Free Churches include all except the Establishment and the Roman Catholic.) The proposition received favour. Manchester was selected as the place for the first meeting. The various denominations of that city united in welcoming their brethren from different parts of the Kingdom. This Free Church Congress will not fail to bring nearer together those who agree in their belief that there should be separation between Church and State. Many have long felt that Congregationalists and Baptists are practically one, and that they should combine their forces. English Baptists are seldom Close Communionists, and where there is recognition of the right of each individual to decide for himself concerning Baptism, both for infants and adults, the chief barrier toward union disappears. That is already often left to individual choice in the English churches, which in this country is made a condition of church membership.

Moreover, in the "Forward Movement," which practically began with the publication of "The Bitter Cry of Outcast London" in 1883, the various denominations of Christians are coöperating in perfect harmony. The leaders of the Baptists, Congregationalists, Wesleyans, are so near together that it would be impossible for a stranger to detect the lines which are supposed to separate. Many Baptists are in Congregational churches; many Congregationalists in Baptist congregations. There is a clear, strong and widespread conviction among the more intelligent members of the Free Churches in favour of ultimate church union and of present coöperation.

We now approach a subject of surpassing significance. It needs no better name than that by which it is known—"The Nonconformist Conscience." This is a crusade whose aim is the creation of a sentiment among the people which will demand pure moral character as a condition of public service. It insists that those who occupy high official positions shall possess not only ability and faculty, but also that their lives shall, at least, be decent, and free from scandal. This movement, as the name indicates, is not limited to Congregationalists, but among its apostles are many of its most eminent leaders.

Two illustrations of the strength of public sentiment in relation to this subject are found in the cases of Charles S. Parnell and Sir Charles Dilke. The one was the uncrowned king of Ireland, and the other a man whose intellectual ability and faculty as a statesman at one time indicated that he would be the successor of Mr. Gladstone in the leadership of the Liberal party. Both men were proven guilty of serious social crimes. Sir Charles Dilke retired to private life, declaring that he would not attempt to re-enter public service until he had established his innocence before a court of law. In spite of that declaration, however, he appeared as a candidate for the Forest of Dean, and the chorus of opposition to his election which arose from all parts of England showed that the Christian faith of the people is even stronger than their political affiliations. Many declared that if Sir Charles Dilke were allowed to assume a prominent position in Liberal politics they would desert the party. And such loyal Liberals as Dr. Mackennal and Rev. Guinness Rogers most emphatically, yet in courteous and Christian ways, served warning of what might be expected if the leaders presumed to disregard the conscience of the people. The electors of the Forest of Dean have returned Sir Charles to Parliament, but he will have to be content with obscurity, for the Nonconformists are a large proportion of the Liberal party, and when the issue concerns a matter of conscience they will endure no trifling. Mr. Parnell presumed upon his supremacy in Irish affairs and upon his great services in the past, but fought a losing battle when he attempted to ignore the conscience of the English people. In his case not only the Nonconformist conscience but also that of the nation was against him. Sir Charles Dilke's bitterest opponents were those who in other conditions would have been his most loyal friends.

A more illustrious example of the power of the Nonconformist conscience was seen in the case of the Prince of Wales, who in the spring of 1891 was found to be not only an occasional but an habitual gamester, accustomed to go from house to house among his friends carrying with him the implements of the gambler's profession. The excitement over this discovery can hardly be exaggerated. Even Mr. Gladstone is reported to have said to a distinguished editor that certain reflections on the course of the Prince of Wales, which that editor had made, if published would imperil the stability of the British throne. The papers were full of the scandal, and when the Prince went to the North on a State occasion in one city he was compelled to pass under a transparency on which were these words: "Welcome to our Prince, but no welcome for gamblers." During the summer of 1891, in most audiences of Nonconformists, no sentiment was more rapturously applauded than condemnation of the course of the heir to the throne. The excitement subsided because it was believed that the Prince had learned his lesson; but he was almost officially warned that if he dared again to violate the conscience of his subjects it would be at the peril of the succession. This may be an exaggerated statement, but in England, under all the apparent reverence for forms, and devotion to position, there is a sturdy reverence for the fundamental principles of righteousness. The old Puritan standards of conduct have by no means disappeared. Faith in God and loyalty to the moral life are deeply imbedded in the English character. No finer tribute to the results of the Puritan Revolution, and few more striking illustrations of the irony of history, can be imagined than the fact that the probable successor of the King who ordered the reading of the Book of Sports in the churches on the Sabbath day, should be notified, by the descendants of the very people whom his ancestor presumed to deride, that his title to the throne, so honoured by his mother, may be imperilled by disloyalty to the principles of Puritan and Christian morality.

The movement designated by the phrase "Nonconformist Conscience" has not yet culminated, and many men in conspicuous positions are being made to realise that, whether the power of the pulpit is waning or not, the teachings of Christ as a force in the life of the people were never so mighty or so vital as to-day. Americans may well pray that that which is symbolised by the phrase "Nonconformist Conscience" may traverse the Atlantic, and do its work in the halls of our metropolis, in the legislatures of our States, and in the Capitol of the nation where ignoble politicians violate the people's liberties with the suggestion that bribes be allowed to determine the issues of questions of national and international importance.

Another significant movement in English Congregationalism results from the new consciousness of imperial relations. A clear idea of the greatness of the British Empire, and the fact that the colonies are fast becoming Empires, is just dawning upon the average English mind. India has been called a "dependency"; so have Canada, Australia and South Africa: but recent events have taught the nation that if it would retain its hold upon its colonies it must appreciate its own imperial privileges and their greatness. Australasia, under the leadership of Sir Henry Parks, has made a great stride toward unity and nationality beneath the Southern Cross. South Africa, under the guidance of Cecil Rhodes, is facing the future with the prospect of speedily becoming an independent Empire; and Canada has long been independent in nearly everything but name. Increased intercommunication has brought to the home government a new conception of the vastness of the dominion of which Westminster is the capital. An imperial consciousness has grown in the minds of all Englishmen.

Springing out of the growth of this imperial idea has also grown a truer conception of the responsibility of English Christians, and of their duty in a world-wide federation. Pastors go and come between England and Australia, Canada and South Africa. Dr. Bevan, after having been in London, came to New York, returned to London, and is now in Australia. The successor of Baldwin Brown was called from Canada. A son of Mr. Spurgeon, long the pastor of a large church in New Zealand, has now been asked to succeed his father in London. The sons of Colonial Nonconformists go to England for education. As the colonies and the mother country are getting nearer together, and better appreciating each other, the consciousness that the English churches have relations which are not insular is disappearing, and their dignity and responsibility as leaders in a world-wide movement for the advancement of the Kingdom of God is being recognised. The International Council of Congregationalists held in London in 1891 stimulated this consciousness. It brought together representatives of the churches from the ends of the earth, and showed that their brotherhood is real and vital. It was once said by way of reproach, of English Independents, that they thought only of themselves, or of interests which were near to themselves. That reproach is no longer merited. They realise that they are part of a world-wide fellowship; that on them rest imperial obligations, and with a fine enthusiasm they are rising to meet their responsibilities.

We now turn from these questions to another which is of greater interest to American thinkers, namely the theological outlook in the English churches. This subject was considered in two papers read before the International Council—one by Principal Simon, of the Theological College at Edinburgh, and the other by Dr. E. R. Conder, of Leeds. Few men were better able to speak on this subject than the accomplished theologian of Scotland, and the eminent representative pastor of the North of England.*

---

* Dr. Conder, who was one of the most scholarly of modern English divines, has died since the meeting of the Council. He was

Principal Simon found little that is encouraging to a theologian in the state of theological science in Great Britain. He says: "The first thing that calls for notice is the pronounced and widespread distaste, not to say aversion or hostility, to the theological and scientific treatment of Christian truth. . . . The theological tone of our colleges is, I believe, higher than it ever was, but the anti-theological, and falsely practical, current is so strong outside that even the best students have difficulty in stemming it—the majority prefer to float with it." He supports these statements by two or three interesting facts. During the last thirty-five years only one work on Systematic Theology has been published by British Congregationalists, and out of six hundred registered Congregational publications, during, say, twenty-five years, scarcely fifty are scientifically theological; and out of upwards of four hundred and fifty discourses by Congregational ministers, printed during the last five years, or thereabouts, in the Christian World Pulpit, scarcely thirty were properly doctrinal. He makes an exception, however, of three doctrines, in his statement that there is little interest concerning theological subjects; those three are, Inspiration, the Atonement, and Future Punishment. He believes, however, that

---

pastor of the Parade Street Congregational Chapel in Leeds. Dr. Simon is no longer in Edinburgh, having been called to the Presidency of the United College at Bradford, Yorkshire, in succession to Dr. Falding.

while in recent times there is less doctrinal preaching than formerly, the tone of the pulpit is more profoundly ethical than ever before. The old Calvinism, he says is entirely gone. There is "no clearly defined doctrine of Inspiration." We are all "at sixes and sevens concerning the doctrine of God." "Stress is no longer laid on His infinitude, His transcendence, His absolute authority, His awful holiness, infallible righteousness and consuming anger: we dwell by preference on their essential affinities as involved for example in the Divine Fatherhood and immanence; in His love and yearning for man; and in the claims which men have on Him." He thinks that more emphasis is put on the humanity than on the divinity of Christ; that "conversion has been well-nigh converted into decision for Christ; regeneration into a process of spiritual culture." On the question of man's future destiny he says that the churches are divided between Universalism, the doctrine of life in Christ, the Larger Hope, and various phases of a non-committal position—the sterner views held a generation ago having well-nigh disappeared.

Here is an interesting sentence: "Compare the heresy-fancier of to-day with the heresy-hunter of the past, and you will scarcely hesitate to apply the word revolution to the change that has come about. Few things, however, are more significant than the fact that Tennyson's lines, the quotation of which in my student days was almost enough to stamp a man a heretic—

> 'Our little systems have their day;
> They have their day and cease to be;
> They are but broken lights of Thee,
> And Thou, O Lord, art more than they'—

now form part of a hymn in the 'New Congregational Hymnal.'"

Principal Simon, commenting on the significance of the change, finds in it a reaction against dogma, and especially against the error which, he says, found classical expression in the words of the Athanasian Creed : " Whosoever will be saved, before all things it is necessary that he hold the Catholic faith." " In view, however, of the stress which is at last beginning to be laid on the distinction between fact and doctrine, of the increasing effort to get face to face with historical actualities, whatever their nature ; of the marked revival of Biblical studies ; of the place that is being assigned to Christian experience in the genesis of Divine knowledge; and of the growth of interest in philosophy, I look forward to a day when under the inspiration of insight into the true functions of theology,— namely, first, to supply the believer with a reason for the faith he already possesses, and thus to add to his capability of bearing strain and witness then of helping to guide non-believers to Christ further, of giving doubters a reason for believing, a very different thing from giving Christ a reason for receiving non-believers and doubters; and, finally, of filling up an otherwise vacant and fatal gap in the circle of sciences—the prevailing indifference will give place to hearty, intelligent and active interest."

This paper of Principal Simon's, and others read at the same time, were discussed by several English ministers, among the number being Principal Fairbairn and Rev. George S. Barrett, both of whom made remarks which are worthy of careful notice.

Principal Fairbairn said: "Now the movement of thought consequent on the new historical method has led to two things; on one side, to the recovery of the Holy Scriptures, and on the other side, to the recovery of their great historical Person. I do not hesitate to say that our theology is marked more than anything by the recovery of Christ." He further said: " I do not think that systematic theology is done with. I believe it is only beginning to be. But there is a vast difference between systematic theology and agglomerated theology. . . The doctrine that we need as the pre-eminent doctrine for Christianity must be on the historical side Christocentric, and on the doctrinal side it must be Theocentric." The substance of Principal Fairbairn's address may be epitomised in the statement that the historical movement has led to the recovery by the modern Church of the Scriptures and of

Christ. Mr. Barrett, in an admirable speech, condensed his survey of the theological outlook as follows: "So far as I know anything of the theological thought of our ministers it may be characterised in two sentences—first: hearty loyalty to the evangelical faith; and, secondly, the utmost freedom in criticism, both of doctrine, and the human side of the Bible."

Turning now to the condensed and luminous paper of Dr. Conder, we find him saying that there are three movements of great importance which indicate the theological changes through which the English churches have passed in fifty years. The first is the disappearance of the old theology known as Calvinism; the second, the upgrowth of an unprecedented sentiment of freedom; and the third, the place personally occupied by our Lord Jesus Christ in theological thought, in preaching—especially evangelistic or mission preaching—and in Christian life. He states his opinion of the first two movements as follows: "We have lost theology, and we have gained freedom." "In our day, instead of looking into himself to see whether he truly believes and understands the Gospel, the penitent is encouraged to bring his ignorance as well as his sinfulness and impotence to Christ, and to put himself unconditionally in the hands of the living and loving Saviour, who was delivered up for his trespasses and raised for his justification."

Dr. Conder is careful in all his statements, and is both a shrewd and wise observer. He believes that the spiritual gains from the transformation of theology are immense, yet does not fail to recognise that there have also been great losses. One statement in the address from which we have quoted is that the old theology did not perish under the assault of a rival system, but expired because an atmosphere had been created in which it could not breathe. He says concerning the doctrine of a Limited Atonement: "We have frankly come over to the ground of our Wesleyan brethren." * Dr. Conder especially commends Dr. Dale's book on the Atonement as indicating the line along which English thought is likely to move. Concerning Eschatology, he says: "Views of Divine government, of the unlimited, undiscriminating punishment of sin, and of the condition and fate of the heathen world, which have never commanded the unanimous assent of the wisest Christian thinkers, yet which were commonly preached without a qualm and with terrific power fifty years since, have become—may I not say to most of us—incredible, because they seem to ascribe injustice to God." He does not indicate, however, any special centre about which the thought of the English churches concerning this subject is crystallising.

---

* Rev. Bryan Dale, commenting on this remark, says: "Long ago, chiefly through Dr. Wardlaw's book."

His summary is as follows: "Our churches have gained in breadth, catholicity, elasticity, activity, sympathy with the temporal as well as the spiritual need and woe of our neighbours, of our nation, of the world. But in personal spiritual life—*q. d.* in faith, fervour, prayer, unworldly simplicity, intense religious conviction, stern loyalty to truth and conscience self-denial, the life of conscious relation to things unseen and eternal, and living communion with our Saviour and our Father by the mighty indwelling Spirit,—glad as I should be to believe it, I dare not assert that we surpass—I doubt if we equal—the Christians whose characters were shaped and toughened by a severer creed in a more wintry social, civil, moral and religious climate."

This is an outline of the doctrinal beliefs of the English churches as indicated by the utterances of some of their most distinguished, and truly representative, leaders. Often quite as accurate an estimate may be formed by an observer from the outside as by testimony from within, and I therefore venture to record some of my own impressions concerning the present theological *status* of English Congregationalists. Without doubt there is relatively little doctrinal preaching in England; and the effort of the pulpit is rather in practical than in theological lines, but there is much Biblical and expository preaching. It is true that in their theological colleges there is but one preëminent theologian, but there are several inspiring and helpful teachers. Even Dr. Fairbairn has won his fame by lecturing and preaching and by occasional articles, rather than by permanent contributions to theological scholarship.* Principal Cave of Hackney has published more than Principal Fairbairn, and is a vigorous thinker and voluminous writer. Principal Reynolds, of Cheshunt College, is a theological instructor who has made a far deeper impression on his students than on the outside world, and is a man of lofty and inspiring spirituality; while Principal Scott, of Lancashire College, has long worthily filled a difficult and honourable position. Professor Duff, of Airedale, has recently published a very valuable book on Biblical Theology which is full of promise for the future. And yet there can be no doubt that Dr. Fairbairn is the only English theologian of any denomination whose fame is world-wide.

In the theological colleges of England there is too little division of labour. The institutions are too numerous for the territory and the endowments; consequently, each professor is burdened with such a variety of duties as makes it impossible for him to find time for much original investigation, and for such contributions to current thought as make a theologian a power among the people as well as

---

* This was written before the publication of his last great work—"The Place of Christ in Modern Theology."

among his students. As Principal Simon and Dr. Conder have said, the ancient type of Calvinism has gone. No single eminent English Congregationalist is, in the old sense, a Calvinist. Dr. Dale distinctly declares that he gave up Calvinism years ago. Concerning the doctrine of Inspiration there is about the same uncertainty as in this country. There is no disposition to slacken the hold on the Bible as the Word of God, but theories concerning it differ, and no one of them is conspicuously representative. Most religious teachers of acknowledged eminence believe in Continuous Inspiration; and in the personal Holy Ghost, who is in as vital relations with Christians in these later day as with the ancient Church. Concerning the doctrine of the Atonement there is not much disposition to dogmatise. McLeod Campbell, Maurice and Bushnell have greatly influenced the thinking of English ministers on this subject. The cross of Christ is central and regulative in their preaching. Calvary is a great and dear name,—every head is uncovered and every voice hushed as thought approaches that sacred place. Dr. Parker did not misrepresent the average English feeling when in his farewell address at the International Council, having referred to the cross and Calvary, and being interrupted by some one who started a cheer, he said: "Stop! The man who would cheer such an utterance as that does not understand it." The great majority of English preachers are firm believers in the essential deity of Jesus Christ.*

When the subject of Last Things is approached there is no doubt but that the old doctrine of Everlasting Punishment has been placed in the background. Some, as Edward White and Dr. Dale, accept the theory known as Conditional Immortality.

Many both among ministers and laity hold to "The Larger Hope," of which Tennyson and Frederick Maurice are the most eminent modern prophets; and perhaps a still larger number do not attempt to formulate their belief concerning the mysterious subject of Last Things.

The English Congregational churches are not moving toward Unitarianism. They were never more evangelical in spirit than to-day.

If their teaching is ethical rather than theological it is because they feel the pressure of life, and in this loud and stirring time there is little opportunity for them to devote their energies to speculation. The English pulpit is manned by men able to do strong and earnest thinking. Joseph Parker, R. W. Dale, Guinness Rogers, Alexander Mackennal, R. F. Horton, George S. Barrett, Charles A. Berry, P. T. Forsyth, Samuel Pearson, Alexander Goodrich, F. H. Stead and others like them, do not

---

* Rev. Bryan Dale adds: "No other could long hold his place in a Congregational pulpit."

turn from the profoundest topics of theology because they are afraid to treat them, but, if at all, because other themes seem for the moment to be of more imperative importance.

The English churches, and English thinkers, as a rule, emphasise the Fatherhood of God; the continuous inspiration of the Spirit; the Deity of Jesus Christ; the cross of Calvary—an eternal and superlative fact; retribution—a reality; the brotherhood of man, so near and so urgent in its demands as to necessitate the interpretation of all other doctrines in its light.

The demands of our subject require that at least an attempt be made to answer the question, What part has Independency yet to play in the religious development of England? As in the past so in the future it will have to lead the Free Churches in their effort to secure Disestablishment. No other denomination has contested with the Congregationalists leadership in this movement. Mr. Edward Miall, M. P., who did more than any other man to give to it the prominence which it deserves as a political question, and Mr. Henry Richard, M. P., another eminent leader in the same cause, were both at one time Congregational ministers. The Pilgrims and their descendants have been in the van in all the long and fierce battle for a free church. Only within a comparatively short period have the Wesleyans been willing to acknowledge that they are really Dissenters. In other communions individuals have taken conspicuous positions as opponents of a State Church; but, from the first, Congregational churches have been at the front.

Disestablishment cannot long be delayed, although there is wide difference of opinion as to how it will be realised. James Martineau believes that, coupled with Disendowment, Disestablishment would be a national disaster. Canon Farrar thinks that Disestablishment will probably come in Wales, but that it will be an illustration of the sins of the parents being visited on their children, because the Church in Wales is now doing a work which, were it not for the mistakes of the past, would make Disestablishment impossible. Mr. Balfour sneers at the selfishness of Nonconformists, but his sneers stimulate rather than obstruct their cause. More and more the English people as a whole are coming to believe that the Church and the State should be separate, and the old leaders in this crusade must remain at its head until the victory is won. Edward Miall, Henry Richard and Sir Edward Baines have gone, but Carvell Williams, Guinness Rogers, Drs. Mackennal and Dale, still remain, and are doing valiant service in the cause of religious freedom.

Futhermore, Congregationalists in England, as around the world, have more or less inspired all the denominations with admiration for the principle of self-government, and therefore have one distinctive mission, namely to keep before the people a polity which makes a true Christian unity possible. There can never be union of the churches on the basis of such an interpretation of the "Historic Episcopate" as would require the descendants of the Puritans to acknowledge that John Bunyan, John Owen, John Knox and John Robinson were not in the apostolic succession and true apostles of God. The Presbyterian polity can hardly be the universal one, because it possesses too much machinery. The Church of the future will recognise the independency of each local company of believers, its right to make its creed for itself, and to determine what its methods of work shall be, while it unites all local churches in the strongest of all bonds—the chains of Christian fellowship. In the United States the Presbyterian church will never have freedom from theological strife until it comes to the Congregational position, namely, that each church may determine for itself its Confession of Faith and its conditions of fellowship. I have no idea that the Church of the future will be purely Congregational; surely it will not be the absolute independency seen in England a century ago, or that modification of it which is now found in America. The coming Church will put more emphasis upon fellowship than any Congregationalists now do, and will devise some wise and consistent plan by which all may coöperate in aggressive movements for the advancement of the Kingdom of God without disloyalty to any one's convictions of truth. Whatever the form or name which the Church of the future may assume it is certain that with the growth of intelligence, with clearer conceptions of the rights and obligations of conscience, no ecclesiastical order will be large enough to meet the needs of all the people which does not guarantee perfect liberty to the local church, and at the same time provide for large and wise coöperation in carrying on charitable and missionary activities. Changes in all the denominations are inevitable. Peculiarities long cherished and musty are being laid aside, non-essentials are receiving less emphasis, and that vital and enduring Christian unity is being realised by growth which it has been found impossible to secure by mechanical contrivances.

Whatever, then, may be the developments of the future, this may safely be predicted: the two poles of the sphere on which the coming Church will turn must be—the independency of the local church, and the fellowship of all the churches. To keep these two thoughts constantly before the people who are passing through what is little less than a great ecclesiastical and theological revolution, is the peculiar mission of English Congregationalism in the immediate future.

We bring this study of spiritual life and ecclesiastical polity to a close with a feeling of inspiration and satisfaction, for we have learned that the children of our fathers who remained in Old England have fought, and are winning, the same battle for liberty of conscience and freedom to think and worship, that has been fought and won in the American Republic. The descendants of Robinson, Brewster and Bradford have done their work in America; the descendants of Thomas Goodwin, Philip Nye, and their associates, have been equally loyal to vital truth in Old England. The principles which have given to Americans their characteristic civilisation have been transforming institutions and bringing in larger liberty among Englishmen. There are sad and discouraging features in the outlook, and many of them have at different times been pointed out with discrimination and wisdom, but there is eternal youth in those principles which have been held aloft by the Pilgrims and their children in Old England; and of their ultimate victory, both in Church and State, there can be little doubt—if what has been is prophetic of what is to be. The contrast between the church in the Bridewell and such churches as are now found in every part of England, the United States, and the British Colonial Empire, is great indeed, but not greater than the contrast between the civilisation of the Elizabethan and the Victorian eras of English history.

I will not finish these lectures without expressing the hope that they may help a little toward a truer and better appreciation of "our kin beyond the sea"; nor without the prophecy that as Christians on both sides of the water learn to understand and appreciate one another, they will compel the politicians to abandon their habit of taking counsel of the ignorant and selfish who are influenced by passion and greed, and thus hasten a truer, more vital, and more enduring union of those nations, which, most of all, ought to be constantly loyal to each other. Great Britain and the United States of America have common interests, a common lanugage, a common religion, a common history. May all that tends to divide and make hostile disappear, and a thousand Christian ministries bind into close and lasting fellowship those nations which seem to be separated by a great dividing flood, but which are in reality one people, with a common mission and a common destiny.

INDEX.

ABOLITION of University tests, 106.
Academies, 158.
Adelbert, 17.
Africa, South, 315-317.
Allon, Dr. Henry, 87, 112, 173-175, 272, 277, 285.
Ambrose, 252.
American Board of Commissioners for Foreign Missions, 133, 140.
American Republic, 7.
Anabaptists, 56.
Andover Theological Seminary, 157.
Anglicans, 25, 26.
Apostles' Creed, 231, 232.
Apostolic Church, 16, 19, 27, 39.
Archdeacons, 99.
Arches, Court of, 98.
Arianism, 67, 261.
Arminianism, 214, 242, 243.
Articles of Faith, 152, 229-231, 234.
Assembly, Savoy, 185, 186, 194, 195, 204, 205, 222.
 Westminister, 184-186, 192, 205.

(*Assembly—continued.*)
 Presbyterian General, 310.
 Associations, County, 169, 170.
 State Local, 150.
Athanasian Creed, 320.
Augustine, 17, 88, 89, 92.
Australia, 315-317.
Awakening, the Great, 206.

BACON, Lord, 255.
Baines, 128.
Bailey, F. T., 231.
Balfour, 329.
Baptism, 13, 311.
Baptist Churches, 180, 181.
 Conditions of Membership, 232, 237.
Baptists, 68, 73, 108, 283.
Baptist Union, 302.
Barbarians in England, 88.
Barnard, Sherman S., 208.
Barnes, '91.
Barrett, Geo. S., 277, 292, 321, 322, 327, 329.
Barrowe, Henry, 60, 61, 63, 69, 80, 253.
Baxter, Richard, 257, 258.
Beecher, Henry Ward, 253, 254, 259, 271.

INDEX.

Behrends, A. J. F., 232.
Bernard, St., 252.
Berry, Chas. A., 168, 229, 277, 292, 327.
Bethune, Dr. Geo. E., 254.
Bevan, Dr., 316.
Binney, Thomas, 267, 268, 271, 272, 275, 276, 279.
Bishops, 12, 46, 75, 90, 99, 105, 162.
    Election of Christian, 43.
    Supremacy of, 47.
Bishop of the diocese, 95.
"Bitter Cry of Outcast London," 134, 135, 303, 311.
Boatmen of Madras, 17.
Boleyn, Anne, 92.
Boniface, 17.
Boot and Shoe Brigade, 135.
Booth, Charles, 135.
Booth, General, 136.
Boston (Massachusetts), 65, 207, 288.
Bradford,(England,) 159, 332.
Bradford, William, 54, 65.
Bradford Observer, 128.
Bradlaugh, Charles, 86.
Brewster, William, 54, 64, 65, 255, 332.
Bridge, William, 185, 186.
Briggs, Professor Charles A., 302.
Bright, John, 280.
Bristol, Albert G., 208.
Brown, James Baldwin, 166, 171, 267, 272, 276, 280.
Browne, Robert, 53, 59, 80.
Brownists, 53, 60.
Brown, John, 45, 292.
Brooke, Lord, 183.
Brooks, Phillips, 254, 259, 279.
Buckingham, Duke of, 55.
Burial Hill, 202, 208, 222.
Burgon, Dean, 109.
Burleigh, Lord, 61, 63.

Burroughs, Jeremiah, 185.
Bushnell, Horace, 254, 260, 326.
Byles, of *Bradford Observer*, 128.

CALVIN, 50, 55, 92.
Calvinism, 70, 75, 181, 214, 299, 319, 326.
Calvinism in England now, 137.
Calvinistic Creed, 242, 243.
    System, 186.
Calvinists, 51.
Cambridge (Massachusetts), 106, 158, 309.
Cambridge Platform, 204.
Campbell, Dr., 267, 326.
Canada, 315, 317.
Canterbury, Archbishop of, 95, 99, 102.
Carpenter, Dr. Boyd, 280.
Caryll, 186.
Cartwright, Thomas, 50, 55, 181.
Case for Disestablishment, 97.
Catechism, Shorter, 203.
    Westminster, 187, 197.
Catharine of Aragon, 92.
Cathedrals, 118.
Catholics, Original Owners of Church Property, 101.
    Failed to unite Church and State, 114.
    Gain seats in Parliament, 106.
Cave, Principal, 292, 325.
Chapel Union, 168, 173, 277.
    Building Society, 134, 140, 158.
    Mark Lane, 260.
    Weigh House, 276.
    Westminster, 267, 268, 270, 276.
Chapels, 168.
Charter, 91.
Charles First, 54, 256.

INDEX. 337

Charles Second, 66, 96.
Cheshunt, 159.
Cheyne, Canon, 301.
Chicago, 207, 288.
Christ, Deity of, 201.
Christian Unity, 309.
Church Aid and Home Missionary Society, 134, 139, 148, 149, 151.
  Anglican, 121.
  Arguments for and against union with State, 109, 110.
  American, 216.
  Branch, 151.
  Congresses, 88.
  Chorlton Road, 168.
  Early Christian, 45-47.
  English, Articles of the, 105.
  Discipline of the, 98.
  Laws concerning property, 100.
  Origin and value of property, 101, 102.
  Entrance to, 47.
  Erection, 140.
  Episcopal, 97, 119.
  Established, 69, 80, 182.
  Free, 22, 25, 28, 120, 138, 162, 181, 301, 328.
  Free, Genesis of, 59.
  Congress of, 310, 311.
  Future, 20, 31, 32, 330, 331.
  Ideal, 14, 15, 20.
  In Antioch, 40,
  In Corinth, 8,
  Independent, 151, 153.
  In Jerusalem, 8, 19, 27, 40.
  Irish, 120.
  Local, 142, 169.
  Mission, 151.
  Order, 196.
  Organisation for work, 167.
  Parish, 110.
  Parties, High and Low, 25, 108.

(*Church—continued.*)
  Polity, Platform of, 192.
  Reëstablishment of, 96.
  Roman, 89, 90, 252,
  and State, Union of, 67, 115.
  Union, 150.
  Universal, 238.
Churches, Basis of Union, 147.
  Members of, 97.
  Number of, in England, Wales and United States, 131,132.
  Organisation of, 148.
  Wealth of, 91.
Churchill, Randolph, 86.
Citations, Statute of, 94.
Civil War in America, 207.
Clapp, Z. E., 231.
Clarkson, W. F., 134.
Clayton, 267.
Clifford, Dr. John, 310.
Clink Prison, 61.
Clyfton, Richard, 64.
Colleges, 69, 131, 132.
  Combining, 159, 160.
College, Harvard, 259.
Collier, Jeremy, 267.
Colliers' Rents, 235.
Colonies, English, 65, 66.
Committee, Standing, 152.
Commonwealth, 25, 67.
Conder, George William, 268.
Conder, Dr. E. R., 317, 322, 323, 325.
Confession, Augsburg, 217,
  Burial Hill, 209-212.
  Heidelberg, 217.
  Savoy, 185-187, 190-197, 200, 202, 206.
  Westminster, 184-186, 190, 195, 196, 200, 202, 203, 216.
Confessions of Faith, 29, 179, 180, 181.
Congregationalism, 67, 68, 73.
  In Great Britain, Modern, 58. 67, 71.

(Congregationalism—cont'd.)
In United States, 71, 72.
Progressive and Conservative, 143.
Strength of English, 165.
Weakness of English, 161-164.
Congregationalist Churches, Work of, 133, 134.
Conditions for Membership, 233.
Salaries of Ministers, 139.
Denomination, 179,
Union, 307; of Cheshire, 308; of Staffordshire, 307; Creed of, 29, 187-191, 197, 198; of England and Wales, 148-150, 166, 170, 274; of England and Wales, Chairman of, 166, 167; Year Book of, 131, 187.
Congregationalists, 56, 108.
English, 128.
Number of, 130.
Doctrinal attitude of, early, 200.
Connecticut, 72.
Consciousness of Imperial Relations, 315-317.
Consociation, 206.
Convention of Congregational Churches, Northwest, 207.
Convocation, 183.
Houses of, 99, 100.
Council Chamber, 184.
Of Denominations, 310.
Fourth General, 207.
National, 150, 213, 215, 219.
Of Nicæa, 297.
System, 308.
Councils, 151.
County Union, 146, 148.
Covenant, 152, 230, 232.
Creed, Athanasian, 320.

(Creed—continued.)
Of 1883, 216.
Of National Council, 219-222.
Creeds and Confessions, 154, 169.
Formulated, 46.
Of Christendom, 196.
Pilgrim, 219.
Cromwell, 28, 30, 31, 56-58, 66, 78, 126, 185, 186, 256-259, 298.
Chrysostom, 251-253.

DALE, Bryan, 27, 156.
Robert W., 16, 18, 22, 24, 26, 87, 112, 228, 229, 240, 266, 275-280, 283, 285, 290, 292, 323, 326.
Darlow, T. Herbert, 163, 164.
Davis, W. H., 230.
Davison, W. T., 302.
Deacons, 12, 19, 27, 28.
Dean, Forest of, 312, 313.
Deans, 99.
Decretals, 93.
Defender of Peace, 49.
Democracy in Church Polity, 73.
Dexter, Henry M., 22, 230.
Dilke, Sir Charles, 312, 313.
Disendowment, 329.
Dissenters, 97, 118, 125, 129, 158, 266, 284, 329.
Dissenting Churches, 131.
Ministers, 255.
Disestablishment, 115, 118-121, 129, 285, 328, 329.
Discipline, 153.
Doctrines, 318-320, 326-329.
Doctrinal Schedules in Trust Deeds, 154, 155.
Doctrinal Tests, 25.
Conditions of Church Membership, 225-248.
Doddridge, Philip, 25, 259, 263, 264.

INDEX.   339

Dods, Marcus, 301.
Dörner, Isaac A., 305.
Driver, Canon, 281, 301.
Duff, Archibald, 292, 302, 325.
Dunbar, Battle of, 31.
Durham, 106.

ECCLESIASTICAL Court, 90.
  Council, 145.
  Commission, 102, 103.
  Life, 129.
Edward Sixth, Second Prayer Book of, 95.
Edwards, Jonathan, 21, 305.
Elders, 12.
Elizabeth, 51, 52, 54, 58, 95.
Elliot, Hon. Arthur, 101.
Emancipation Act, 105.
Empire, Religion of the, 43.
  Seat of the, 44.
Endowments, 118.
Environment, 6, 9, 10, 16.
Episcopal systems, 162.
  Authority, 45.
  Conditions for Mem'ship, 233.
Episcopalians, 29, 118.
Episcopate in Methodism, 73.
  Historic, 330.
Episcopacy, 299.
Episcopius, 256.
Erastian Church, 25.
Establishment, 30, 87, 111, 114 –116, 127, 160, 163, 266, 275, 283, 305.
  Present, 89, 92.
  A Failure, 108, 163.
Established Church, Evolution of, 88–90.
Ethelbert, 89.
Evangelical, 214.
Evans, Herber, 292.

FAIRBAIRN, A. M., 2, 3, 13, 19, 22, 27, 31, 160, 277, 281, 292, 301, 302, 309, 321, 325.

Fairchild, James H., 208.
Farrar, Canon, 109, 118, 280, 329.
Fellowship, 169, 170, 172, 331.
Fisher, George P., 207, 216, 218.
Fiske, J. O., 207.
Fitchburg, Church in, 234.
Forward Movement, the, 134, 311.
Forsyth, P. T., 327.
France, 107, 115.
Fraternal Complaints, 213,
Free Synod, 183,
Fytz, Richard, 59, 69.

GAINSBOROUGH, 54, 63.
Gale, Nahum, 207.
Genevan Theology, 70.
Germans, 304, 306.
Germany, 107.
Gibbon, Edward, 2.
Gibson, J. Monroe, 310.
Gilmour, the Missionary, 141.
Gladstone, 120, 174, 312, 313.
Goodrich, Dr., 168, 229, 292. 327.
Goodwin, E. P,, 230.
  Thomas, 185, 186.
Green, John Richard, 97.
  Dr. Thomas, 155, 157, 307.
Greenhill, 186.
Greenwood, John, 60, 61, 69, 77, 80.
Gregg, David, 230.
Gregory the Great, 89, 92.
Gulliver, John P., 212.
Guthrie, Thomas, 254.

HALF-WAY Covenant, 72.
Halifax, Harbour of, 306.
Halley, Dr., 268.
Hamilton, Dr. Richard Winter, 267.
Hampden, John, 182, 183.

Handley, S. B., 307.
Harris, Dr. John, 267.
  Samuel, 208.
Harrison, Joshua, 277.
  Robert, 60.
Hart, John C., 208.
Harwood, W. Hardy, 306.
Hatch, Dr., 251.
Haven, Joseph, 208.
Haweis, H. R., 109.
Heads of Agreement by the United Ministers, 308.
Heath, A. H., 232.
Hebrews, 114.
Henry the Eighth, 51, 89-95, 298.
Hood, Paxton, 271, 272.
Hooker, Richard, 97.
Hopkins, Mark, 218.
Horne, C. Silvester, 278.
Horton, Robert F., 229, 277, 281, 292, 327.
Howe, John, 255-257, 259, 265.
Hubert, 91.
Hughes, Hugh Price, 138.
Hunter, John, 267, 277.

INCE, 305.
Independency, Atlas of English, 185.
  In England, 126, 161, 169, 170.
  Federated, 171.
  Idea of, 138, 172, 187, 307, 328, 330.
Independent Theory, 306.
Independents, 24, 26, 28-31, 56, 57, 76, 127, 128, 137, 158, 180, 184, 199, 284, 299.
  During Commonwealth, 192.
India, 315-317.
International Council, 18, 35, 143, 309, 317, 326.
Ireland, Home Rule for, 120.

JAMES First, 54-56.
James, John Angell, 268-269, 276, 277, 280.
Jay, William, 267.
Jesuits, 17.
Jewish Disabilities Removal Act, 105.
Jews Admitted to Parliament, 106.
John, Griffiths, 141.
John, King, 91.
Johnson, Francis, 61, 63.
Johnson, Dr. Samuel, 261.
Jones, Thomas, 268.

KEBLE, 109.
Kingsley, 109, 254.
Knox, John, 50, 55, 181, 252.
  Dr. Vicesimus, 262.

LABOUCHÈRE, Henry, 86.
Lacordaire, 252.
Ladd, H. M., 232.
Lambeth Conference, 310.
Lancashire College, 159, 162.
Langdon, Stephen, 91.
Laud, Archbishop, 185, 258.
Lawrence, 232.
  E. A., 207, 208.
Laws, William G., 141.
Leader, 128.
Leeds Mercury, 128.
Leyden, University of, 255.
Liberal Party, 112.
Liberation Society, 119.
Liddon, Canon, 279, 280.
Life, 5, 7, 9, 10, 13, 14, 16.
Liturgy, 183, 184.
Livingstone, 141.
Locke, John, 261.
London, 135, 159.
London Congregational Union, 134, 135, 136, 140.
  Missionary Society, 133, 140, 141, 142, 150.

INDEX. 341

(*London,—continued.*)
 University, 131.
 Lord's Supper, 106.
 Table, 152.
 Lord Privy Seal, 95.
 Luther, 43, 49, 50, 92, 252.

MACFADYAN, Dr., 68.
Mackennal, Dr. Alex., 167, 277, 292, 310, 313, 327, 329.
Magee, Dr., 279.
Mahaffy, Professor, 252.
Manchester, 98, 159, 160, 310.
Manor House of Brewster, 255.
Mansfield College, 69, 159, 162, 301, 309.
Marlborough, Duke of, 86.
Marsiglio, John, 49, 50.
Martin, Samuel, 267–270, 275.
Martineau, James, 329.
Mary, Queen, 51, 95.
Massillon, 250.
Mather, Cotton, 233.
Maurice, J. F. D., 109, 254, 273, 280, 305.
McAll, Robert S., 266, 269, 276.
McKenzie, Alexander, 231.
McLaren, Dr. A. 282, 310.
McLeod, Norman, 254, 326.
Mearns, Andrew, 134–136.
Medhurst, Walter H., 141.
Mellon, Enoch, 267.
Membership, Church, 41, 151–153, 169, 229, 230.
 Conditions of, 225–248.
Memorial Hall, 135.
Meredith, R. R., 231.
Methodism, 70, 130.
Methodist Conditions for Membership, 233.
Methodists, 112.
Miall, Edward, 284, 328, 329.

Milman, Henry Hart, 88.
Ministry, One Man, 163, 164, 168.
 Methods of Entering, 144,
 Training for, 144.
Ministers' Fraternal Union, 146.
Ministerial Standing, how Certified, 146, 147.
Mint District, 135.
Missionary Work in London, 138.
 Home, 133, 134, 139, 140.
Moffat, the Missionary, 141.
Moody, Dwight L., 287.
Morley, John, 86.
Morris, A. J., 268.
Mosheim, J. L., 2.
Mozley, James B., 305.
Mulford, Elisha, 32.
Munger, T. T., 231.
Mystics, 56.

NATIONAL Council of the United States, 149, 166, 167.
Nestorius, 17.
New College, 162.
 Colonies, 165.
 England, 202.
 Hampshire Confession, 181.
Newcastle, 98.
Newman, John Henry, 118, 254, 281, 282.
Newspapers, 127, 128.
Nineteenth Century Review, 161.
Noble, F. A., 230.
Nonconformist Ministers, 87, 129, 130.
Nonconformists, 67, 69, 111–113, 118, 119, 127, 128, 159, 166, 172, 184.
" Nonconformist Conscience," 312, 313, 315.
Noyes, Daniel J., 207.
Nye, Philip, 185, 186.

OBERLIN, 213, 214, 216, 222, 236.
Officers of Early Church, 12.
Organisation, 6, 9.
   Ecclesiastical, 172.
Owen, John, 186, 255, 257, 258, 265.
Oxford, 106, 158, 160, 301, 309.

PARISH, the Larger, 168.
Park, Edwards A., 208, 305.
Parker, Dr. Joseph, 167, 229, 278, 279, 280, 306, 326, 327.
Park Street Church, 234.
Parks, Sir Henry, 316.
Parliament, 86, 117, 182.
   Acts of, 93-99.
   The Long, 55.
Parliamentary Forces, 57.
Parnell, Charles S., 312.
Parsons, Edward, 268.
Parsons, James, 267, 268, 270.
Pastors, 12, 287.
Patronage, 103.
Pearson, Samuel, 292, 327.
Penny Dinner, 135.
Penry, John, 61-63, 69, 77.
Peter, Primacy of, 44.
Pilgrims, 21, 23, 27, 28, 32, 36, 58, 65, 66, 78, 79, 80, 81, 127, 298, 328, 332.
   In United States, 71.
Plymouth, 65, 76, 208, 213, 256.
Poor Relief, 135.
Pope, The Head of the English Church, 51.
Porter, Noah, Jr., 208.
Presbyterianism, 181, 307, 330.
Presbyterians, 16, 29, 112, 184.
   Scotch, 182.
Presbyterian Church, Conditions for Membership, 232.
   State, 183.
Presbytery, 30.
Priesthood, 18.

Puritanism, 23.
Puritans, 25, 28, 58, 71.
Puritans, Presbyterian, 53, 55, 65, 66, 75, 80.
Puritan Clergy, 183.
Puritan Revolution, 30, 74, 181, 190, 205, 298, 314.
Pusey, Dr. Edward B., 109, 280.
Pym, John, 182.

Quakers, 112.
Queensberry, Marquis of, 86.

RAFFLES, Thomas, 267, 276.
Raleigh, Dr. Alex., 268.
Ramea, Island of, 63.
Rationalism, 67.
Recognition Service, 146.
Redford, Dr., 198.
Reed, Dr. Andrew, 267, 268.
Reformation, 48, 101, 252, 297.
   Under Henry VIII., 93.
Republican Theory, 7.
Restraint of Appeals, Act for, 94.
Revival, Evangelical, 67, 200, 201.
Review, British Quarterly, 174.
Reynolds, 292, 325.
Rhodes, Cecil, 316.
Richard, Henry, 328, 329.
Richards, C. H., 231.
Rippon, 94.
Rippon, House of Roger, 61.
Robertson, 109, 254.
Robinson, John, 54, 64, 77, 78, 80, 332.
Rogers, J. Guinness, 277, 292, 312, 327, 329.
Rome, 42, 43, 90.
Rowland, Thomas, 59, 69.
Royal Commissions, 88.
Royalists, 56.

INDEX. 343

SACRAMENTS, 18.
Salem (Massachusetts), 65.
Salvation Army, 135.
Sanday, Professor, 281.
Sankey, Ira P., 287.
Savage, George S. F., 208.
Savoy Confession, 29, 185-187, 190-197, 200, 202, 206.
Schaff, Dr. Philip, 196.
Schleiermacher, 305.
Scotch Bond, 182.
Scott, Principal, 292, 325.
Scotland, Doctrinalism of, 187.
Scotland, 75, 89, 107, 299, 300.
Scrooby, 54, 63, 255.
Seminaries in England, United States and Wales, 131-132.
Separatists, 53, 54, 57, 58, 59. 61, 62, 63, 67, 74, 75, 77, 81, 126, 255, 299.
Separation of Church and State, 53, 57, 59.
Sermons, Traffic in, 116.
Sheffield Independent, 128.
Sherman, James, 267.
Sherrill, F. H., 327.
Simon, Principal, 292, 317, 318, 320, 321, 325.
Simony, 103-104.
Simpson, Sidrach, 185.
Smith, Henry B., 305.
  Pye, 305.
Smyth, John, 63.
South, Robert, 253.
Southey, Dr. Robert, 262.
Southwark, 54, 61.
Southwell, 98.
Sparke, Bishop of Ely, 102.
Speculation in England, 137.
Spurgeon, C. H., 253, 254, 270, 278, 282, 302.
  Thomas H., 316.
Stanley, Dean, 17, 97, 109, 174.
State, The, 4, 6, 7, 9, 10.
  Supremacy of, 48.

(*State—continued.*)
  Theocratic, 114.
  And the Church, 83-121.
St. Albans, 98.
St. Louis (Missouri), 216, 222.
Stead, F. H., 327.
Stimson, H. A., 232.
Storrs, Dr. R. S., 218, 231, 271, 272.
Stoughton, Dr. John, 182, 196, 197, 198.
Students in England, United States and Wales, 131-132.
Stubbs, Bishop, 93.
Sunday Service, 168.
Supremacy, Act of, 52.
Swain, Leonard, 208.
Synod, Cambridge, 204-205.
  Of Boston, 204-206.
  Of Saybrook, 206.

TAYLOR, Jeremy, 253.
  Dr. W. M., 230.
Tennyson, 319.
Theology, Science of, 300, 318.
  Systematic, 318, 321.
Theological Agitation in England and America, 301, 302.
  Colleges, 325.
  Outlook, 317.
  Status, 324.
Theologians, Speculative, 303-304.
Thirty-nine Articles, 29, 52, 59, 184.
Thomas, David, 268, 307.
Thompson, Joseph P., 207.
Thrall, J. B, 231.
Thwing, C. F., 230.
Toleration, 20, 67-68, 125.
  Act, 105, 283,
Toynbee Hall, 136.
Truro, 98.
Trust Deeds, 155, 156, 157, 180, 198, 222.

ULFILAS, 17.
Uniformity, Act of, 52, 58, 95, 96.
  Of Worship, 111.
Union, Baptist, 310.
  County, 150, 151.
Unitarians, 112, 147, 148, 156, 234.
Unitarian Controversy, 233, 235.
Unitarianism, 67, 75, 261, 327.
United College, 159.
United States, 107, 151, 156, 165.
  Religious Life in the, 125.
Unity, 13, 15.
University of Aberdeen, 264.
  Dutch, 259.
  Of Oxford, 300.
  Tests, Abolition of, 106.
Universities, 69, 87, 112, 144, 158, 255, 309.

VANE, Sir Harry, 57, 182, 186.
Vaughan, Dr., 267.
Virgin, Dr. S. H., 231.
Virginia, 65.
Voluntary Principle in America, 115.
  System, 118.

Vose, J. G., 232.

WACE, 305.
Wakefield, 98.
Wales, 88–89.
  Prince of, 313, 314, 315.
Walker, George F., 231.
Wardlaw, Ralph, 305.
Watts, Isaac, 259–265.
Weiss, 305.
Wesley, John, 67, 69, 200, 259, 262, 283.
Wesleyans, 112, 130.
Westminster Assembly, 57.
  Confession, 29, 73.
White, Edward, 277.
Whitefield, George, 67, 69, 200, 259, 262, 283.
Whitgift, Archbishop, 62.
Williams, Carvell, 284.
  John, 141.
  Roger, 66, 76.
Witenagemot, 90.
Worcester, Dr., 234.
Wycliffe, John, 50, 91, 252.

XAVIER, Francis, 17.

YORK, Archbishop of, 99, 102.
Yorkshire Union, 156.

" Opens up a central ana to many unknown truth—admirably and unanswerably. The Church is full of Ephesian Christians, who ' have not so much as heard whether there be any Holy Ghost.' "— LYMAN ABBOTT, D.D.

SPIRIT AND LIFE.
THOUGHTS FOR TO-DAY.
BY
AMORY H. BRADFORD, D.D.,
First Congregational Church, Montclair. N. J.

CONTENTS: *The Holy Spirit the Fundamental Doctrine of Christianity; The Holy Spirit in Individual Experience; The Holy Spirit and Christian Work; The Holy Spirit a Constant Factor in the Problem of Progress; Conditions of Spiritual Sight; Theological Thought of Our Time; The Incarnation; The Vicarious Principle in the Universe; The Appeal to Experience; The Life the Light of Men; The Invisible Realm; The Endless Growth.*

"In the flood of this kind of literature, it is a pleasure to find one book which deserves the printing. . . . Those who have heard Dr. Bradford preach need not be told of the intellect and spiritual vigor which these sermons show. . . . Will give light and life to the minds and spirits of those who read it."—*The Christian Inquirer* (Baptist), N. Y.

"Well-nigh unequaled work upon his high theme. . . . If a student will glance at the bound volumes of the Bibliotheca Sacra, during its first fifty years, he will be astonished to find with what completeness this subject of the Third Person of the Trinity has been let alone. . . . The sermons here are strong and vital and of permanent value."—*The Golden Rule* (Cong.), Boston.

"Dr. Bradford's reverent spirit, intellectual independence and pure tastes have rendered his writings very agreeable and profitable to me. . . . I shall feel that I am doing my friends a favor by commending it [his 'Spirit and Life'] to their attention."—CHARLES F. DEEMS, D.D., *Pastor, Church of the Strangers, N. Y.*

"Eloquent and thoughtful, singularly free from cant, and altogether outside of the ordinary theological rut."—*News and Courier*, Charleston, S. C.

"The best phase of current Christianity. . . . Not controversial, but in sympathy with progressive theology and the best modern thought."—*Providence Journal.*

"Have directness and point. . . . Sympathetic and helpful in character."—*Boston Transcript.*

"Dr. Bradford belongs to that increasing class of clergymen whose teaching defies the scientific classifier, because it takes on such a new form and is so thoroughly the outgrowth of his own personal experience. . . . Without a common understanding or a common symbol, this modern school of thinkers are all agreed in giving great prominence to the doctrine of the divine immanence in nature and in human experience. . . . We commend his volume heartily to those of our readers who desire to get an appreciative and wholly uncontroversial interpretation of the Bible which God is writing continuously in human hearts."—*The Christian Union*, N. Y.

1 Vol. 16mo, 266 pages, Vellum Cloth, $1.

☞ *Sold by all Booksellers, or mailed to any address, on receipt of the price by the Publishers.*

FORDS, HOWARD, & HULBERT,
47 East Tenth St., New York.

"A power of thought enabling him to grapple with the most difficult subjects with no ordinary skill; a power of expression which crystallizes his ideas into the most incisive and vigorous phrase."—*Leicester (Eng.) Post, in a notice of* DR. BRADFORD *as one of the Delegates to the International Congregational Conference,* 1891.

OLD WINE: NEW BOTTLES.
Some Elemental Doctrines in Modern Form.
By AMORY H. BRADFORD, D.D.
First Congregational Church, Montclair, N. J.; Author of "*Spirit and Life,*" etc.

White Leatherette, 35 Cents.

Four discourses, on "The Living God;" "The Holy Trinity;" "What is Left of the Bible;" "The Immortal Life." The sermons were delivered during Lent and on Easter Sunday, 1892, the topics selected as being essential—or, as Dr. Bradford phrases it, elemental—in Christianity.

This preacher is one of the men of the day, in that he does not insist on the old bottles of formulation which are being so sadly rent by the new spirit of inquiry, but rather prefers to conserve what he thinks to be the beliefs necessary to Christian thought and life as found in the Scriptures, by putting them into the forms compelled by modern thought and the experience of mankind.

"Dr. Bradford is one of the best exponents, in a practical way, of the modern spirit sometimes miscalled New Theology. He does not expound theology; he is a preacher of righteousness. He does not construct bottles; he brings wine to thirsty souls. . . . The volume is to be commended alike for its candor, its reasonableness, and its perception of, and ministry to, spiritual needs."—*Christian Union,* New York.

"These subjects are handled by Dr. Bradford in his fearless, frank and serene manner, and always with a hopeful attitude toward the thought and speculation of the present day. . . . Superb and eloquent assertions and definitions of the common faith."—*Independent,* New York.

"In the writer of this pamphlet we have an eloquent preacher, and in the four discourses these pages contain we find a frank acceptance of what science has demonstrated combined with a bold and earnest proclamation of the convictions modern thought and experience have produced on an intense but open-minded nature. . . . Lofty spiritual teaching enforced in a fit eloquence all the nobler because free of narrowness, enriched by wide reading and enforced by a clear, sound and reverential mind."—*The Modern Church,* Glasgow, Scotland.

"Four admirable discourses of practical Christian doctrine. . . . Models of conciseness and lucidity."—*Newark (N. J.) Advertiser.*

"Quite suggestive of some of Professor Drummond's best works, the style is effective and attractive, and it well deserves the commendation given by another: 'It would be difficult to find more good sense, sound morality and lofty spiritual teaching than are condensed in this little book.' It deserves a wide circulation, and is just the book to put in the hands of a friend.'"—*Public Opinion,* Washington, D. C.

FORDS, HOWARD, & HULBERT,
47 East Tenth St., New York.

Notable and Interesting Religious Books.

SIGNS OF PROMISE.

Sermons Preached in Plymouth Church, Brooklyn, 1887-1889.

BY LYMAN ABBOTT, D.D.

Eighteen Discourses. 12mo, cloth, gilt top. Price, $1.50.

"'Signs of Promise' is the fit title of the first volume of sermons preached in Plymouth Pulpit since its greatest occupant passed from earth. By all logical and intellectual inheritance, that pulpit is now worthily filled. . . . The Plymouth preacher of to-day shows us that God is, and not merely that he was. His words thrill with the currents of hope born of a survey of the past and making contact with the unseen future. . . . . All of these sermons are strong, helpful and suggestive, and reveal the true prophet."—*The Critic*, New York.

"Clear and compact, and palpitate with the influences of the time. . . . One cannot read these sermons without being impressed with the ability with which the subjects are handled, and with many glowing passages which are eminently spiritual and uplifting."—*Christian Intelligencer*, New York.

"One of the favorite assertions of that supremely irritating created thing, the infidel who has not sufficient strength of mind to believe in aught but himself, is that Christianity is behind the times, is incapable of grappling with the problems of every-day life, and, indeed, blinds itself to their existence; and as this kind of infidel is common, and his cuckoo cry is all but continuous, it is a pleasure now and then to encounter a volume of sermons showing the keenest sensitiveness to current topics of interest. One need not agree with the author's theology; one may be a Buddhist or a Mohammedan and yet enjoy the manner in which such an one will attack and rout this species of infidel."—*Boston Herald*.

"Dr. Abbott is no copyist, but a man strong in his own peculiar powers and gifts."—*Christian Register*.

"Full of earnest and vigorous thought and are eminently stimulating. Even those who do not altogether agree with the author's theological positions will find much to be admired here and little to be condemned."—*Congregationalist*.

"A clew to Dr. Abbott's Beecher-like reception of all revelation, in Scripture nature or life, and to his ability to keep abreast with the stream of such revelation as it widens continually between the opposite but not opposing banks of theology and science."—*Brooklyn Eagle*.

SPIRIT AND LIFE.

Thoughts for To-Day.

BY AMORY H. BRADFORD, D.D.,

First Cong. Church, Montclair, N. J.

Twelve Discourses. 16mo, vellum cloth. Price, $1.00.

"It is evident to the laical mind that a certain tender, serious, humane spirit possesses men of this class, urging them to work for the good of man and the glory of God in nobler fashion, broader ways, than purely metaphysical schemes can ever hope to instigate"—*Boston Post*.

"We commend his volume heartily to those of our readers who desire to get an appreciative and wholly uncontroversial interpretation of the Bible which God is writing continuously in human hearts."—*The Christian Union*, N. Y.

"Rarely has there been published in this country a finer volume of sermons, or sermons more worthy of publication, or better fitted to be of actual helpfulness to Christian thought and the spiritual life.'—*The Advance*, Chicago.

"The best modern preaching deals with spiritual wants and vital truths. Judged by this test, the sermons before us are worthy to be classed among the best sermons of the day."—*New Englander and Yale Review*.

FORDS, HOWARD, & HULBERT,
47 East Tenth St., New York.

"*Here is a clear, cogent presentation of those views which are of the progressive type of theology. It is a book of the day.*"—PUBLIC OPINION, Washington, D. C.

UNTO THE UTTERMOST.

BY
JAMES M. CAMPBELL.

CONTENTS: *Unto the Uttermost; A Castaway Reclaimed; Grace Conquering Nature; A Pessimistic View of the Moral Condition of Man; The Limits of Evolution; Moral Miracles; The Higher Environment; The Universality of the Divine Purpose of Redemption; The Forthputting of Redemptive Effort a Necessity of the Divine Nature; The Sin that Shuts the Door of Mercy; The Chief Danger-point; The Fluidity of Character; Judicial Blindness; A Common Spiritual Disease; Past Feeling; Bartering the Birthright; Death a Loss; The Finality of the Present.*

"Mr. CAMPBELL stands firmly by the Bible, but uses it with breadth and freedom of interpretation. . . . They [*i. e.*, the essays which make up the book] fall wholly within the lines of orthodoxy, for which indeed they make a stout and in some respects original defense, and are a valuable contribution to the questions of the times."—*The Independent.*

"Composed of chapters which are suggestive, full of hints, and notable especially for their spiritual exegesis, their inlook into texts, and the discovery of the real and deeper meaning of Scripture. . . . More than usually worth reading by the fireside or as a means of spiritual quickening in the pastor's study."—*Christian Union.*

"This book carries in it the reason for its being. Its matter is excellent. The style is trenchant. The points project themselves so conspicuously that you find them, and they find you. The author is no 'picker up of unconsidered trifles.' It is such a volume as a thinker upon religious matters would like to have with him in the cars. It is decidedly stimulating."—*The Golden Rule.*

"There is not a dull line. Truth that is old and familiar is exhibited with a new luster glorifying its face. . . . It is altogether too rarely that one comes on a volume from which he realizes both a distinct mental stimulus and a devotional glow. It is particularly because of this double office it performs that Mr. Campbell's book will find a welcome place on the study-table."—*The Northwestern Congregationalist.*

"Packed with truth eloquently uttered. Certainly the book is vigorous."—*The Evangelist, N. Y.*

"New, thoughtful, healthful interpretations are given, which give new light."—*Christian Inquirer, N. Y.*

"Discourses of remarkable clearness upon living themes about which the Christian world is at this time doing much thinking."—*Chicago Inter-Ocean.*

"Full of the fire of conviction."—*Evening Wisconsin.*

"The book has many bright and true things."—*New York Observer.*

"A new work which is attracting considerable attention in theological circles. . . . Brings some fresh thinking to bear on important subjects."—*The Universalist*, Chicago.

"It is a book that it profits one to read, and to read carefully and studiously. There is many a sentence full of suggestive thought. It will stimulate the Christian thinker."—*Public Opinion.*

1 Vol. 16mo, 254 pages, Vellum Cloth, $1.25.

☞ *Sold by all Booksellers, or mailed to any address, on receipt of price.*

FORDS, HOWARD, & HULBERT,
47 East Tenth St., New York.

> "A prophet foretells . . . because he sees more clearly than his fellows the nature of truth, the movements of Providence, and so the tendencies and probable fruition of events. Of these principles a remarkable and interesting illustration is [here] afforded. . . . These sermons to a considerable extent anticipate the results of modern criticism, and at the same time indicate the method in which those results can be practically employed . . . for spiritual ends."—LYMAN ABBOTT, *Editorial in the Christian Union.*

BEECHER'S BIBLE STUDIES.
1878—1879.

Readings in the Early Books of the Old Testament (Genesis to Ruth), with Familiar Comment. Prefaced by two characteristic sermons: "The Inspiration of the Bible," and "How to Read the Bible." By HENRY WARD BEECHER. Edited, from Stenographic Notes of T. J. ELLINWOOD, by JOHN R. HOWARD. 438 pp. 8vo. Garnet cloth, $1.50.

"One of the very best works which has ever come from Mr. Beecher's fertile brain. It is learned enough for the scholar, and popular enough for the layman. . . Its spirit is reverent and devotional, and it is distinctly positive and constructive in its method."—AMORY H. BRADFORD, D.D., *First Cong. Church, Montclair, N. J.*

"Models of clear, vigorous and instructive exposition. . . The dry bones of the old days of Israel have a living soul given to them by this rare preacher. . . The book is admirably compiled."—Rev. ALMON GUNNISON, *Worcester, Mass.* (Universalist).

"I do not regard Mr. Beecher as an authority in theology or creed-statement, but I do regard him as an authority in the ethical interpretation of the Bible. . . Marked by his characteristic insight, freshness, good sense and spiritual robustness."—GEO. DANA BOARDMAN, D.D., *First Baptist Church, Phila.*

"His elevation of thought, his kindly humor, his unexpected flashing wit, his deep devotion, his keen practical sense, his philosophical analysis of character, his helpful ethical instruction, his lofty and impressive eloquence, have constant themes. It is many a day since so suggestive and stimulating a volume has appeared."—*Brooklyn Citizen.*

"As rich in vital thought, fresh suggestion and poetic entertainment of the oldest themes of human interest as any preceding one by its author."—*Brooklyn Eagle.*

"A great treat to me. . . . A mind perfectly free, and perfectly devout, is *rara avis*, and its genuine heartfelt reflections on the ancient Scriptures must carry valuable help to thoughtful men and women."—CHAS. H. HALL, D.D., *Rector Church of the Holy Trinity, Brooklyn, N. Y.*

"An admirable presentation of the facts of ancient Hebrew history in the light of modern ideas."—Pres. WM. DEW. HYDE, *Bowdoin College.*

"It is bright with the light of his genius, warm with the love of his great heart, and altogether admirable reading for our times. You have done a worthy service to all students of the Bible by the publication of these inimitable Readings."—GEO. A. GORDON, D.D., *Old South Church, Boston.*

"Henry Ward Beecher was a remarkable expositor of the Bible . . . in a peculiar sense a prophet of modern religious tendencies. . . Rare insight and luminous candor."—*New York Tribune.*

"Insight, sanity, spiritual sympathy, profound faith in God, and contempt for the pettiness of cloister commentators."—*Literary World, Boston.*

"He had a rare faculty of stripping a difficult subject of technical and scholastic rubbish. I wish the first two discourses, on 'Inspiration' and 'Reading the Bible,' might be in the hands of every Bible reader. . . . Commend themselves alike to *common sense* and *scholarly* sense."—PROF. MARVIN R. VINCENT, *Union Theological Seminary, New York.*

FORDS, HOWARD, & HULBERT,
47 East Tenth St., New York.

PLYMOUTH PULPIT SERMONS

BY

HENRY WARD BEECHER

Four Volumes, covering the period from Sept. 1873 to Sept. 1875.

About 600 pp. each, Garnet Cloth, $1.50 per vol.

"The late HENRY WARD BEECHER was, take him all in all, the most remarkable preacher and orator of this generation. His fertility of mind was inexhaustible. The publishers have rendered a public service in reprinting in a convenient form these sermons. . . . Printed on good paper and in good type, they are issued at a price which will put them within the reach of hundreds of young ministers and thousands of laymen, who retain their relish for original and vigorous thought presented with fervid eloquence."—*New York Evangelist.*

Vol. I.—*Religion in Daily Life; Forelookings; Heroism; New Testament Theory of Evolution; The Atoning God; Prayer; Man's Two Natures; All-Sidedness in Christian Life; Fact and Fancy; Cuba; Moral Teaching of Suffering; How Goes the Battle? Nature of Christ; Working and Waiting; What is Christ to Me? Science of Right Living; Religious Constancy; Soul Power; Riches of God; St. Paul's Creed; The Departed Christ; Naturalness of Faith; Spiritual Manhood; The Debt of Strength; Special Providence; Keeping the Faith.*

Vol. II.—*Charles Sumner; Saved by Hope; The Primacy of Love; Foretokens of Resurrection; Summer in the Soul; Hindering Christianity; Soul-Relationship; Christian Joyfulness; Liberty in the Churches; The Temperance Question; God's Grace; Ideal Christianity; Problem of Life; Unjust Judgments; Immortality of Good Works; The Universal Heart of God; Delight of Self-Sacrifice; Truth Speaking; The Secret of the Cross; Resolving and Doing; Triumph of Goodness; Following Christ; Prayer and Providence; What is Religion? Christian Sympathy; Luminous Hours.*

Vol. III.—*Law and Liberty; Faint-Heartedness; As a Little Child; God's Will; Present use of Immortality; The Test of Church Worth; Peace in Christ; The Indwelling of Christ; The End and the Means; Saved by Grace; Soul-Rest; The World's Growth; Foundation Work; The Bible; The Work of Patience; Divine Love; Unworthy Pursuits; True Righteousness; Things of the Spirit; Christian Contentment; Moral Standards; Trials of Faith; Old Paths; Meekness, a Power; Extent of the Divine Law; Soul-Growth.*

Vol. IV.—*Christ Life; The Courtesy of Conscience; Love, the Key to Religion; Christianity Social; Morality and Religion; Law of Soul-Growth; Sources and Uses of Suffering; God's Dear Children; Grieving the Spirit; Working and Waiting; The Sure Foundation; Nurture of Noble Impulse; Sowing and Reaping; Soul Statistics; Secret of Christ's Power; The Communion of Saints; Christian Life a Struggle; The Prodigal Son; Universality of the Gospel; Economy in Small Things; Good Deeds Memorable; Divine Indwelling; Claims of the Spirit; The Kingdom Within; The New Birth; Perfection Through Love.*

RECENT OPINIONS.

"They cover the period of Mr. Beecher's deepest trouble, 1873-1875, and the period in which his preaching had perhaps the ripest thought and the deepest spiritual life, . . . the ripest and best portion of his ministry."—*The Christian Union.*

"As one turns these wonderful pages, it is hard to think that the mind which speaks through them with such ever fresh power to interest, and often with such tremendous vitality and suasive strength, has ceased to act on earth."—*The Congregationalist,* Boston.

FORDS, HOWARD, & HULBERT,
47 East Tenth St., New York.

A BOOK OF PRAYER.

By HENRY WARD BEECHER.

Compiled from Unpublished Notes of his Pulpit Ministrations,
By T. J. ELLINWOOD,
Who was for upwards of thirty years Mr. Beecher's Special Stenographer.
With Portrait. 32mo, Cloth, 75 cts.; Cloth, gilt, $1.00.

"It is often declared, especially by transient hearers, his prayer was more than his sermon."
"The prayers published with the sermons are as remarkable as the sermons themselves."

The above remarks were made by two papers, one secular, one religious, when reviewing some of the original volumes of "Plymouth Pulpit Sermons." And, to persons accustomed to the perfunctory petitions which too often arise in public service, the beauty and fragrance of spirit shown in Mr. Beecher's praying—as genuine a development of his nature as oratory—never failed to appeal with irresistible attraction. His public prayer was free and delightful communion with his people and with God, and in it he poured out aspiration, gratitude, encouragement, petition, manly pride, humility, tender sympathy—whatever his prolific soul brought to his lips, that could "raise the fallen, cheer the faint," or help any of his flock to better life and higher thoughts.

"As a treasury of suggestion to young Christians who have yet to learn the naturalness and ready helpfulness of prayer, this little book will be invaluable. The brief introduction, compiled from various expositions by Mr. Beecher in his lecture-room talks, will give a new and happy view of prayer to many, while the prayers themselves must prove sources of strength, of comfort, of light, and of radiant hope to any thoughtful reader."—*Epworth Herald*, Chicago.

"While the spirit is simple, the language is exalted."—*The Christian Advocate*, New York.

"Multitudes who have been led to the throne of grace by the great preacher will desire this volume, and multitudes more, through the warm spirit of devotion that breathes in its pages, will pour out their souls unto God."—*The Golden Rule*, Boston.

"Helpful and delightful devotional reading. . . . There is throughout the wonderful variety of mood, of thought, of illustration and of expression characteristic of the man when at his best."—*Herald and Presbyter*, Cincinnati.

"A volume meriting careful study."—*Boston Traveller*.

"Nothing in the collection is more striking than its simplicity. . . . The play of feeling and freshness of form in them is marvelous."—*Independent*, New York.

"His prayers were seldom perfunctory or stereotyped. More often they were joyous, trustful, tender, devotional outpourings of a great heart. . . . Though some of them suggest local occasions, the most of them are fitted to the deeper wants of humanity."—*Christian Register*, Boston.

"Aside from their devotional expression there is a versatility and wide sweep of thought that no man ever made more impressive than did Mr. Beecher."—*Inter-Ocean*, Chicago.

"Well worthy of study by ministers and laymen."—*Western Christian Advocate*, Cincinnati.

"An admirable book for the culture of devotion and for the development of a restful spirit. . . . We know of nothing in devotional literature which seems to us more suited to modern needs, the needs of undevout, restless, eager, self-sufficient America, than the prayers and meditations of Henry Ward Beecher."—*Christian Union*, New York.

FORDS, HOWARD, & HULBERT,
47 East Tenth St., New York.

Books by Henry Ward Beecher.

Bible Studies.
Sunday Evening Discourses on Inspiration, and Bible Readings, with Characteristic Comment. A new volume from unpublished notes of T. J. ELLINWOOD. Edited by JOHN R. HOWARD [1892]. Garnet cloth, $1.50.

A Book of Prayer.
Introduction on the universality and varied phases of Prayer. Invocation, Prayers before Sermon, and Closing Prayers arranged by topics from unpublished stenographic notes of T. J. ELLINWOOD [1892]. Cloth, 75 cts.; cloth, gilt, $1.

Comforting Thoughts.
For those in Bereavement, Illness and Adversity. Compiled by IRENE OVINGTON. With Vignettes. Cloth, limp, 75 cts.; cloth, gilt, $1.

Sermons.
Four volumes, 1873-4. Ellinwood's Reports. Garnet cloth, per volume, $1.50. (*See also Evolution and Religion, A Summer in England, and Patriotic Addresses.*)

Plymouth Pulpit, single sermons, 5 cts.; assorted lots, 50 cts. per dozen. No complete volumes Send for list.

The Original Plymouth Pulpit, 1868 to 1873. Ten volumes (originally $25) in five volumes. Octavo, garnet cloth, $12.50, net.

Evolution and Religion.
Part I.—Theoretical and Doctrinal; paper, 50 cts. Part II.— Practical and Vital; paper, $1. The two Parts in one volume, garnet cloth, $1.50.

Patriotic Addresses and Sermons.
On Slavery, Civil War (including the Speeches in England, 1863), and Civil Liberty in the United States—from the reply to Henry Clay to the Eulogies on Lincoln and Grant. With a Review of his Life, Personality and Public Influence, by JOHN R. HOWARD. 8vo, 858 pp. Cloth, $2; cloth, gilt, $2.50; half mor., $4.

A Summer in England.
Addresses, Lectures and Sermons delivered there in 1886. With account of the trip by Maj. JAS. B. POND. Photo-artotype portrait; MSS. notes, etc. Cloth, gilt top, $2.

Yale Lectures on Preaching.
I.—Personal Elements; II.—Social and Religious Machinery; III.—Christian Doctrines and their Use. Thirty-three Lectures. 960 pages. Three volumes in one. Vellum cloth, $2.

The Life of Jesus the Christ.
Completed Edition, 2 vols., 8vo. Cloth, $5.50; half mor., $9.50. Either vol., singly—cloth, $3; half mor., $5.

Lectures to Young Men.
On Various Important Subjects. Cloth, $1.50.

Royal Truths.
Reported from his Spoken Words. Fourth American from Sixth English Edition. Cloth, $1.25.

Beecher as a Humorist.
Selections of Wit and Humor from his Works. Compiled by ELEANOR KIRK. Vellum cloth, $1.

Norwood.
A TALE OF VILLAGE LIFE IN NEW ENGLAND. Mr. Beecher's Only Novel. Cloth, Popular Edition, $1.25; paper, 50 cts.

Faith.
Last Morning Sermon preached by Mr. Beecher, Sunday, Feb. 27, 1887. *Portrait.* Embossed paper, 20c.; leather, 45c.

FORDS, HOWARD, & HULBERT,
47 East Tenth St., New York.

www.ingramcontent.com/pod-product-compliance
Lightning Source LLC
Chambersburg PA
CBHW031422230426
43668CB00007B/401